WEB SITE GRAPHICS

NAVIGATION

THE BEST WORK FROM THE WEB

Jeff Carlson | Toby Malina | Glenn Fleishman

GLOUCESTER MASSACHUSETTS

ROCKPORT PUBLISHERS

Rockport Publishers, Inc.

First published in the United States of America by:
Rockport Publishers, Inc.
33 Commercial Street
Gloucester, Massachusetts 01930-5089
Telephone: (978) 282-9590
Facsimile: (978) 283-2742

Distributed to the book trade and art trade in the United States by:
North Light Books, an imprint of
F & W Publications
1507 Dana Avenue
Cincinnati, Ohio 45207
Telephone: (800) 289-0963

Other distribution by:
Rockport Publishers, Inc.
Gloucester, Massachusetts 01930-5089

ISBN 1-56496-518-X

10 9 8 7 6 5 4 3 2 1

Designer: The Design Company
Cover Image: StudioMotiv, p. 73

Printed in Hong Kong

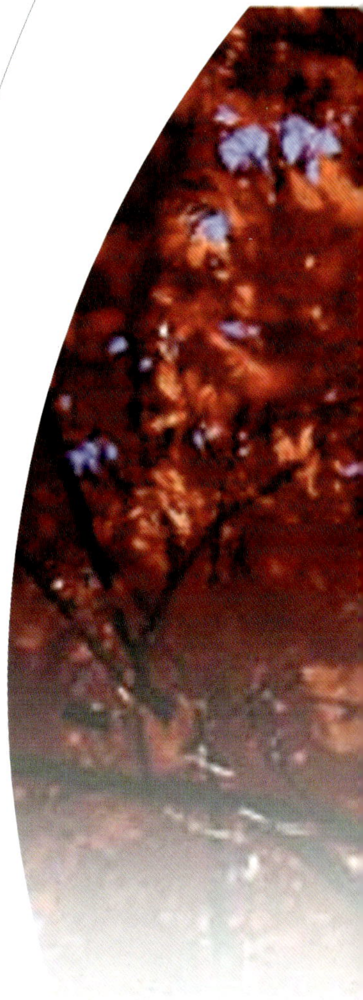

URI

out | pr

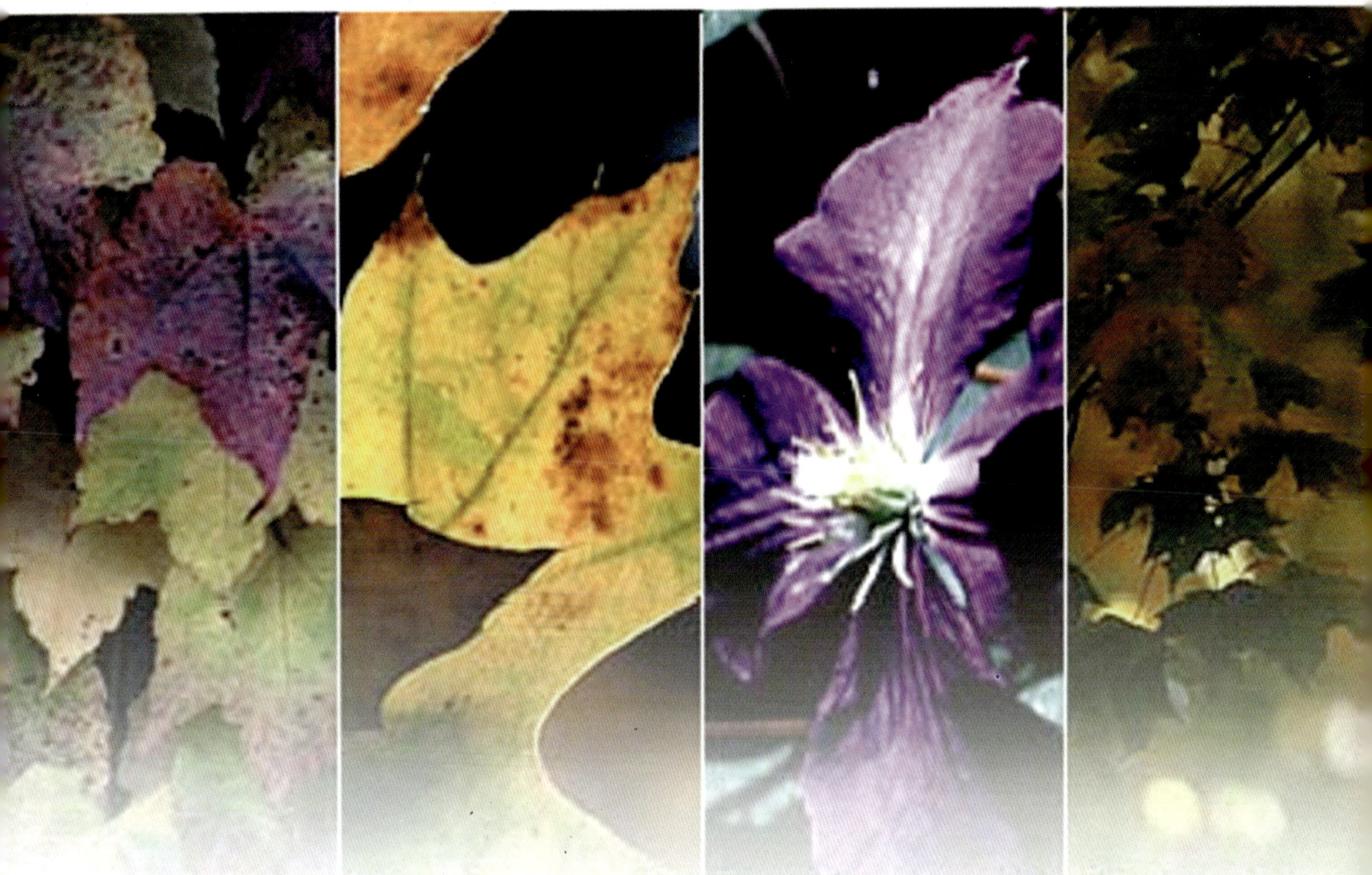

ICULAR COMPUTIN

cipals | projects | venture fund | workshops | sites

introduction

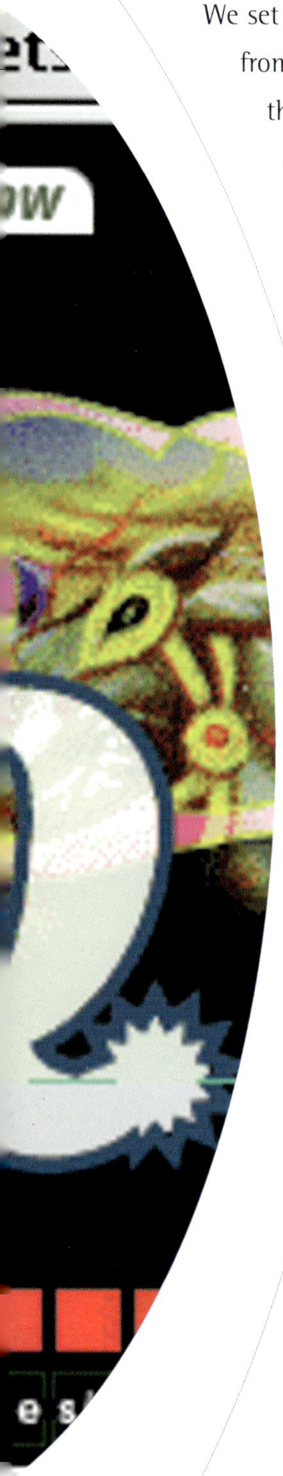

Developments in browsers and Web-publishing tools notwithstanding, the one constant in most Web sites appears to be the colored navigation bar running down the left side of the page.

We set out with this book to unshackle ourselves from this standard by finding examples of sites that were both richly navigable and (as often as possible) used other techniques to lead the user through the site. There's nothing wrong with the left-side, colored navigation bar per se, but with countless pages to look at already—starting with c|net's mustard yellow—we thought we'd break with this new "tradition."

The left-side navigation bar became a feature of the Web landscape because of the idea that every page should, by its nature, lead you to every other page on a site. It's a common desire on the part of marketing folks who want to make sure that the valuable investment made in the Web site isn't lost on the user.

But most designers featured in this book have chosen a different tack, using context to provide navigational aids. In some cases, sites are deliberately unnavigable—but it's still useful to learn from these positive examples of contrary design. Some of the most obscurely engineered sites, like Eye Candy and Funny Garbage, are incredibly compelling—much more so than expensive commercial sites where you would rarely venture deeper than the home page.

What might seem contradictory, however, is that many of our favorite sites include excellent site maps, a number of which you'll find here. Good site design should make navigation seem self-evident. However, assuming the principle that every page doesn't necessarily lead you to every other, a site map can, in the best cases we present here, short-circuit the clicking process, propelling you in a hyperspace leap from deep in one part of the site, through the site map, to the depths of a different level.

This is thinking both inside and outside of the box: the structure is still hierarchical and navigable through navigation bars, text links, or other elements (inside the box), but the site map jumps you into a super-observer position (outside the box) where you can decide exactly where you want to go today.

Navigation is not just a set of links: it is a way of thinking about and structuring a site so that information, illustrations, or documents always feel like they are within reach, not buried far away or impossible to find. Even when you may have to click four or five times, a good design keeps you interested while you're navigating, and keeps the prize (the page you're trying to get to) within your grasp.

"Most designers featured in this book have chosen a different tack, using context to provide navigational aids. In some cases, sites are deliberately unnavigable—but it's still useful to learn from these positive examples of contrary design."

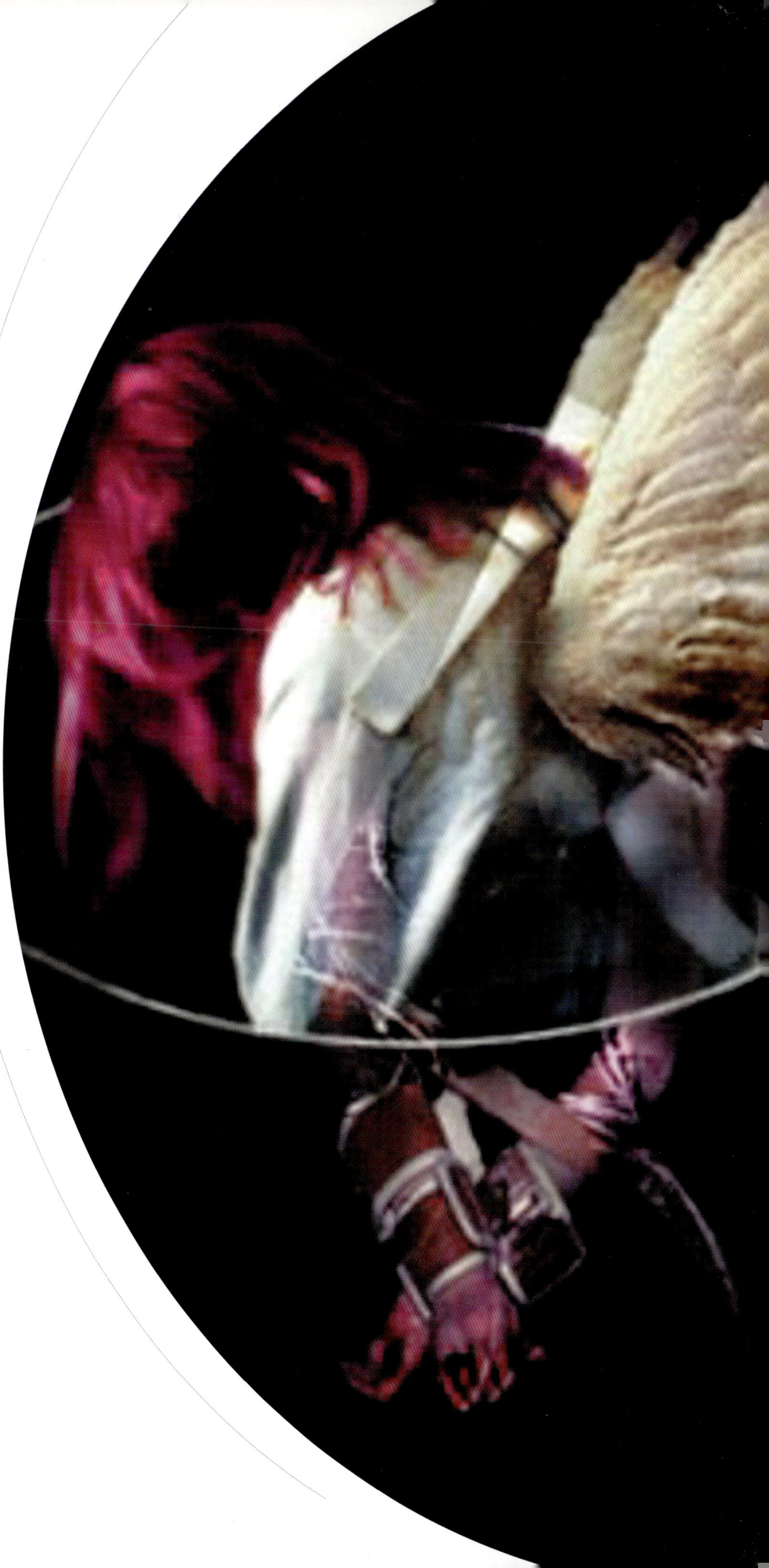

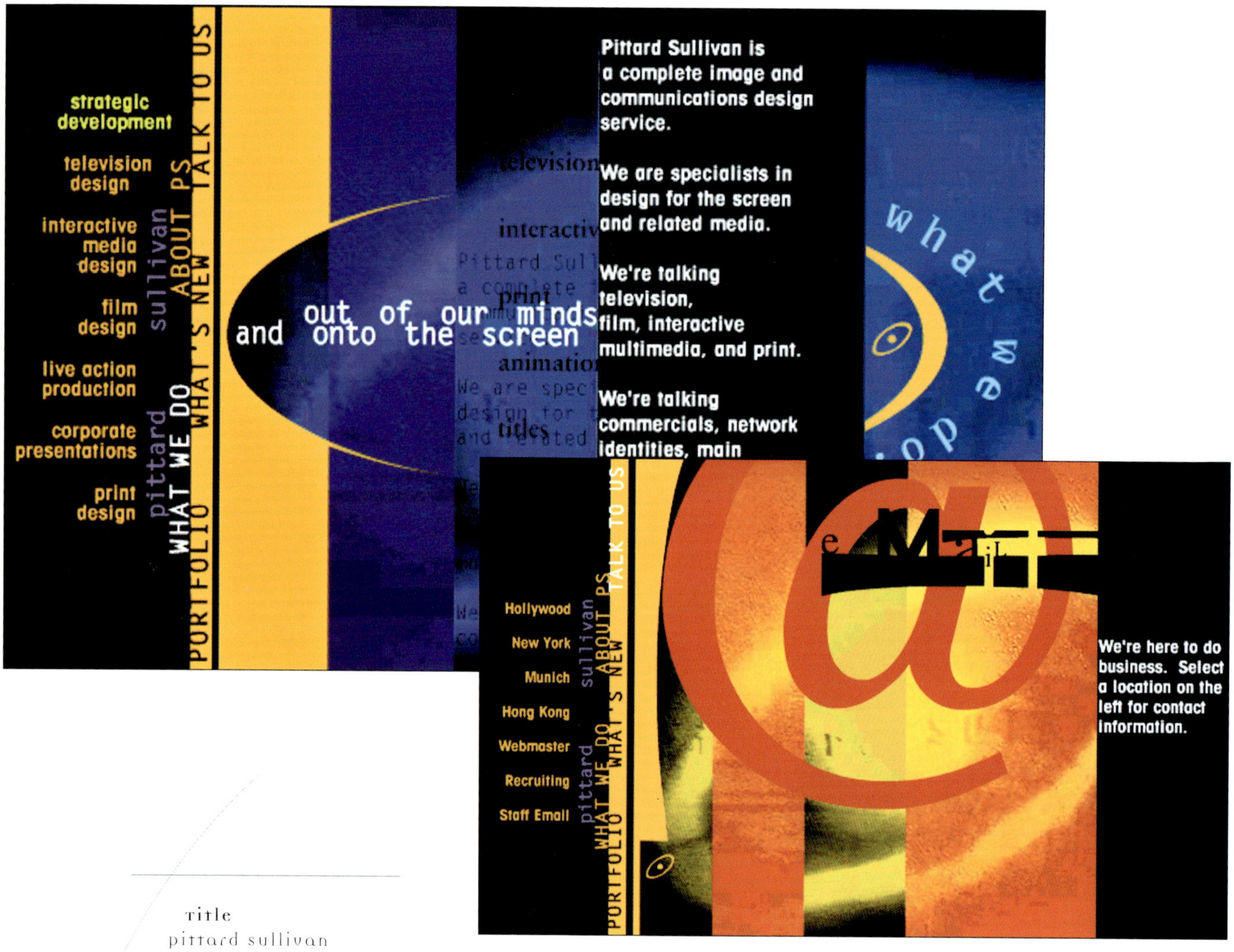

Title
pittard sullivan
URL
http://www.pittardsullivan.com/
Design Firm
pittard sullivan
Designers
Aaron King, Soo Chyun, Ron Romero
Programmers
Bryan Keeling, Marvin Price

Many Web sites direct visitors the way cities direct cars: via a series of icons and symbols. The Pittard Sullivan site, however, directs visitors like a tour guide. Here, text links are not an alternative navigation system, they are the primary methods of getting around. Since the site relies on text for its visual design as well, getting around is pretty easy.

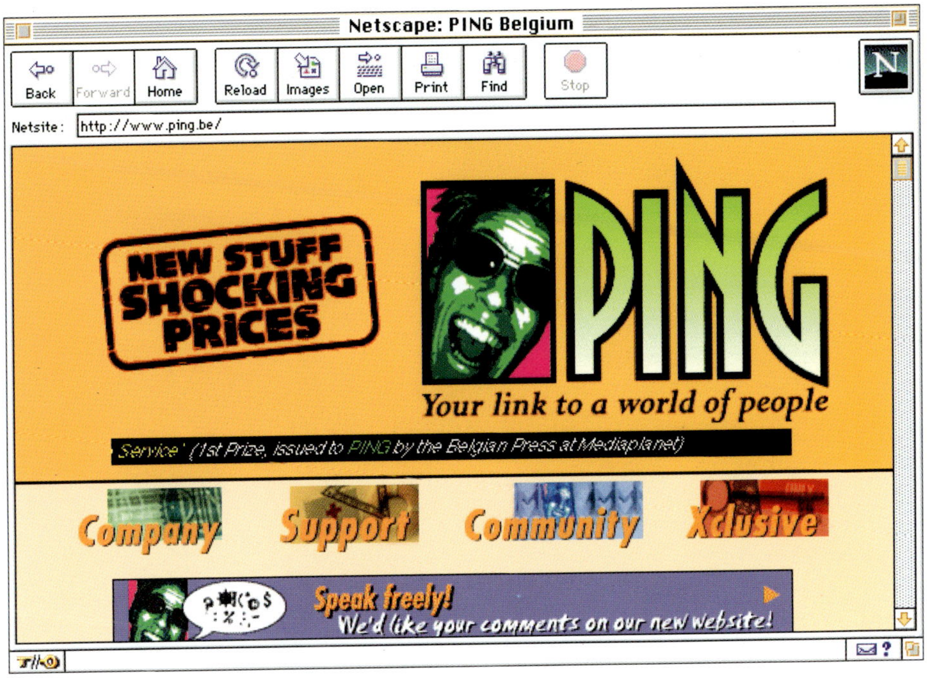

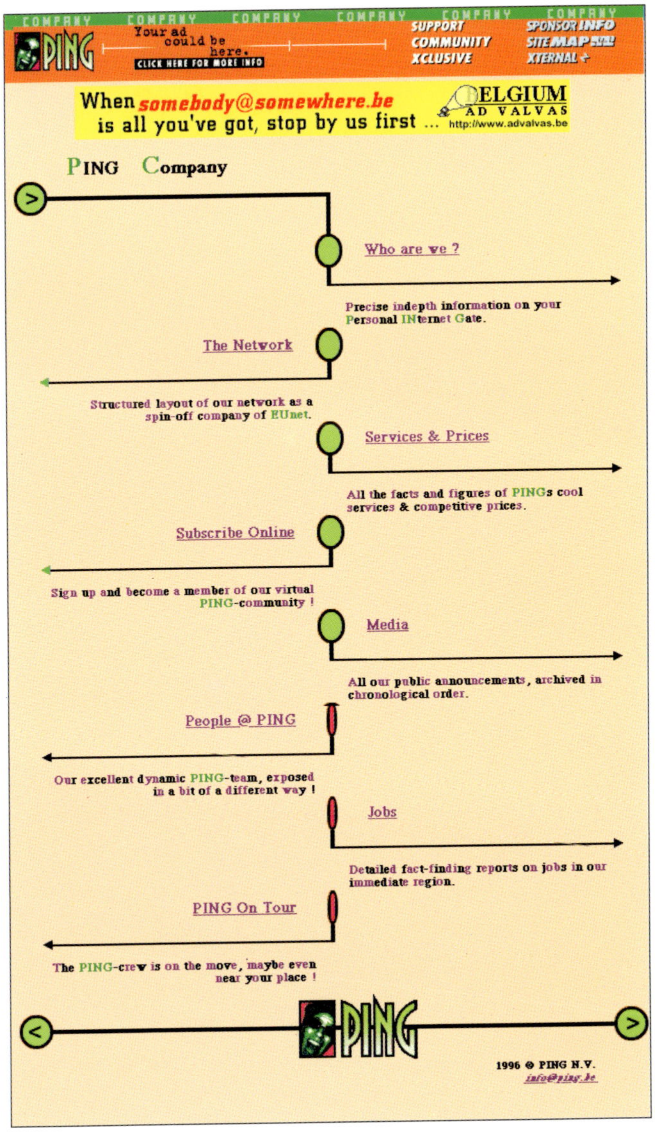

title
PING Belgium
URL
http://www.ping.be/
design firm
PING Belgium
designers
Dirk Zurngenter, Peter Van Hees,
Bernard Gillbrecht
illustrator
Bart De Neve
photographer
Peter Van Hees
programmers
Mark Van Hamme, Peter Van Hees,
Marchteet Garrels

One of the main difficulties in site navigation is expressing many directions in a compressed, easy-to-understand format. The designers at Ping chose to use frames to build trees of subdirectories that are always on screen; going back a level does not require reloading and redrawing a page.

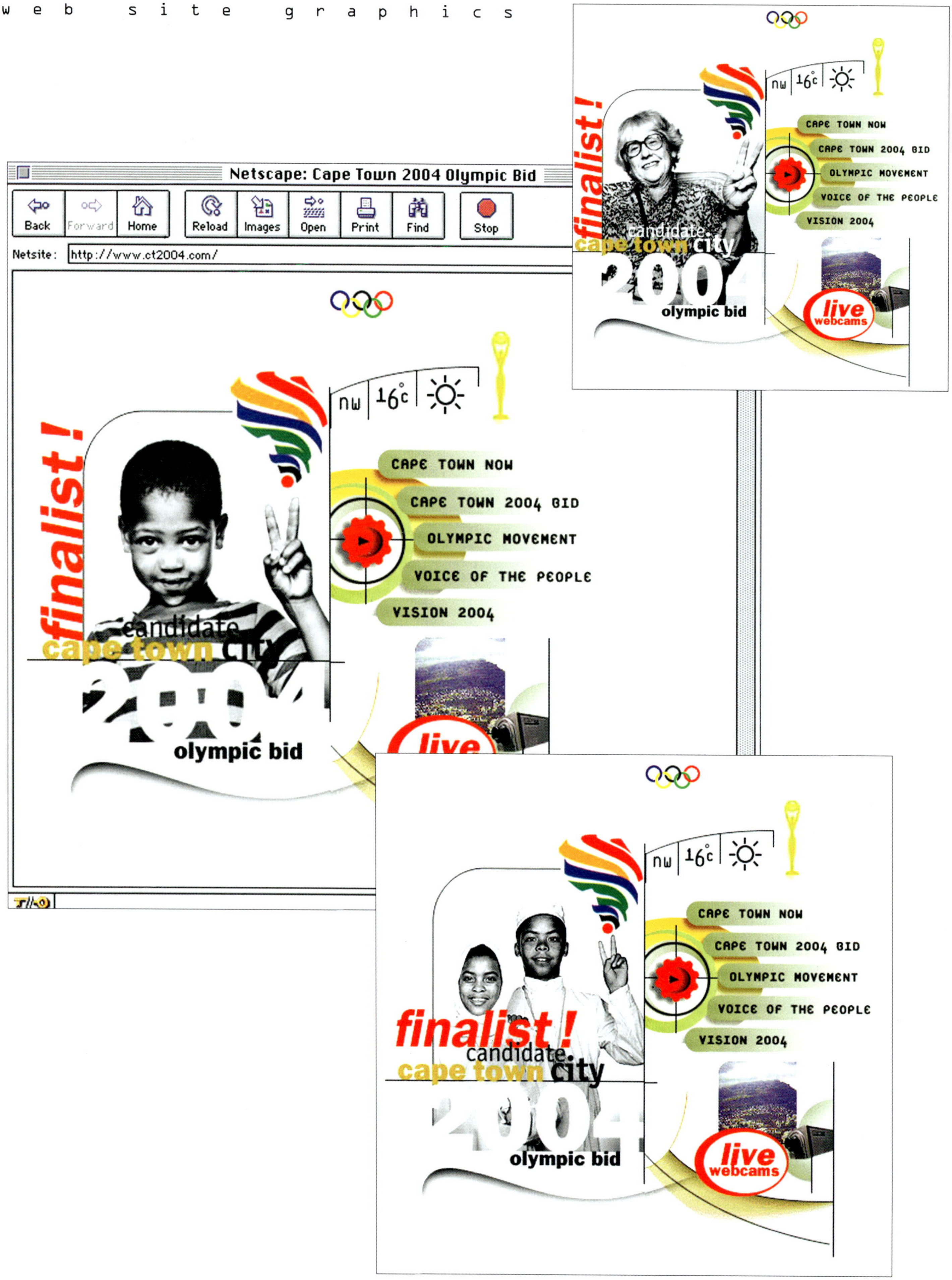

Netscape: Cape Town 2004 Olympic Bid
Back
Forward
Home
Reload
Images
Open
Print
Find
Stop
Netsite:
http://www.ct2004.com/
finalist !
candidate
cape town city
2004
olympic bid
nw
16°c
CAPE TOWN NOW
CAPE TOWN 2004 BID
OLYMPIC MOVEMENT
VOICE OF THE PEOPLE
VISION 2004
live
webcams

title

Internet Underground Music Archive

URL

http://www.iuma.com/

designers

Brandee Selck, David Beach

programmer

Jeff Patterson

Although it can be tempting to devise new and intricate navigation methods, sometimes you just need a few links to do the trick. To spice things up a bit, the IUMA designers chose to create a number of different button bars that reflect the character of a particular page's content. Changing the look is easy—if you use the same file names for the new images, you may not have to adjust each page's HTML code.

title

Cape Town 2004

URL

http://www/oct2004.com/

design firm

Electric Ocean

designer/illustrator

Nicholas Wittenberg

programmer

Stephen Garratt

In its bid to secure Cape Town as the home of the 2004 Olympics, the designers managed to pack a great deal of information into a small space by using a circular navigation system keyed-in by a knob similar to one found on a household stove. Using JavaScript, the selections are highlighted when the arrow on the knob points at the correct direction.

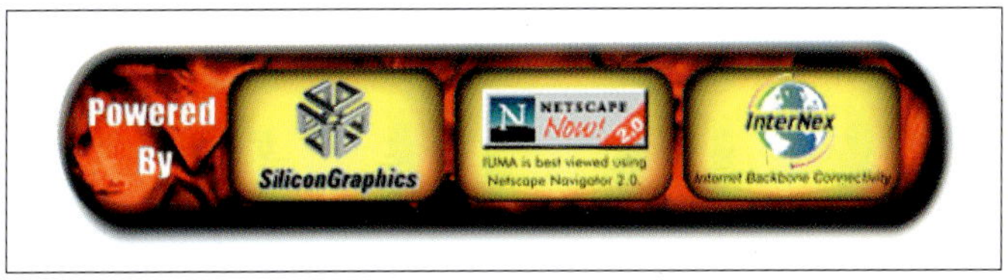

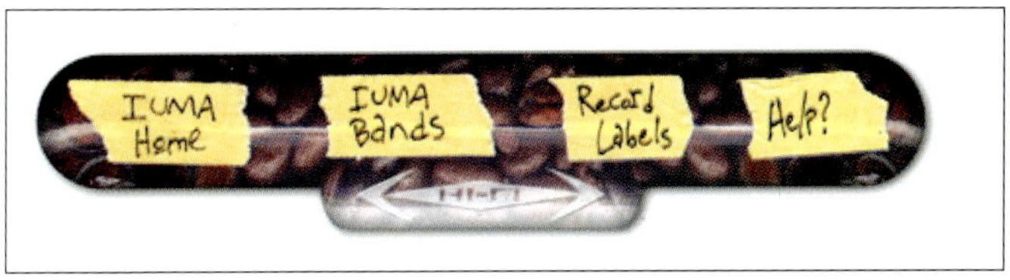

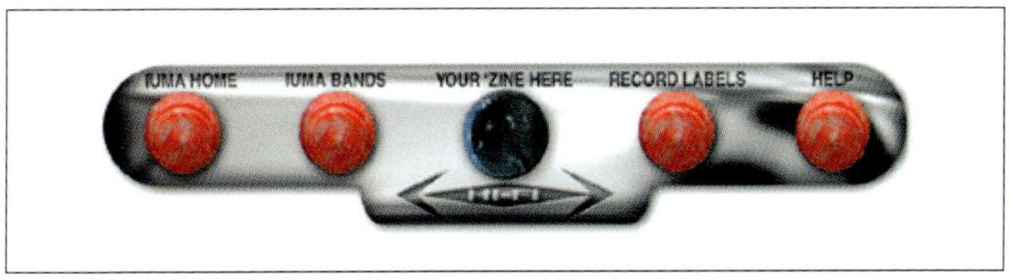

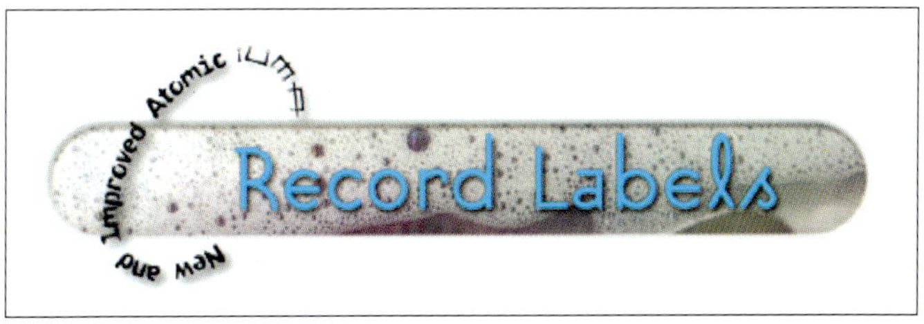

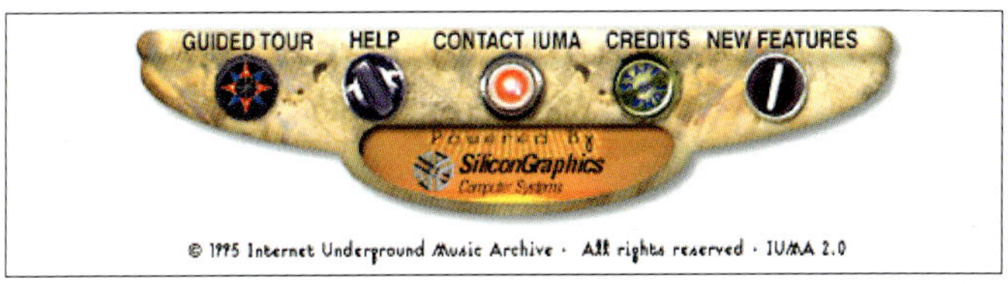

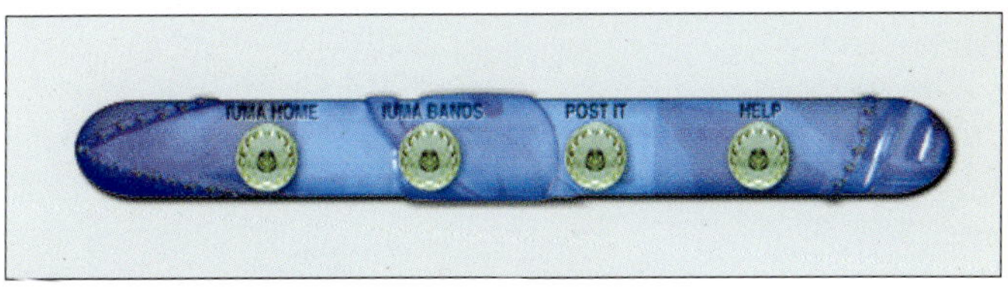

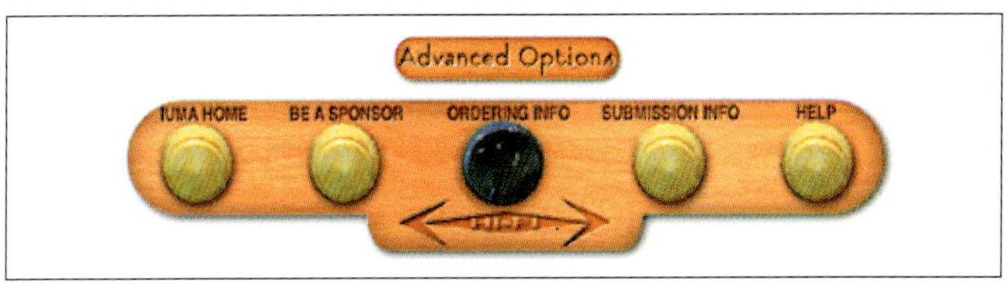

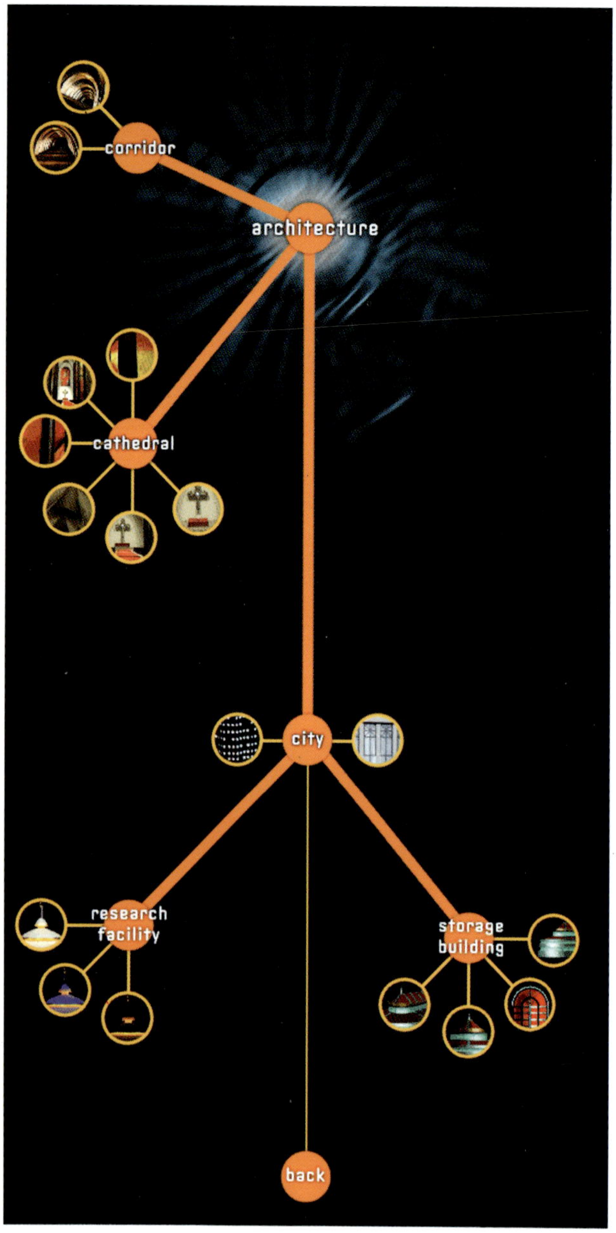

Title
Kjetil Vatne Graphics + Design
URL
http://www.prodat.no/personer/kjetil_vatne/
Design Firm
Kjetil Vatne Graphics + Design
Designer
Kjetil Vatne

Another circular navigation system, this exploration of a designer's skills and achievements is simple to understand and uses half the space that a traditional list-based navigation would use. A straightforward site map groups the main sections in pods, which makes it easier for the visitor to tell where he is located.

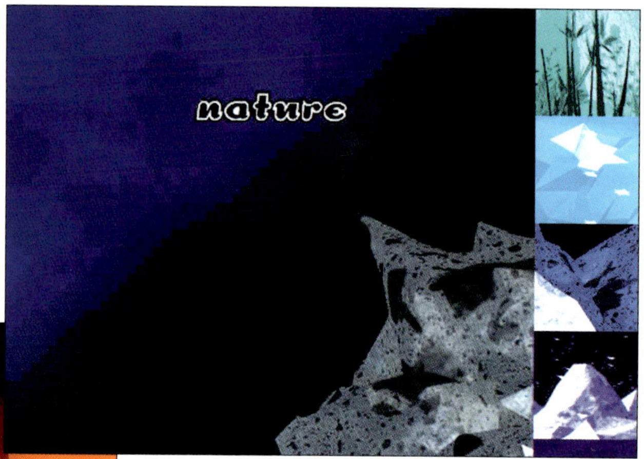

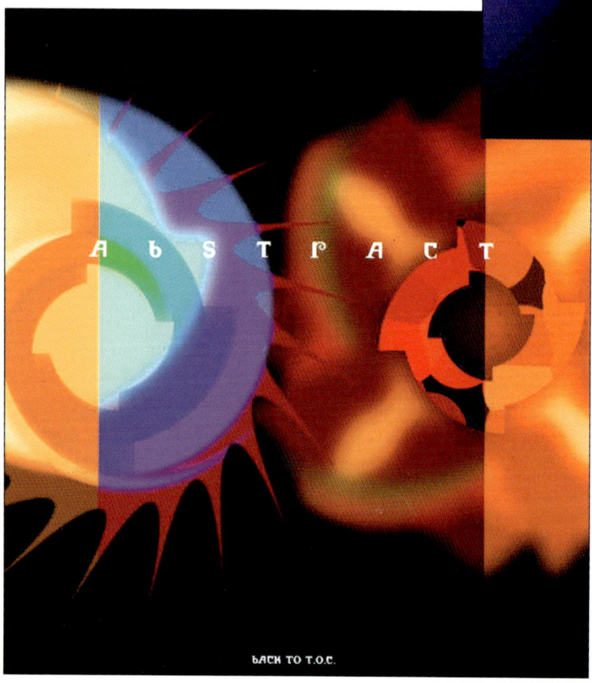

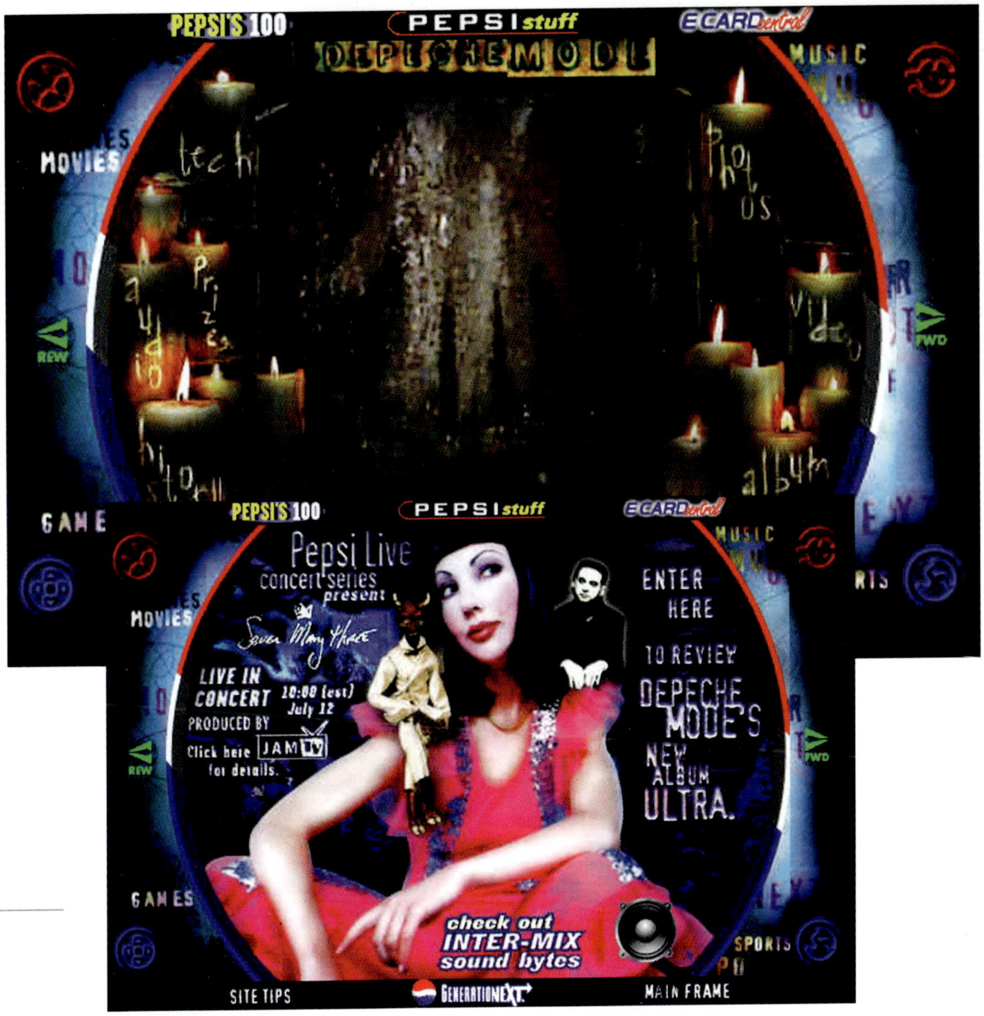

Title
pepsi world
URL
http://www.pepsi.com/
design firm
DDB Interactive
designers
chris Hess, Frances Ko, Mike gonzales, Tricia Elliot
photographer
jill green
programmers
Thomas Jeffry, shelley shay, sal Torneo

List-style and circular navigation styles crop up often on the Web, but it's fairly unusual to find four-corner navigation. The Pepsi World site, which has to incorporate Web sites from other designers in its main "viewer" window, keeps its own set of links at each corner of the screen: easily accessible, yet out of the way.

Title
Qaswa Shockwave Hub
URL
http://www.qaswa.com/shock.html
Design Firm
Qaswa Communications
Designer
Ammon Haggerty

The circular navigation of the Qaswa Shockwave Hub makes it easy to quickly see where each option will lead to, but the designers added another helpful element. When the cursor passes over an icon, the banners above and below the hub give more information about the current selection.

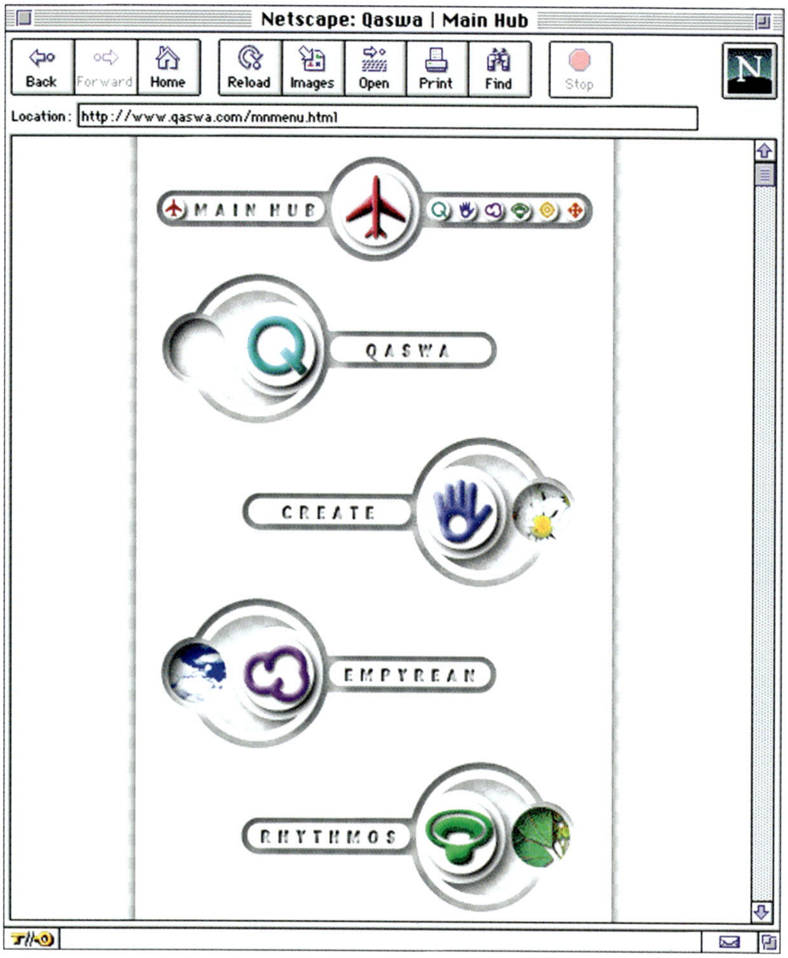

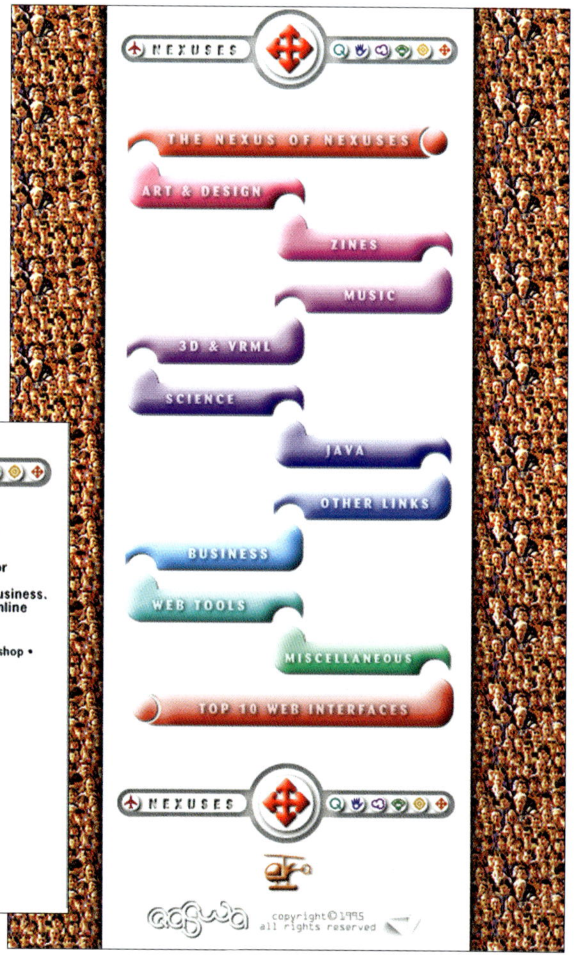

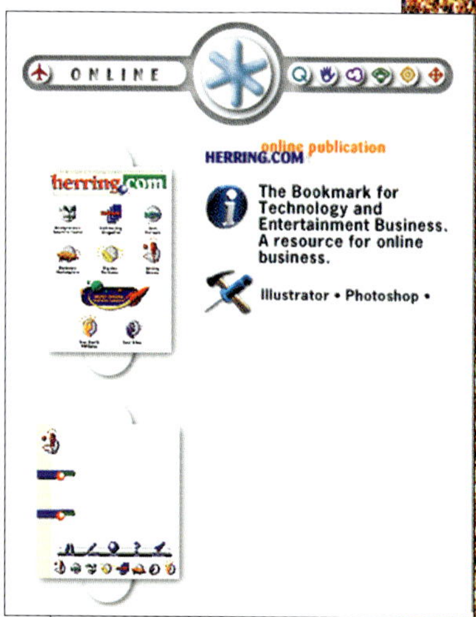

Title
core77
URL
http://www.core77.com/
Designers
Eric Ludlum,
Stuart Constantine

Sometimes it's hard enough dealing with one tree of links, but what about when you have two or more? The Core77 site covers industrial-design issues, but also provides resources such as articles, employment resources, and more. The solution for tackling it all was this combination of circular and hierarchical navigation systems.

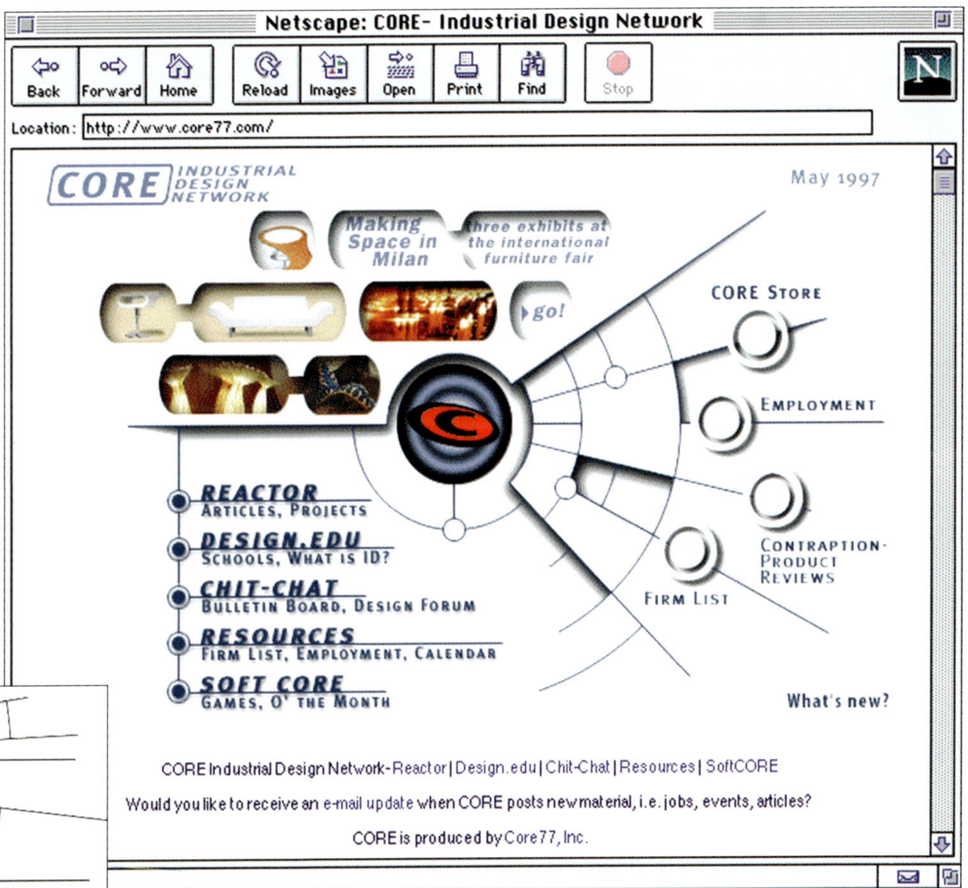

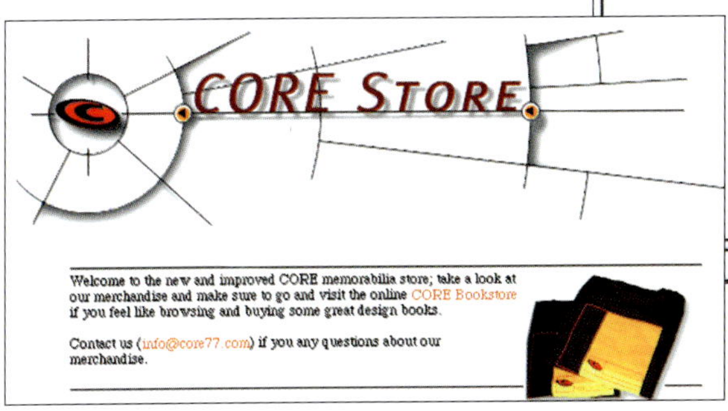

Title
women's wire
URL
http://www.women.com/
Design firm
Lisa Marie Nielsen Design
Designer
Lisa Marie Nielsen

If you reduce the placement of links on this page to their text-only essentials, the result would not be very exciting. As presented here, however, the numbered, colored sections are given identity without succumbing to the desire to fashion a navigation system around the site's content. Yes, sometimes simple is better.

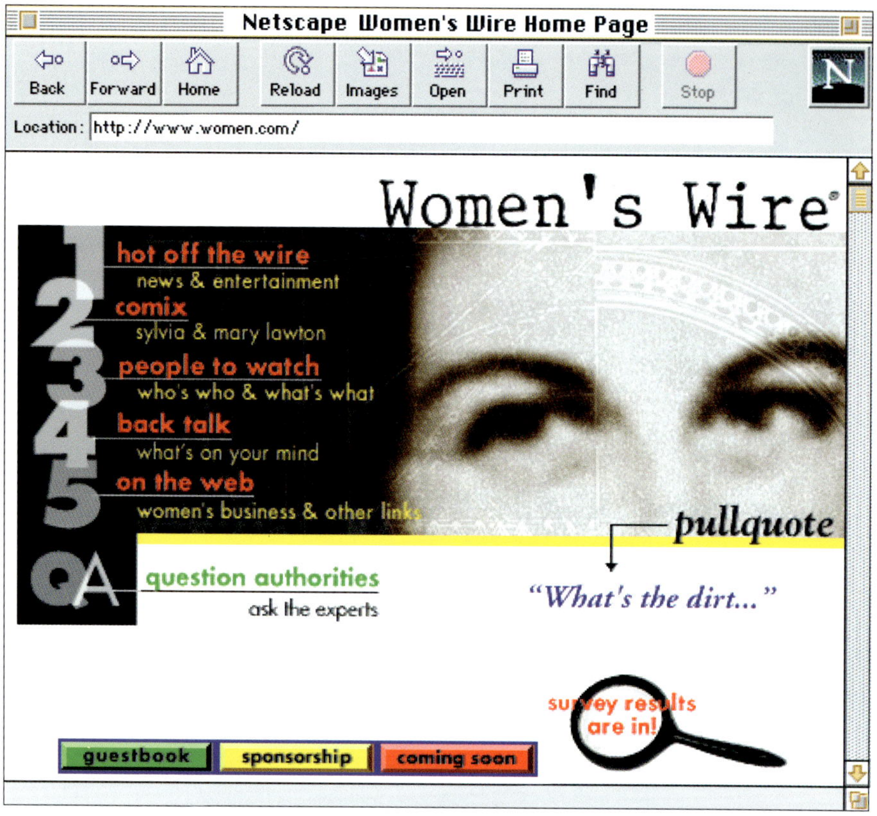

Title
eyescream interactive, inc.
URL
http://www.eyescream.com/
Design firm
eyescream interactive, inc.
Designer
Mark Grimes
Icon Illustrator
Jeffrey Zeldman
Programmer
Eyescream Staff
Authoring platform
PC

A very spare site, it holds interest by emphasizing small type, used for navigation, in the middle of large, color fields. Moving around the site is simple enough: Click a section name, and a new color scheme and large type in the upper right identifies the location. Click a subcategory, like a staffer's name, and the type in the upper right becomes a link to take you back to that section's main page.

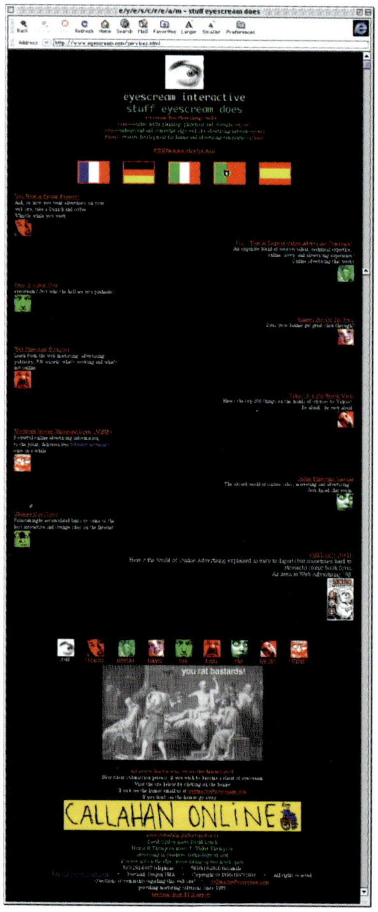

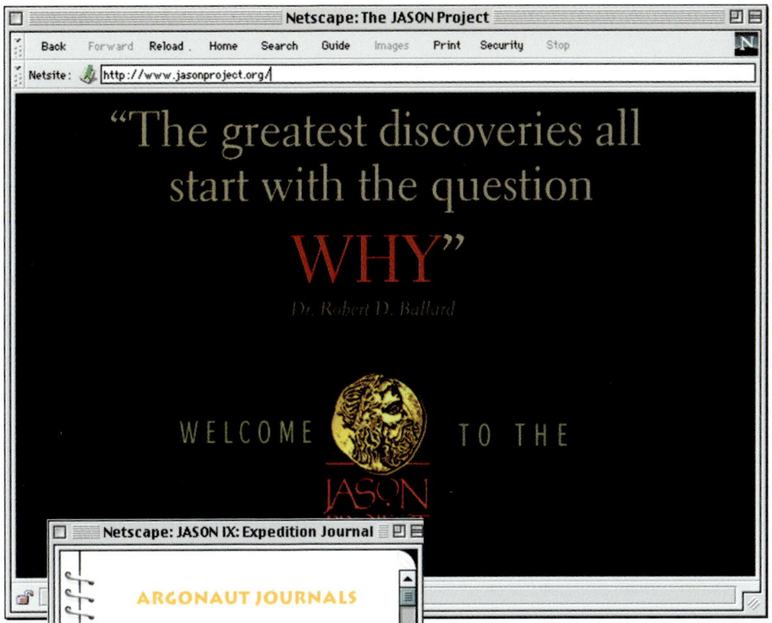

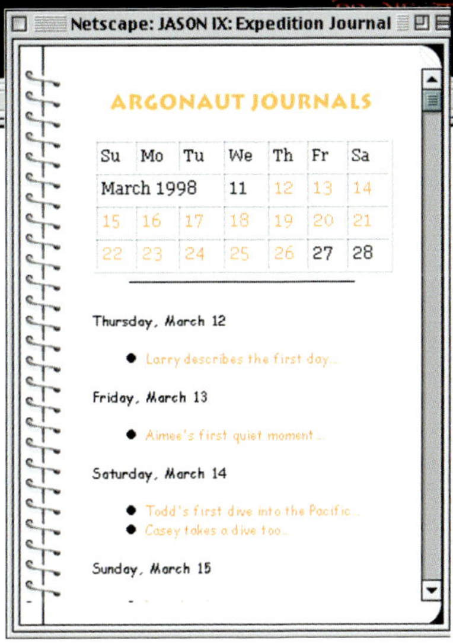

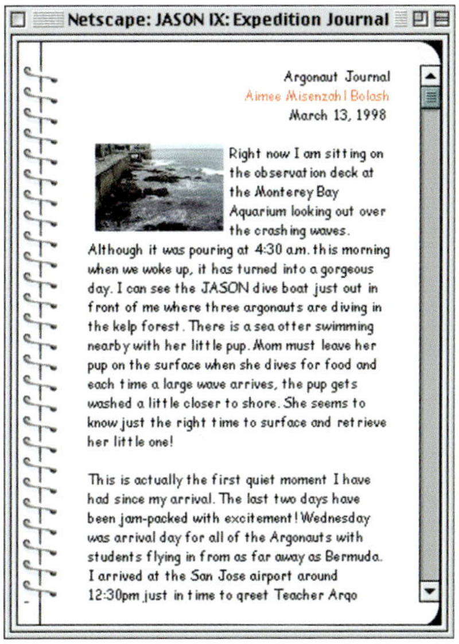

Title
JASON project
URL
http://www.jasonproject.org/expedition.html
Design Firm
Stolte Design (home page); JASON Foundation (all other pages)
Designers/Illustrators/Programmers
Christian Stolte (home page); Patrick Shea, Todd Viola (all other pages)
Authoring Platform
PC (all except home page)

One indicator of a good Web-navigation system is how well the directional elements are integrated within the site. Many creative layouts become diluted when the designer tosses a list of text links in a corner of the page. Here, the links are discretely placed around the page's borders. Moving your mouse to one reveals JavaScript rollovers that visually enhance each link with pictures that blend into the background's swelling ocean imagery.

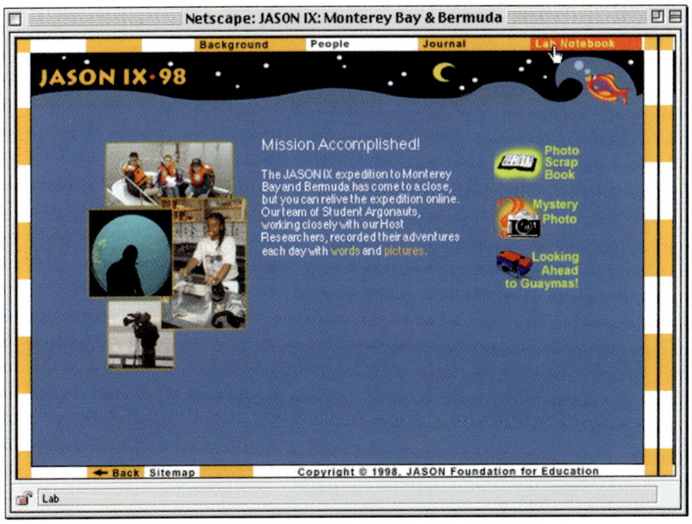

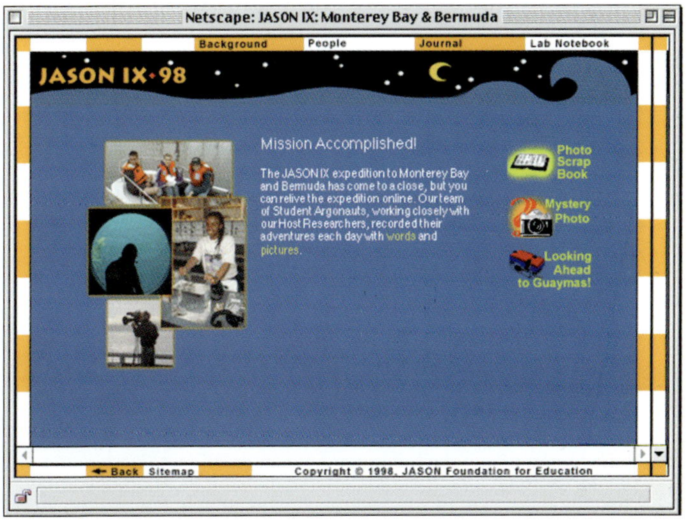

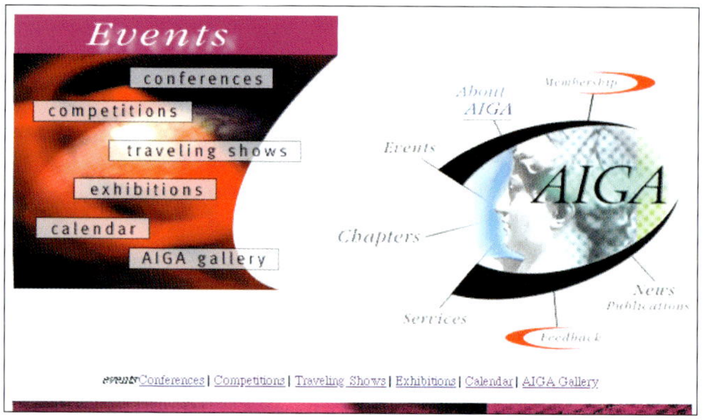

title
AIGA (American Institute of Graphic Arts)
URL
http://www.aiga.org/
design firm
graffito/Active8
designers
Tim Thompson, Jon Majerik
photographer
Morton Jackson
programmer
Jon Majerik

You do not have to rely on just one navigation method. Without hogging precious screen real estate, this site uses both circular and block navigation to quickly point visitors deep into the site. The slanted elliptical grouping to the right leads to main categories, while the blocked-out subsection titles are displayed to the left.

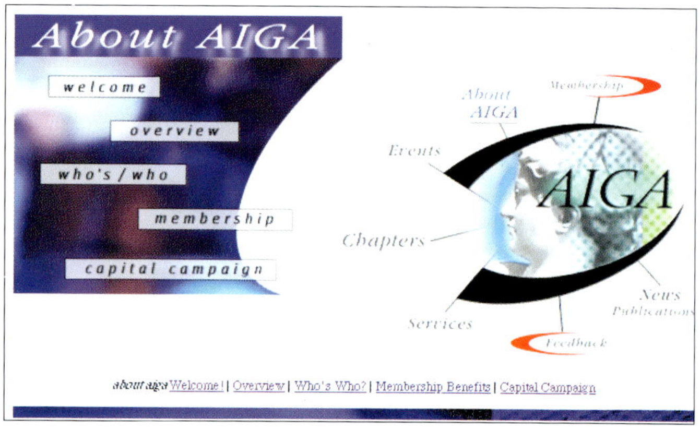

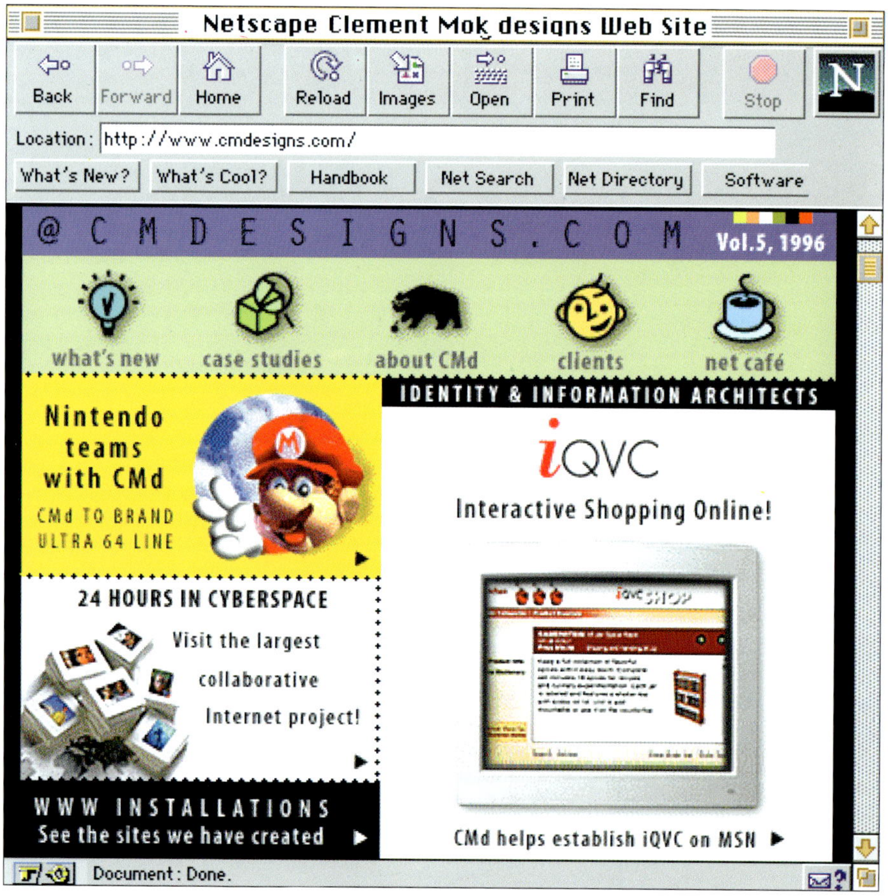

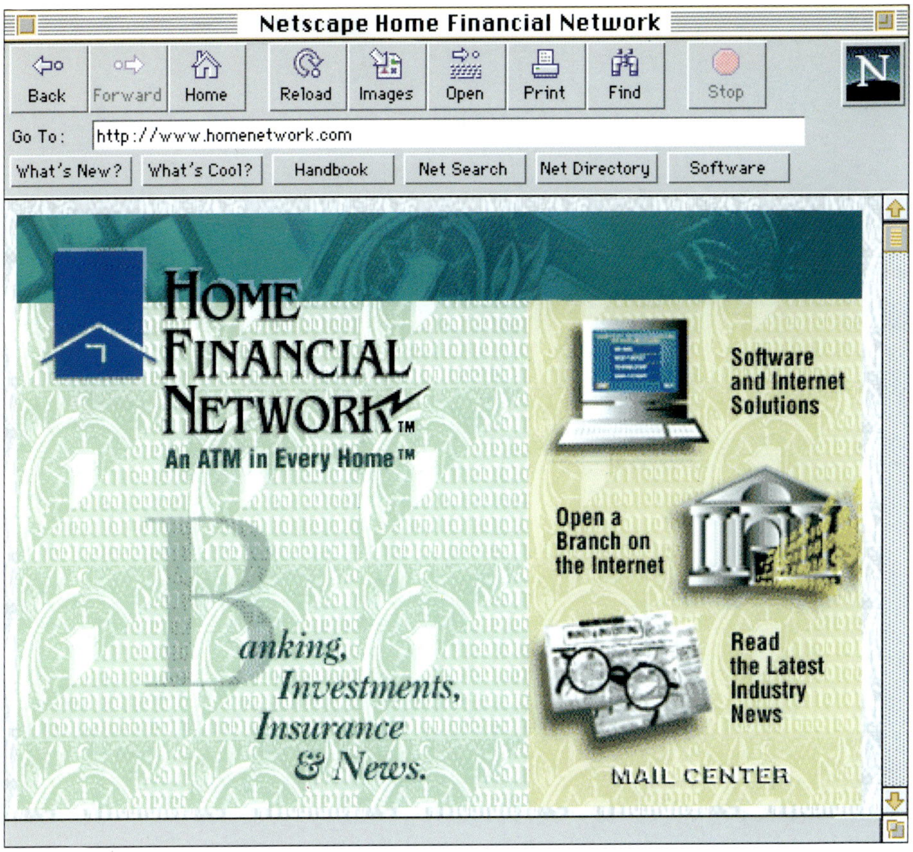

Title
Home Financial Network
URL
http://www.homenetwork.com/
Design firm
The Design Office Inc.
Designers
Yung Beck, Dave Green, Andrea Flamini, Joe Feigenbaum
Programmer
Andrea Flamini

Although this site primarily uses money-related icons to denote features and sections, the beauty of its navigation lies in its consistent use of repeating visual elements. All pages include the top bar that varies only in color, retaining its image and placement.

Title
Studio Archetype (formerly Clement Mok designs)
URL
http://www.cmdesigns.com/
Design firm
Studio Archetype
Producer
Sheryl Hampton
Creative director
Clement Mok
Associate creative director
Claire Barry
Illustrator
Andrew Cawrse
Programmers
Mark Anquoe, Michael Clasen, Stephan Bugaj

This flexible site employs a variety of navigational elements. In addition to line-art icons relating to each main section, colors are assigned to the categories, which include offshoot colored frames that break the navigation bar away from the content slightly. The upper-right corner provides an easy, space-conserving set of section links.

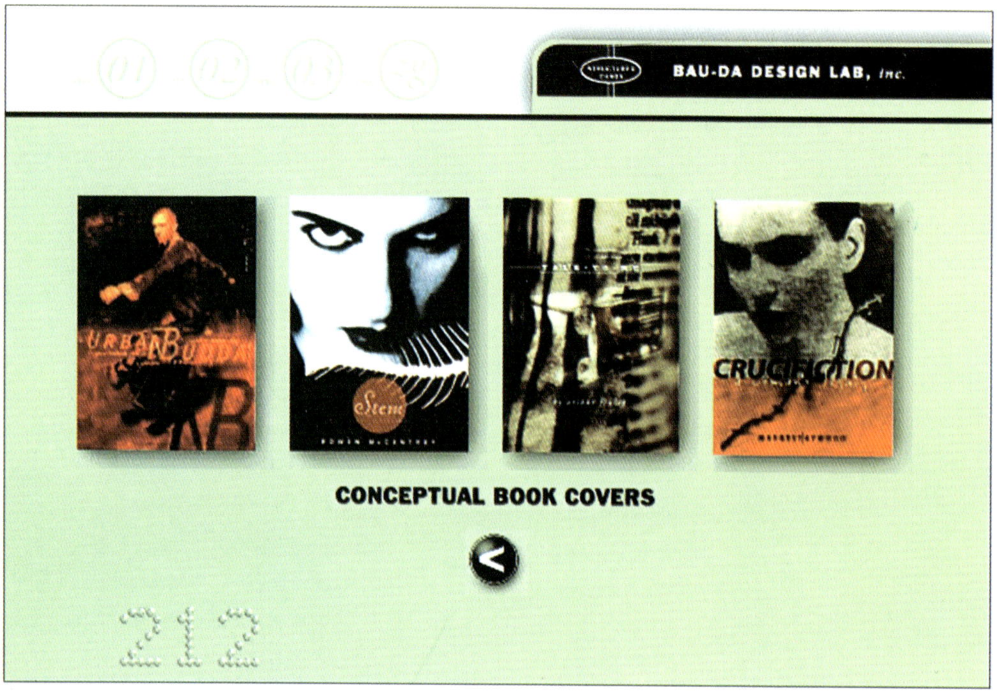

title
Bau-Da Design Lab, Inc.
URL
http://www.bauda.com/
design firm
Bau-Da Design Lab, Inc.
programmers
Eric Brown/Readynetgo
authoring platform
HTML, JavaScript

Why be content with just one set of navigation elements on a given Web page? As you can see here, the site's main page opens with the square buttons on the left, as well as the grayed-out corresponding numbers above. JavaScript rollover effects help to give the reader a sense of where they are in the site.

title
Frank Ford
URL
http://www.frank-ford.com/
designer
Frank Ford

Web design may be a cutting-edge field, but its two-dimensional medium limits it to something one still can't touch. As if reaching out to the viewer, the hand-shaped navigation (and the similarly-shaped portfolio-page graphic resembling a wind-blown inkblot) offers clear navigation using a form familiar to any viewer.

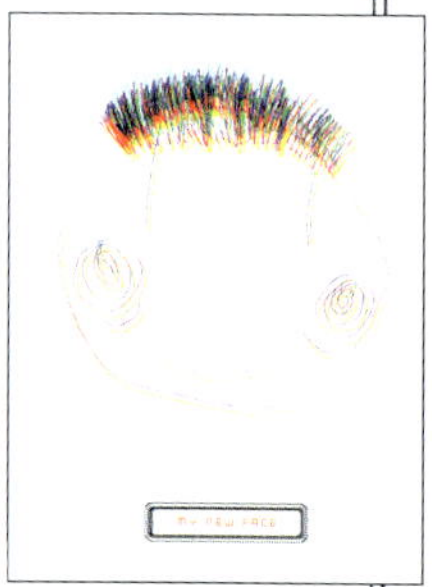

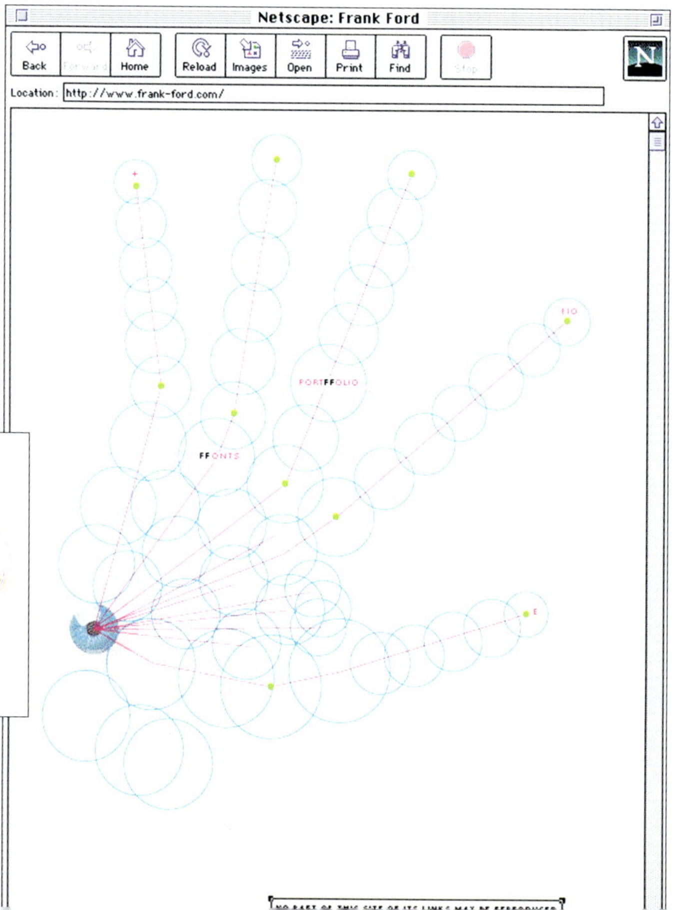

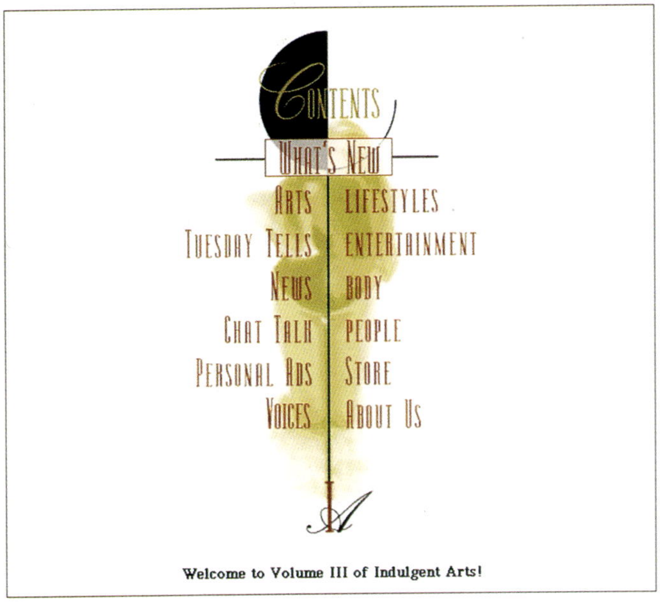

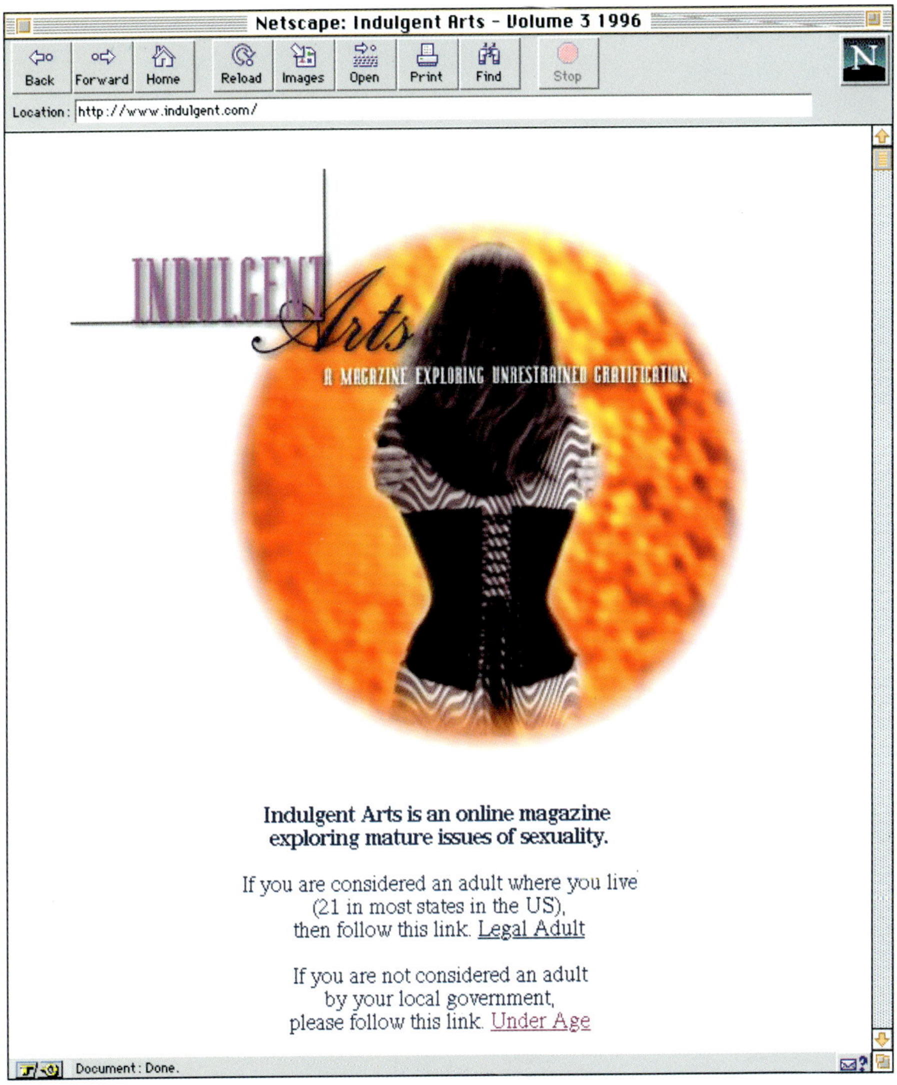

Title
Indulgent Arts Magazine
URL
http://www.indulgent.com/
Design firm
C.A.P.
Designer/Illustrator
Rhonda Anton
Photographer/Programmer
Craig Bramscher

Even without the provocative cover image of a woman's back, the contents page for Indulgent Arts suggests a view of a person's back, with links running up and down the spine. Access to all main areas of the site is expressed in a conservative amount of space, which leaves room for content and breathing room.

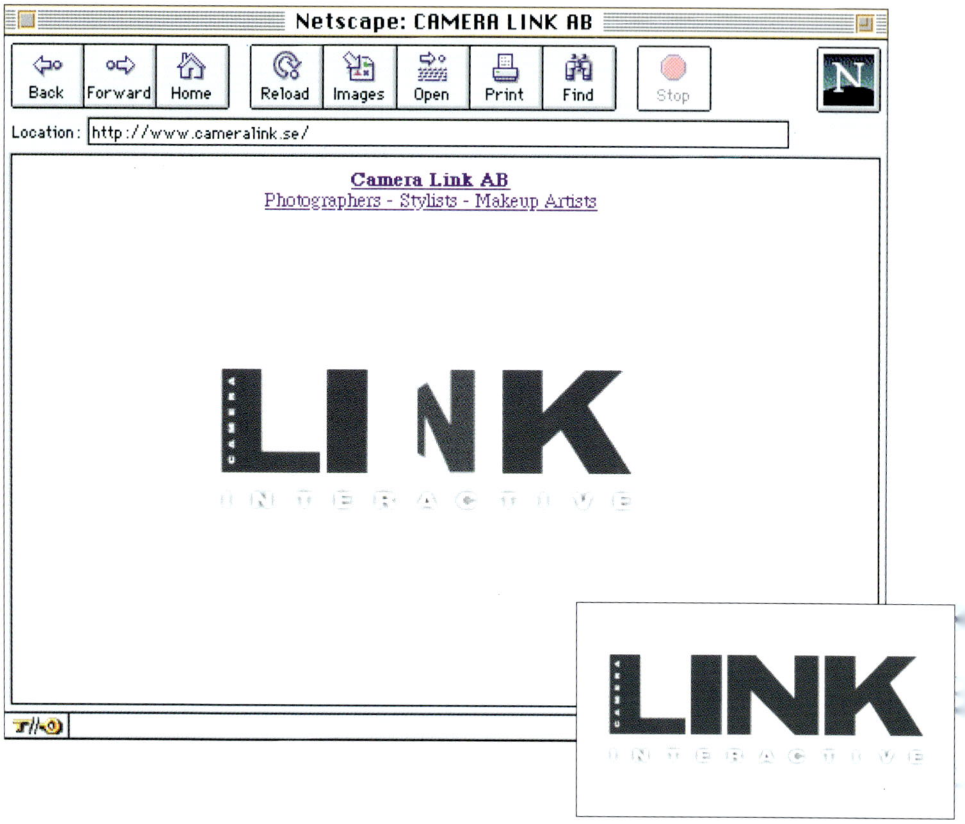

Title
Camera Link AB
URL
http://www.cameralink.se/
Design Firm
Robot
Designer
Raket/Robot
Programmer
Jesper Weissglas

Providing direction to a Web site does not mean that you have to give people "dumb" buttons and still pictures. Real people ask questions and offer advice, which the designers here have emulated.

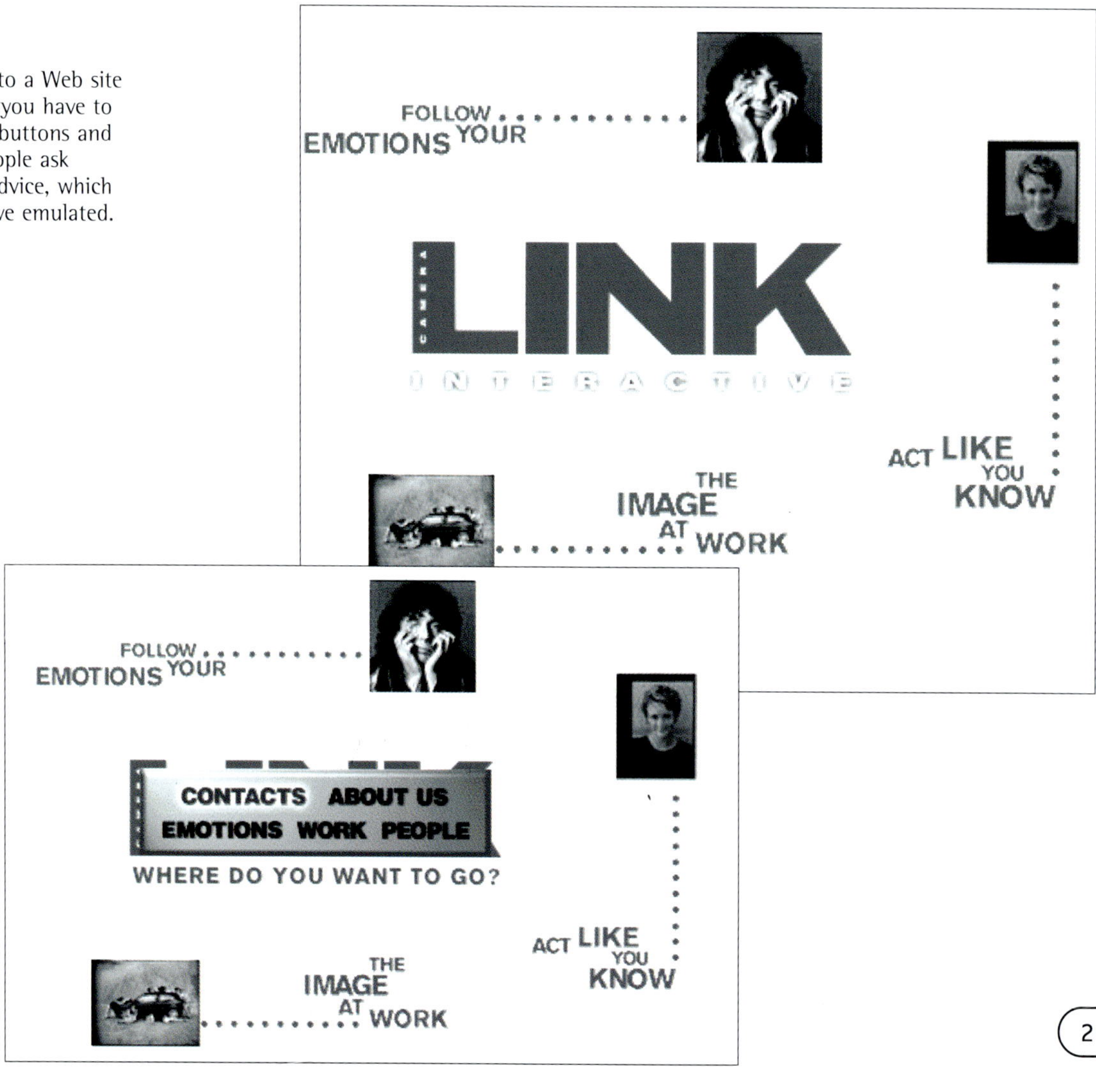

Title
Radio Real World
URL
http://realworld.on.net/
Design firm
Real World Multimedia
Designer/Illustrator/
Photographer/Programmer
York Tillyer
Authoring platform
Mac

Good navigation often means that the viewer must always know where she's headed before committing to a direction. This approach, however, takes away a lot of the fun of exploration. On this site's home page, you're presented only with colored bands (for the text-inclined, positioning one's cursor over a color displays the link's destination at the bottom of the browser window). Consistent use of color quickly makes an initially enigmatic navigation system understandable and familiar.

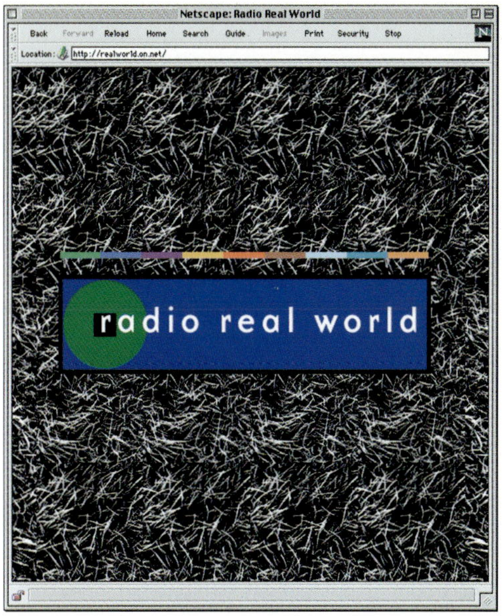

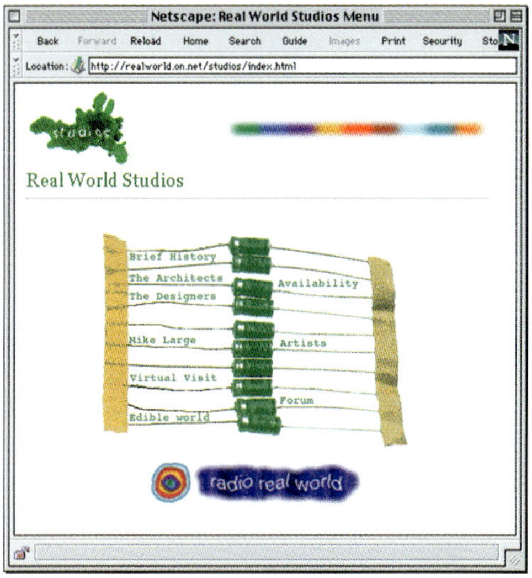

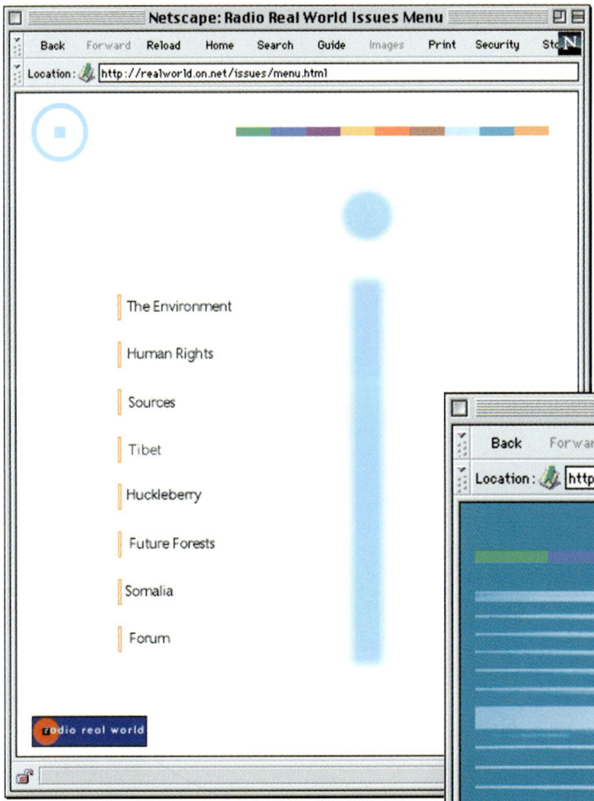

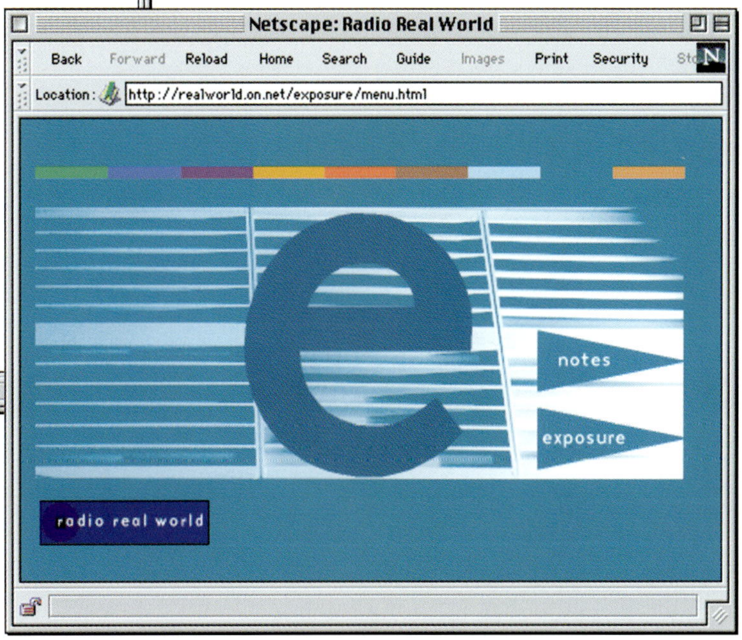

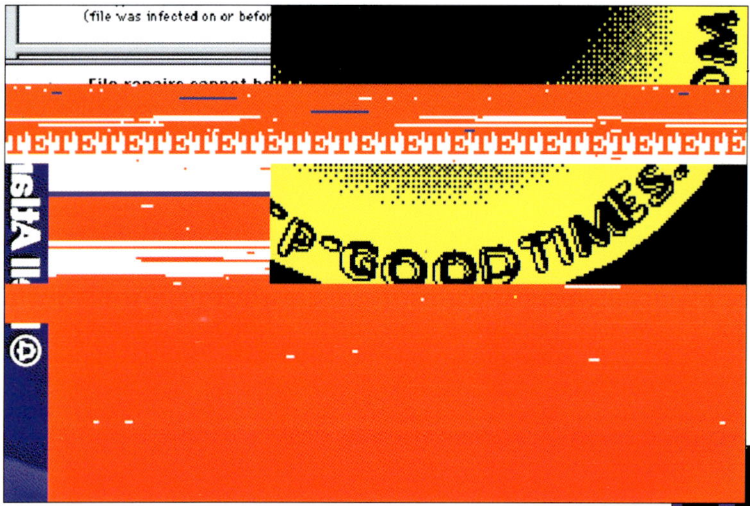

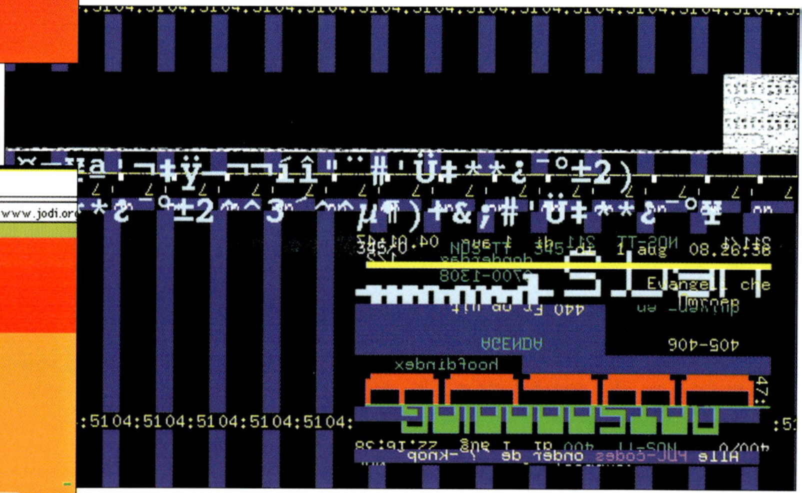

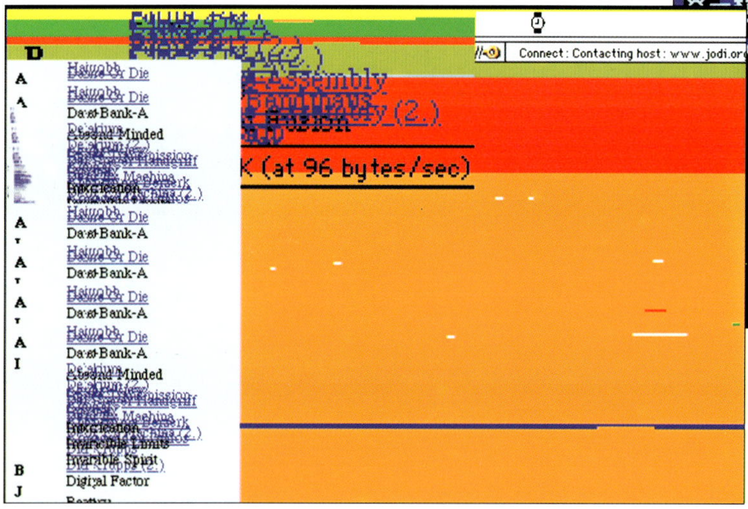

Title
Jodi.org
URL
http://www.jodi.org/
Designers
Joan Heemskerk, Dirk Paesmans

There are times when a visitor wants to stumble onto a new site, then explore it for all it's worth. Then there is Jodi.org, a Web site that seems to throw all the rules about site navigation out the window. Clicking on links (or random URLs) takes you to another aspect of the simulated machine that appears on screen.

Title

Nerve° Magazine

URL

http://www.nervemag.com/

Designer/Illustrator/Programmer

Joey Cavella

Photographer

Walt Chrynwski

Authoring Platform

Mac

Navigation depends on direction, and to establish direction, you need to create a sense of place. The opening page of Nerve° presents a cluttered living room whose objects lead to other parts of the site. What's unique here, though, is the drop-down highlights window shade, which obscures the setting with some context, instead of a list of links off to one side. The animated dangling pull-cord just begs to be clicked.

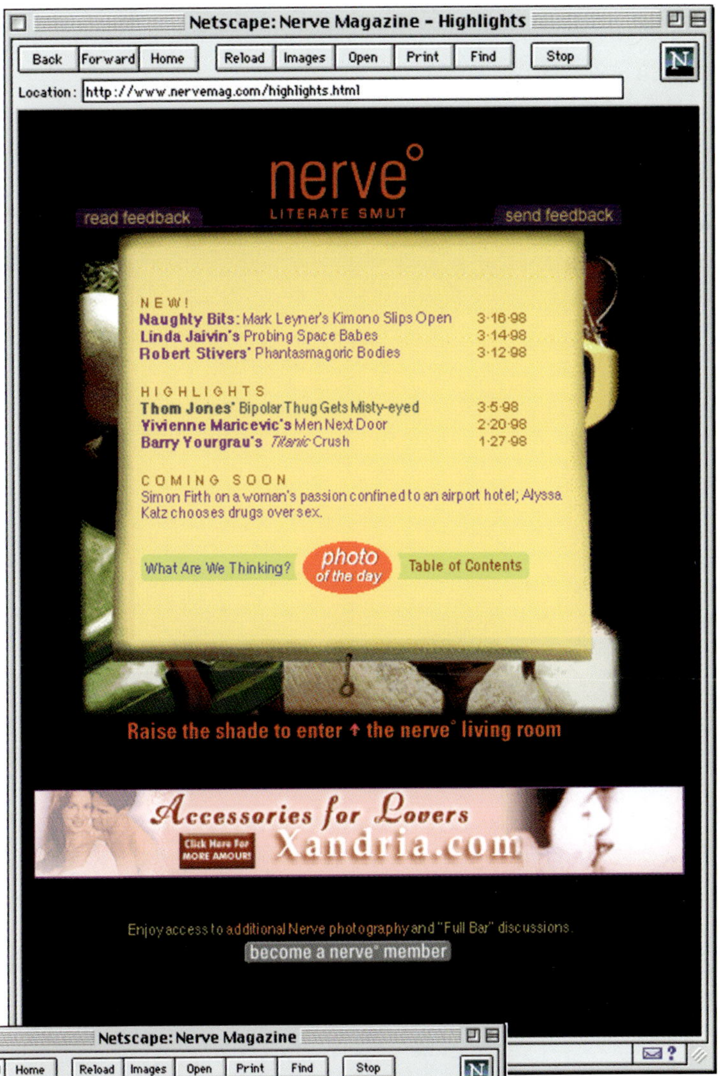

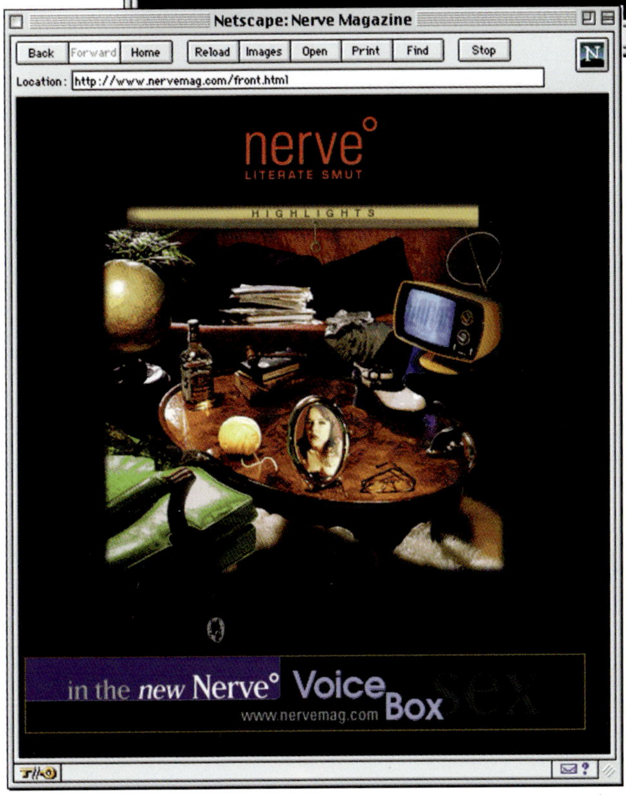

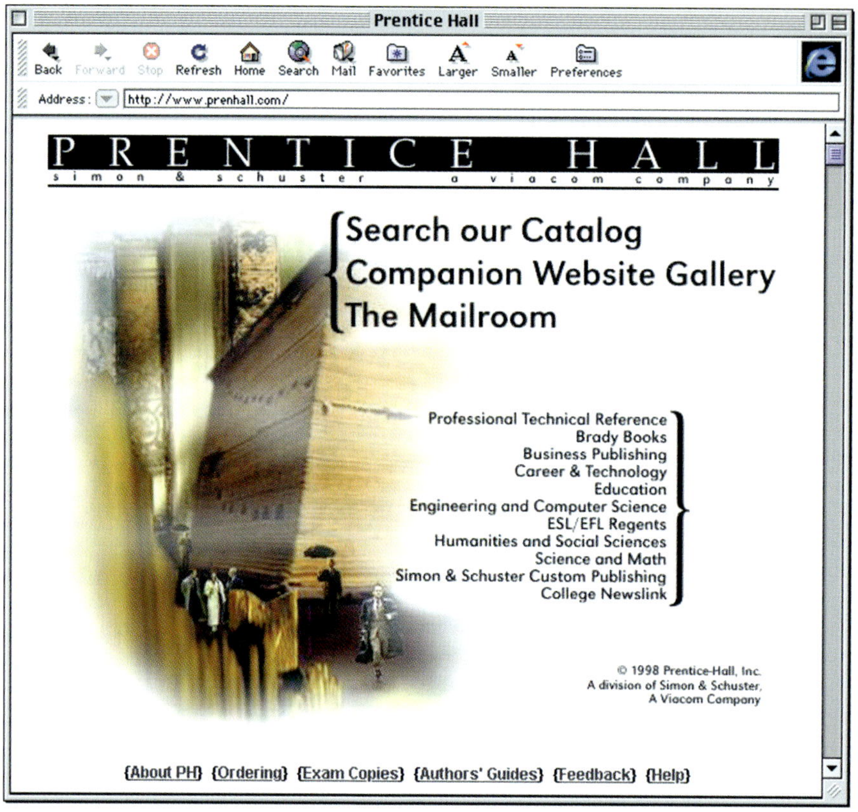

Title
Prentice Hall Higher Education Website
URL
http://www.prenhall.com/
Design Firm
Media Technology Group, Simon & Schuster Higher Education
Designers
Ray Henderson, Daniel Beck
Illustrators
Daniel Beck, Carolyn Wagner
Programmers
Daniel Beck, Paul Pekar, Carolyn Wagner
Authoring Platform
Mac, Unix, PC

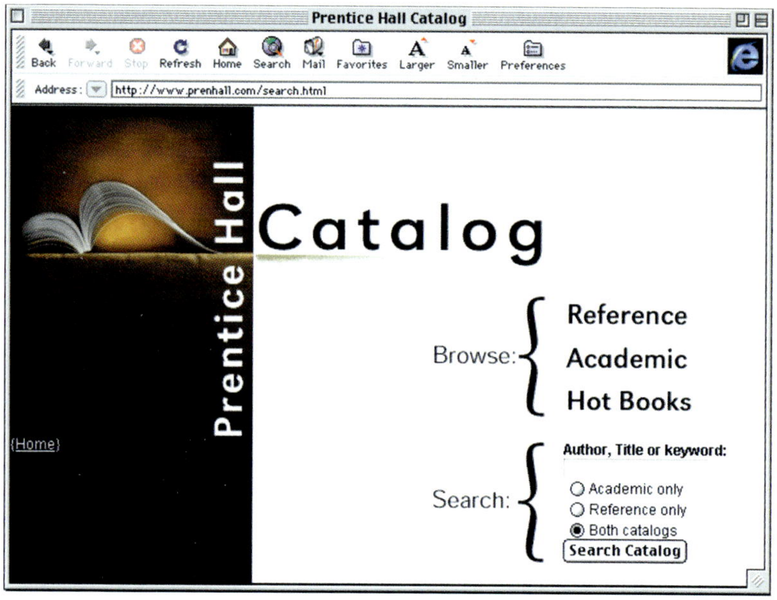

Braces are used as an organizing principle for items in the same category in this site. It helps these items hang together without requiring colors or other visual cues. Larger categories are placed higher on the page and in a larger type size, but it's surprisingly effective to stick a big brace to the left or right as a method of defining categories. This theme is picked up by using braces in text on the bottom navigation bar.

Title

Entropy8

URL

http://www.entropy8.com/

Design Firm

Entropy8 Digital Arts

Designer

Auriea Harvey

Programmers

Auriea Harvey, Marc Antony Vose

Authoring Platform

Mac, PC

With such a graphics-intensive site as this one, screen real estate is a valuable commodity. To provide navigation without distraction, a separate floating window pops up containing gateways to the rest of the site.

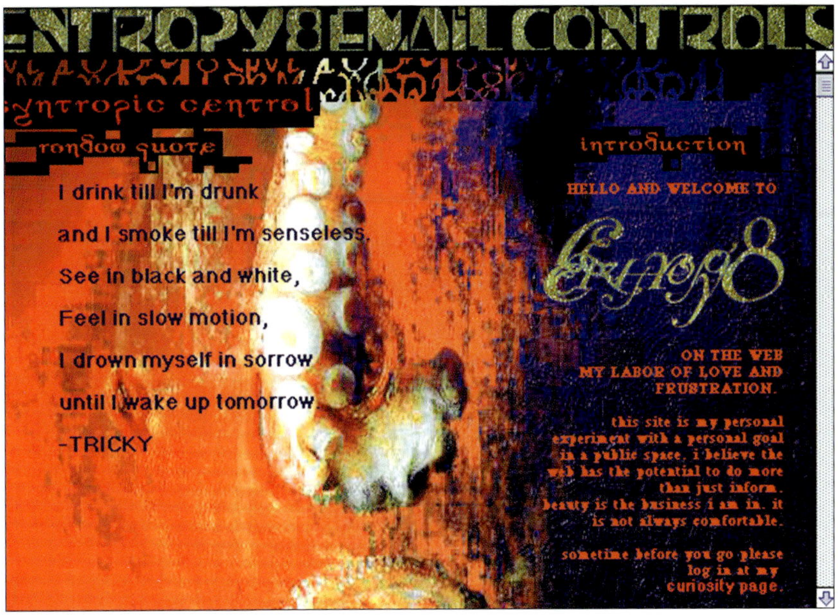

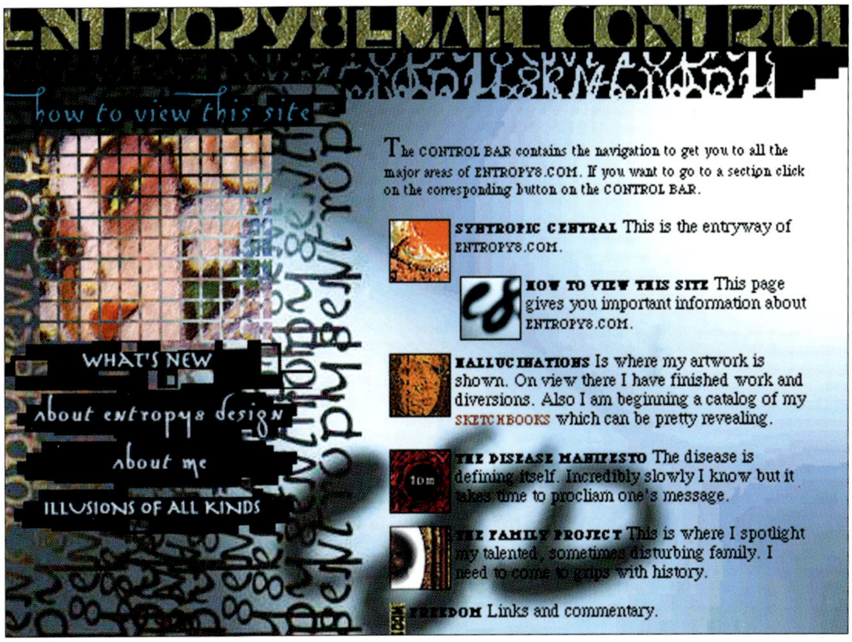

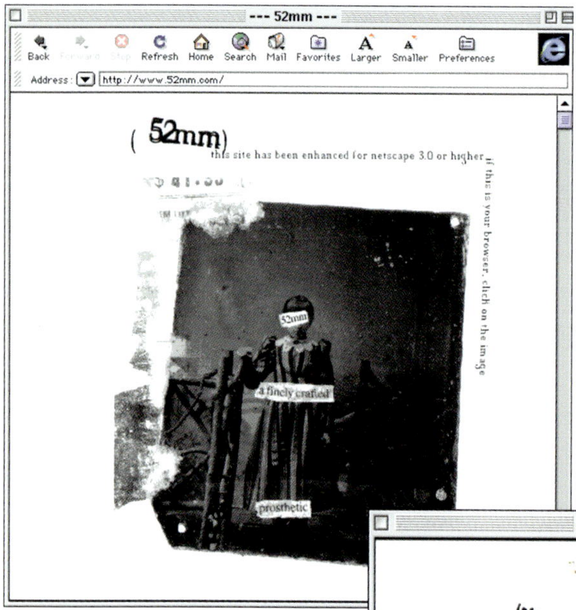

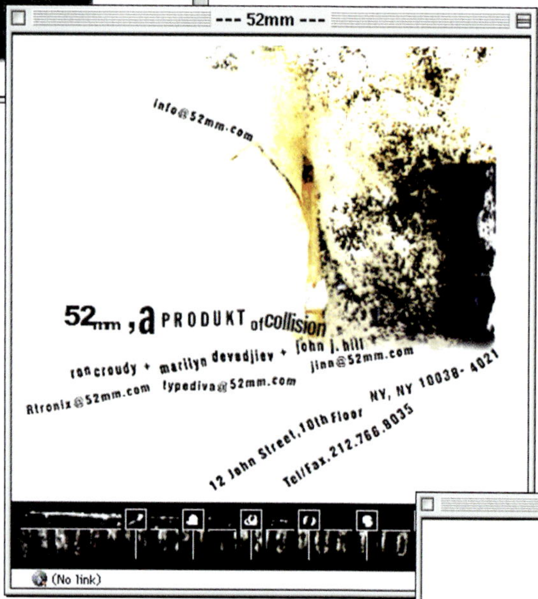

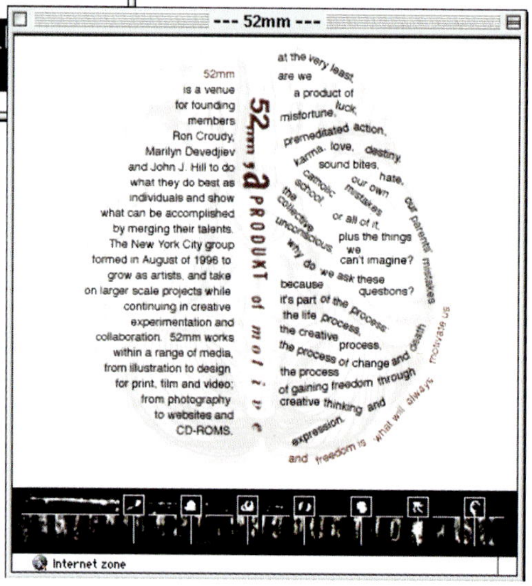

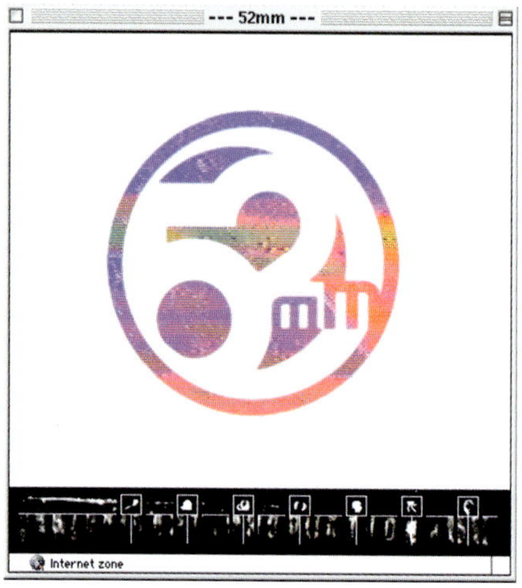

Title
52mm
URL
http://www.52mm.com/
Design Firm
52mm
Designers/Illustrators
John J. Hill, Marilyn Devedjiev, Ron Croudy
Photographers
John J. Hill, Marilyn Devedjiev
Programmer
John J. Hill
Authoring Platform
Mac

52mm doesn't ask you to resize a window; they control the vertical and the horizontal, and their entire site (absent the home page) fits into the space they define. The site is deep, but the only navigational tool is a bar at the bottom. Nonetheless, clicking the links is rewarding: With some exploration, you find comic books, logo experiments, and a deep portfolio of work in many media.

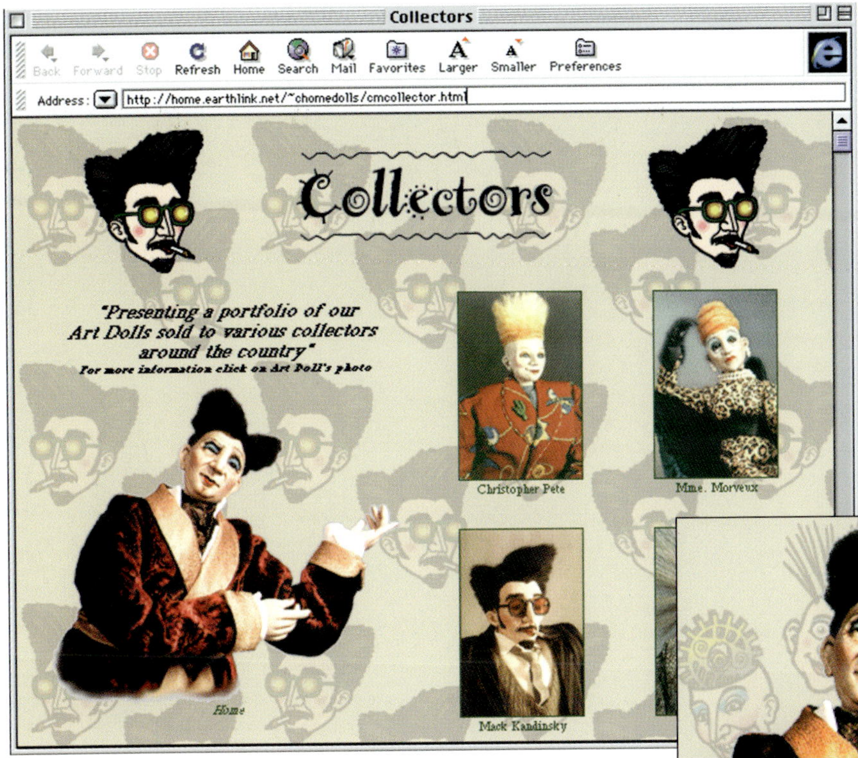

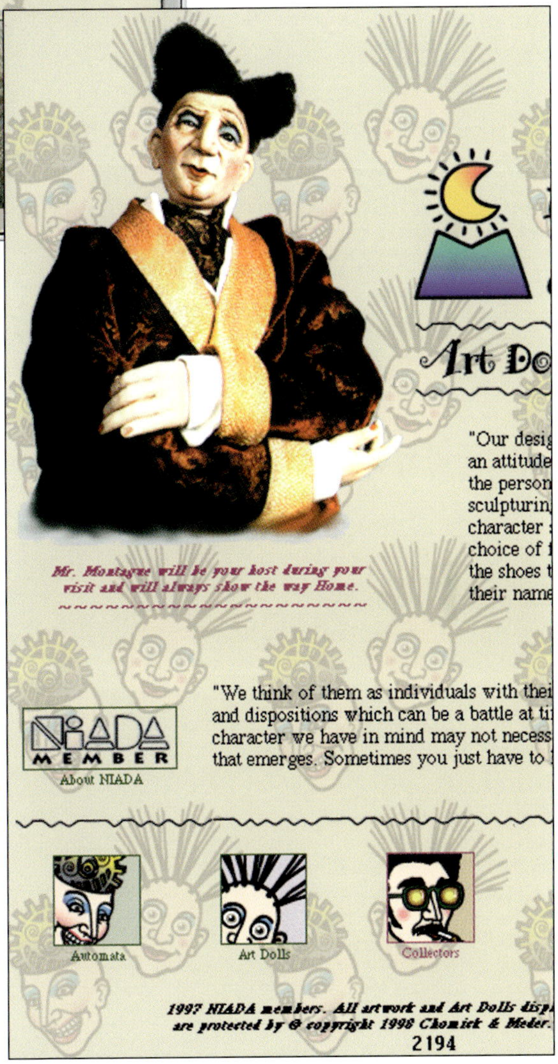

Title
We Make Art Dolls and Automata
URL
http://home.earthlink.net/~chomedolls/cmcollector.html
Designer/Illustrator/Photographer
Chris Chomick
Authoring platform
PC

A site designed for collectors uses graphics to enhance the presentation of the expensive dolls they are marketing. Graphics that abstract the dolls' faces are used for some of the navigation (notably the bottom navigation bar), while the breezy, red-velvet-jacketed host always brings the user back to the home page.

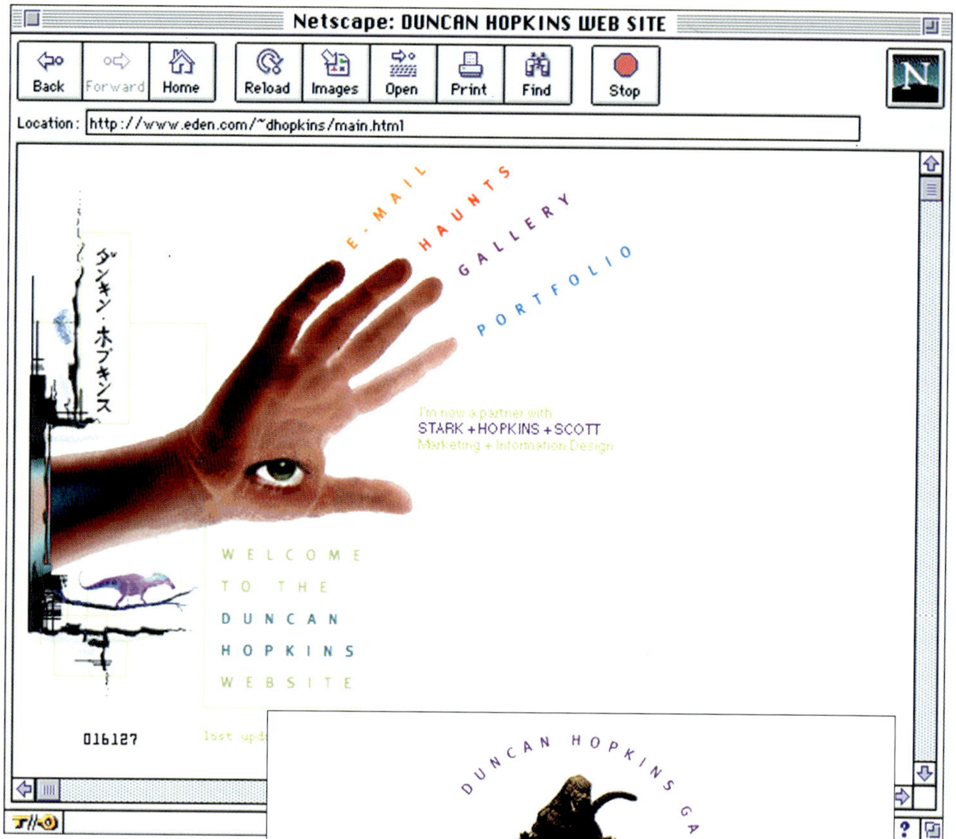

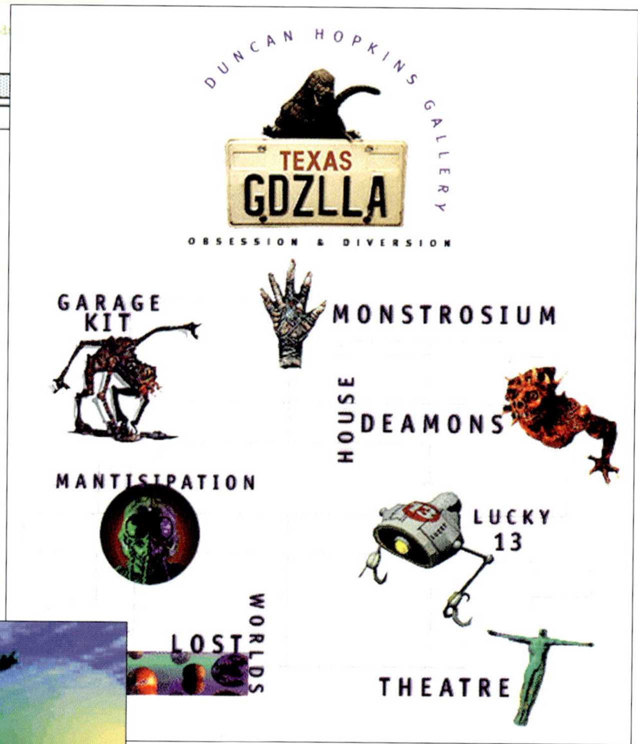

Title
Duncan Hopkins web site and gallery
URL
http://www.syndeticdesign.com/dhopkins/main.html
Design firm
Syndetic Design
Designer
Duncan Hopkins

Around the world, the best method for getting and receiving directions is by pointing. Duncan Hopkin's is outstretched hand of links takes that familiar gesture and uses it as a clean, slightly skewed way of pointing to the inside of his site. You'll notice, however, that on subsequent pages he uses whichever navigation method is most appropriate (or clever) for each section.

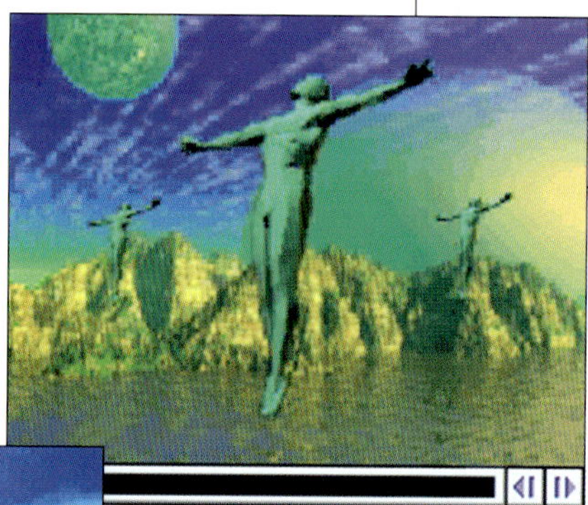

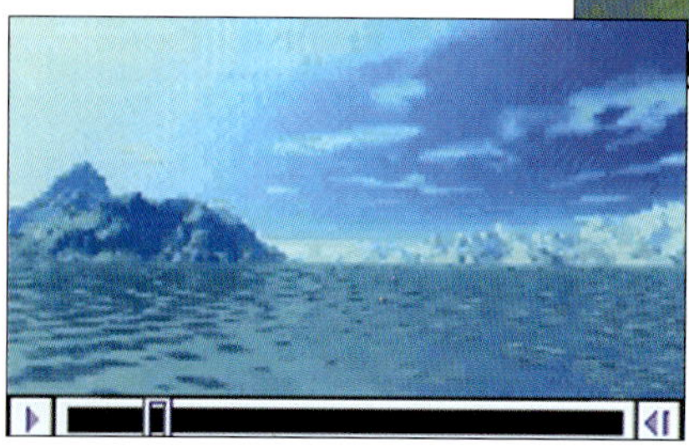

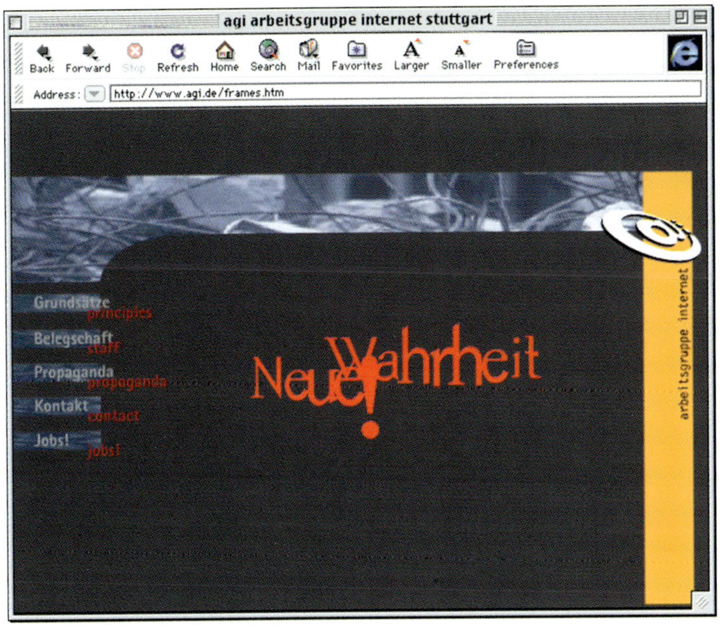

title
agi business media productions gmbh
URL
http://www.agi.de/frames.htm
design firm
agi business media productions
designers
Tim Ruetz, Bernd Fessler, Arwin Hambasic
photographer
Thomas Möller
programmers
agi technology—Gaylord Aulke, Oliver Schmid, Tim Ruetz
authoring platform
Mac, PC

The site makes best use of its bilingual nature (German and English) by incorporating both languages into all the navigation, rather than having two separate sites. The English sits slightly subsidiary to the German in placement, tone, and size, but this does not affect your ability to read it or move about. A rollover on the left navigation bar lights up the white German and red English text. In the Grundsätze (principles) area, hovering over large numbers in circles lights up the numbers and displays that particular principle without the need to click. Every page features a Zurück (back) button to return.

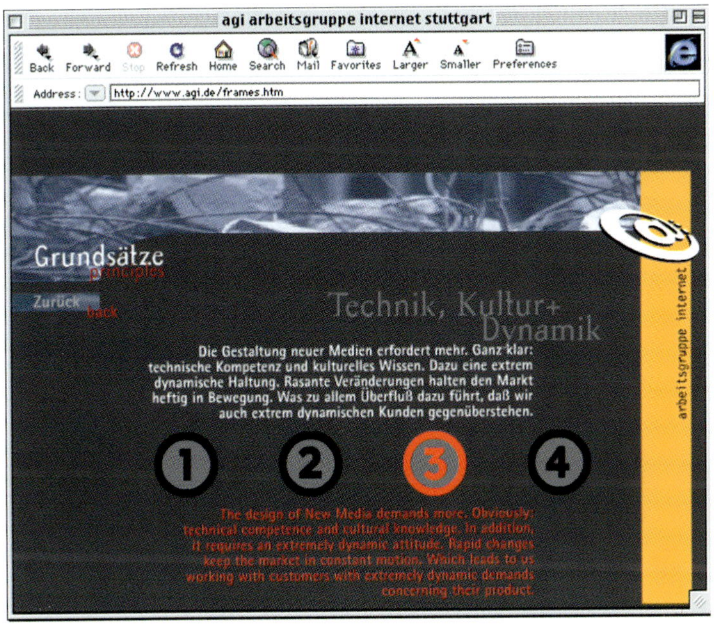

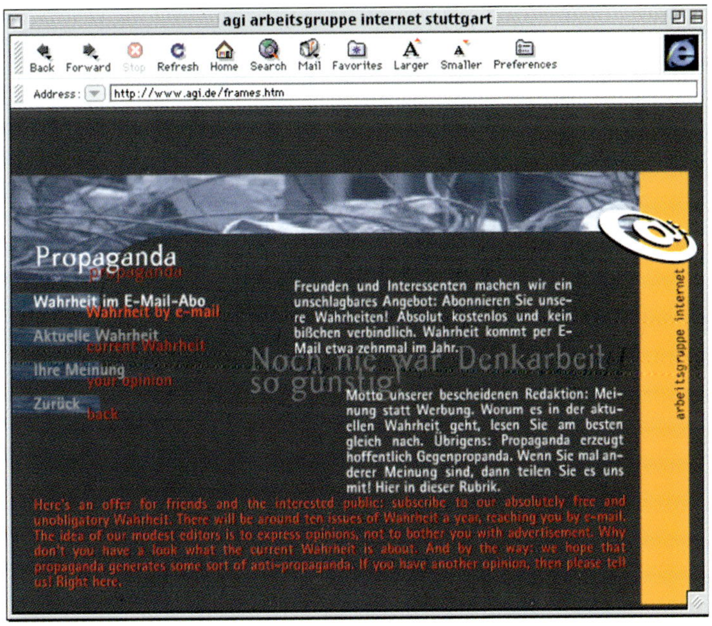

Title
Brett Snyder: personal portfolio
URL
http://www.brettnet.com/
Designer/Illustrator/Programmer
Brett Snyder

The site is constructed on the idea that you are manipulating some strange audio-visual device. The buttons on the left are straightforward enough: each icon, when clicked, gives a brief impression of being depressed like a physical button. Better hidden is the music track: clicking the speaker starts it playing. The portfolio page has a distorted lens at the center. Portfolio images change as you hover over each of the lights on the lens' circumference.

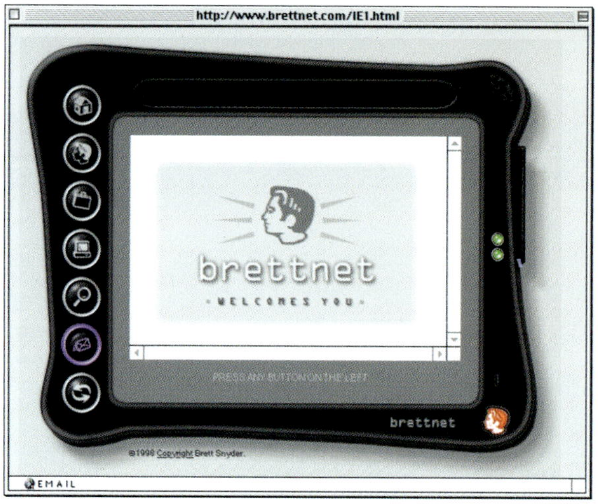

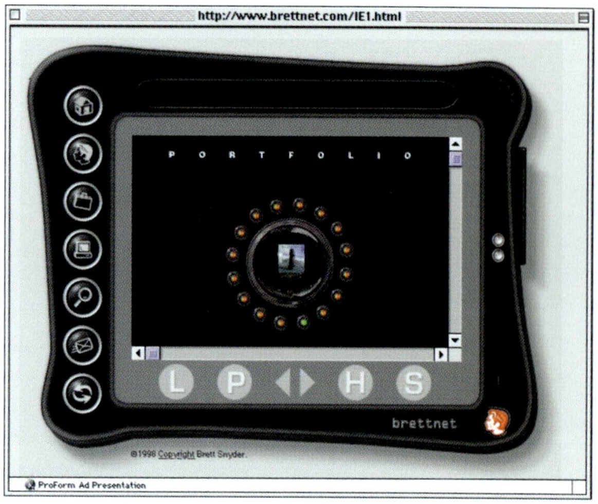

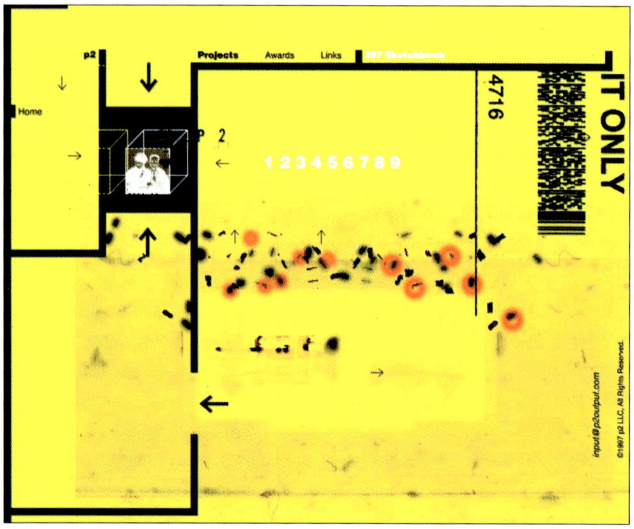

Title
p2 output
URL
http://www.p2output.com/
Design firm
p2
Designers
Christopher Pacetti,
R. Matthew Pacetti
Programmer
Christopher Pacetti

The designers here aren't interested in neatness or order, and the look and navigation of the p2 pages reflects this. Project examples exist as highlighted smudges, while the main navigation on the contents page almost seems pushed to the right as an afterthought. Subsequent navigational elements on other pages appear to lie where they've fallen. Irreverent, yet professional, calculated, and compelling.

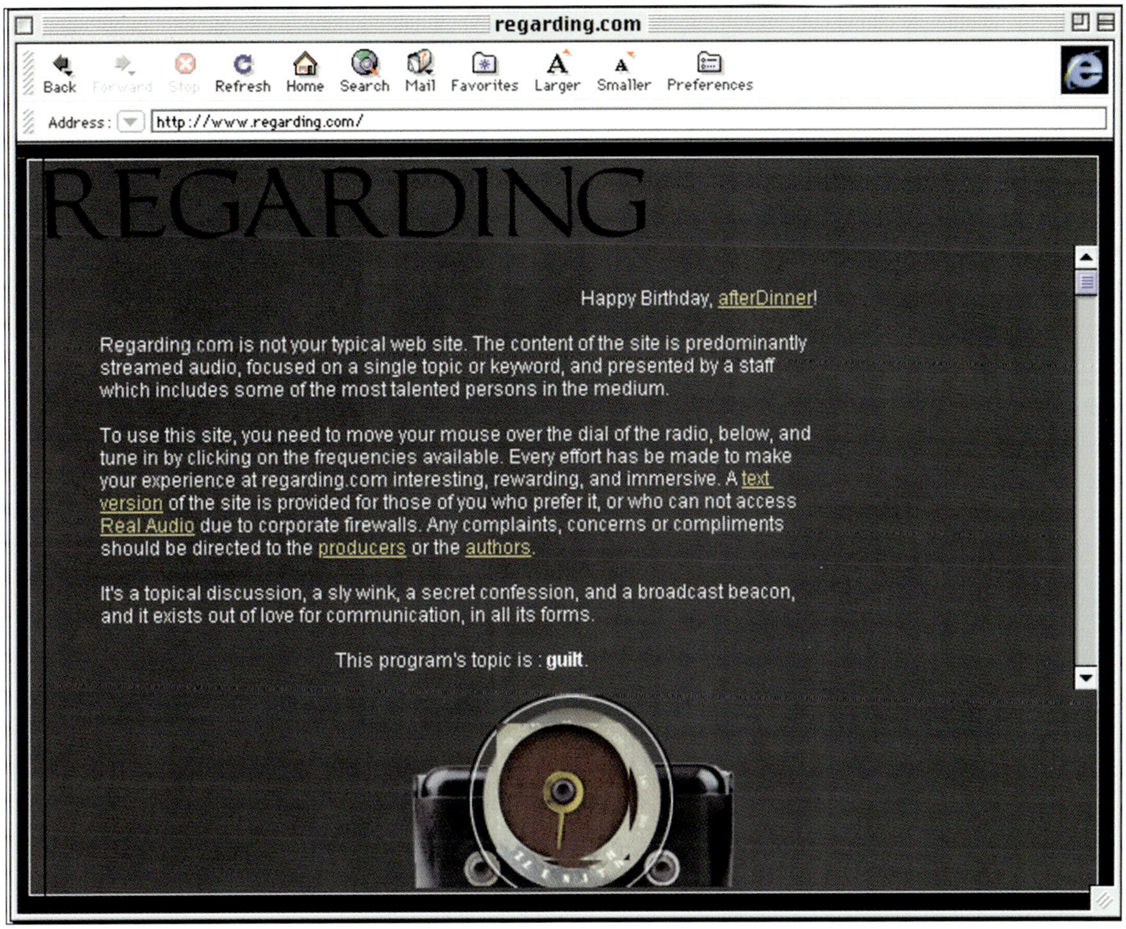

Title
Regarding.com
URL
http://www.regarding.com/
Design Firm
Hushville Interactive
Designers
Alexis Massie, Gregory Alkaitis-Carafelli
Authoring Platform
Mac

The key to Regarding is the radio dial. The site focuses on audio clips, and the radio uses rollovers to point its dial. When you hover over a given area, the dial points there and the status bar displays a text message for that location.

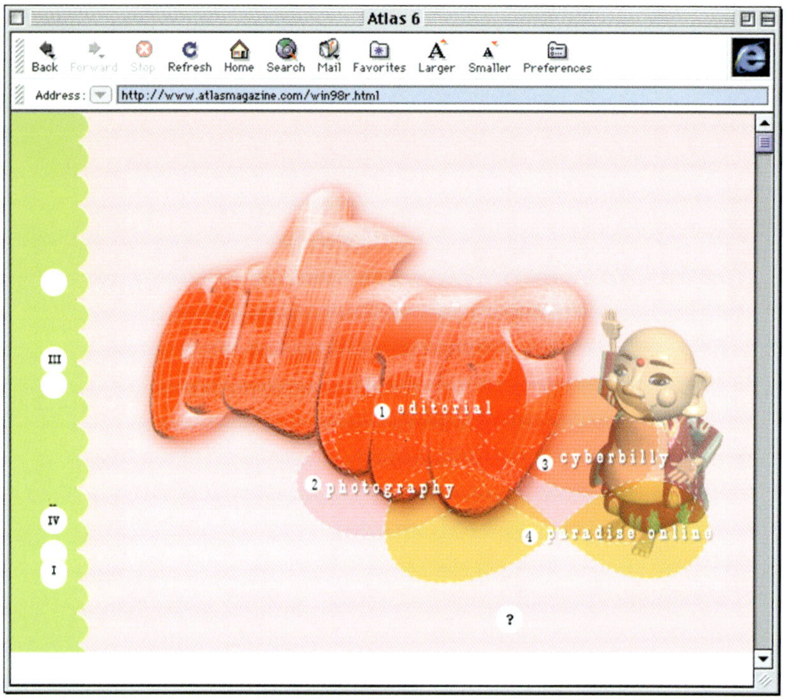

Title
Atlas Magazine
URL
http://www.atlasmagazine.com/win98r.html
Design Firm
Atlas
Designer/Illustrator
Amy Franceschini
Photographers
Olivier Laude, Catherine Karnow, Bob Sacha, Adam Kufeld, et al.
Programmer
Michael Macrone
Authoring Platform
Mac, PC

The home page of this site, in Internet Explorer at least, flashes, jumps, and disappears on cycle so that navigating becomes partly a video game. But the site is visually rewarding enough to pursue. Placement of links is aesthetic, but JavaScript rollovers help identify where you are going when you hover over section names.

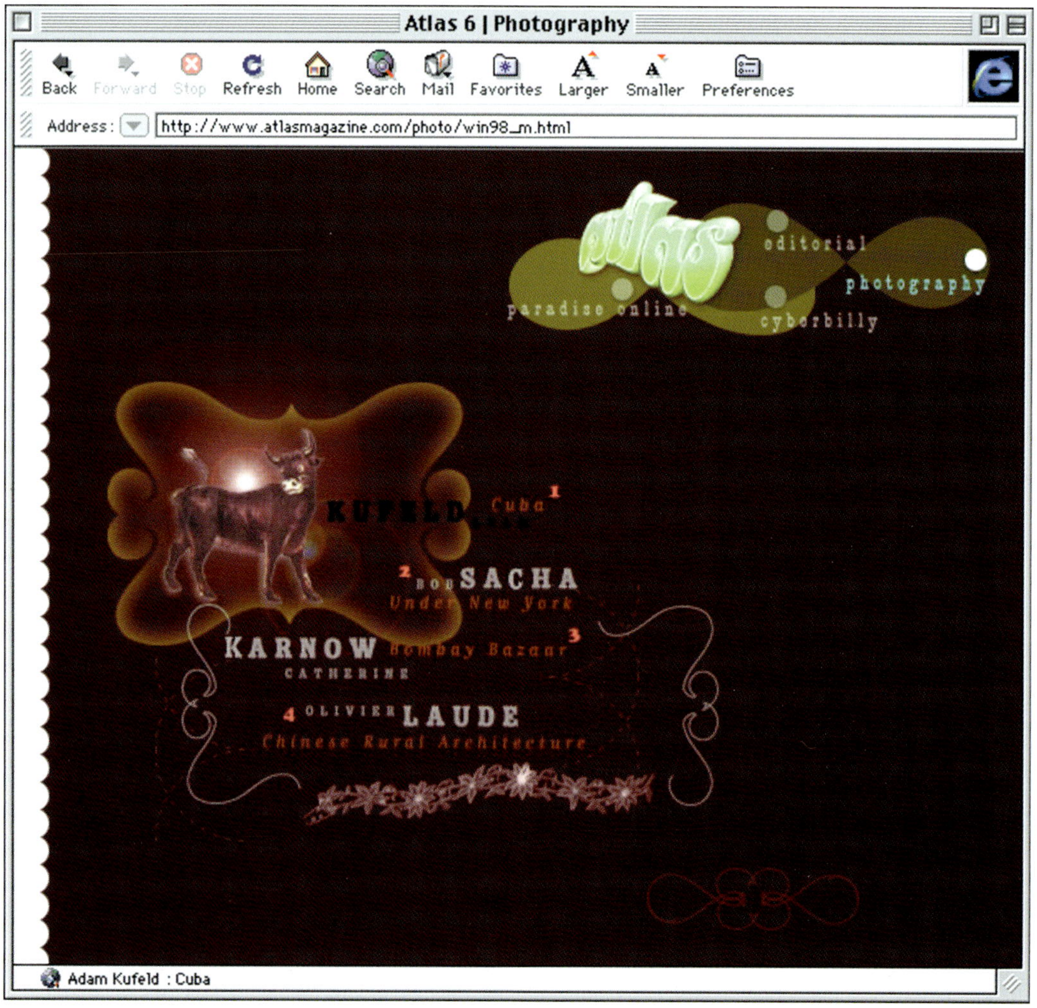

Title
Artseensoho
URL
http://www.artseensoho.com/
Designer/Illustrator
Tim Trompeter
Photographers
Peter Cunningham, Tim Trompeter
Authoring Platform
Mac

The site is geographically centered, and each map page is as long as the street or section of it. Crosstown blocks, not very long when you get to Soho, take up pages by themselves, but downtown blocks run as deep as they need to. Clicking on directional text, like "Turn West on Prince St." takes you to the appropriate page.

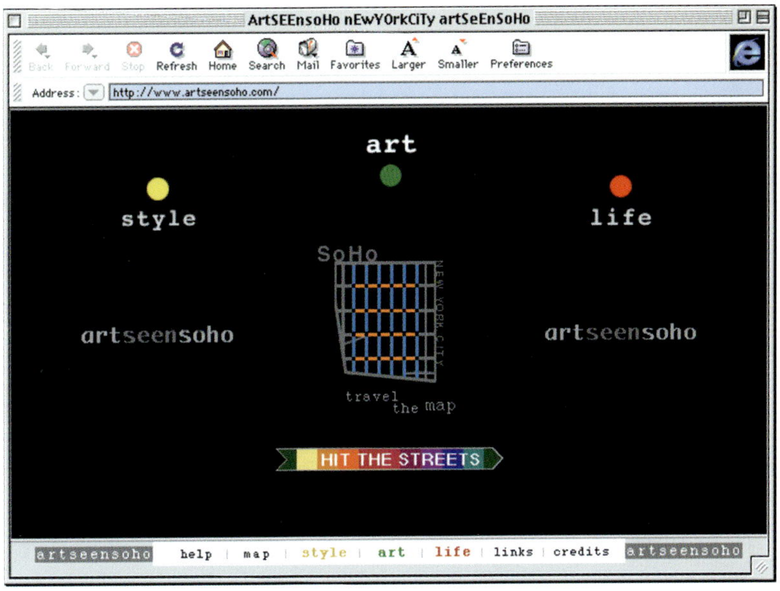

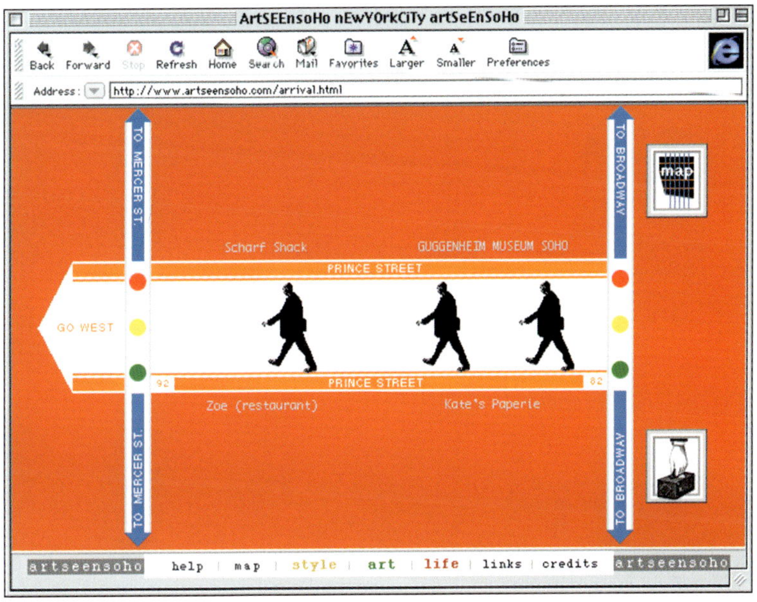

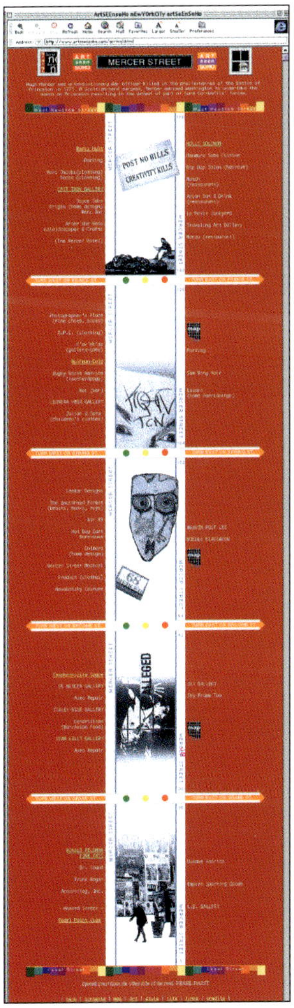

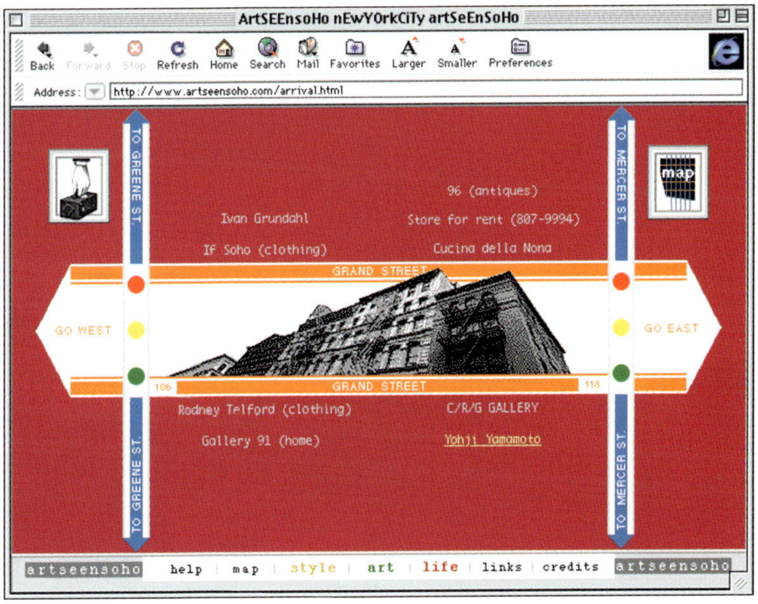

title
beyondexpress.com
URL
http://www.beyondexpress.com/index.html
design firm
pageworks
designer/illustrator/programmer
Kip Shaw
photographer
chris jones
authoring platform
Mac

Beyondexpress.com shows one of the best examples of a good left-side navigation bar. The items are organized with little hierarchy and differentiation, but serve two different purposes: the top half takes you to subsections; the bottom half lists downloads. On subsidiary pages, a clever iconography takes you home, to the top of the page, to the previous page, or lets you leave a comment. Text labels are added to icons in the first occurrence at the top, but the icons (and their purpose) are repeated for the depth of the page.

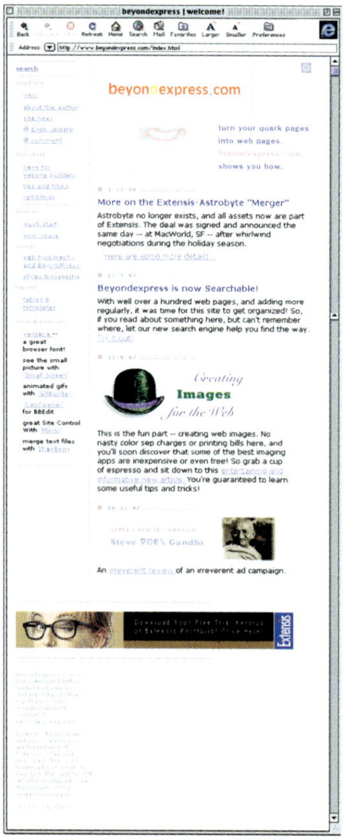

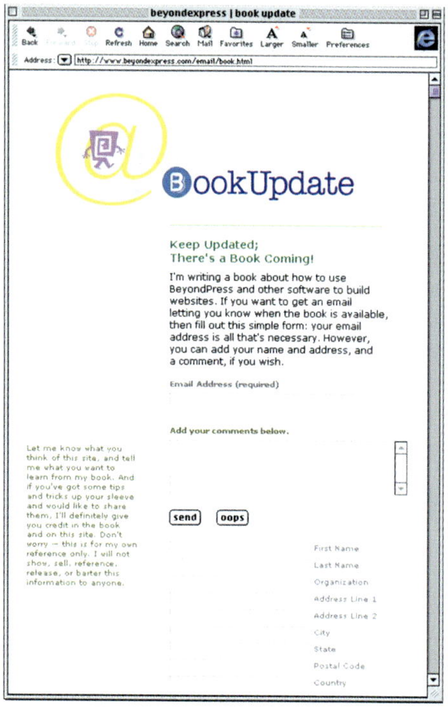

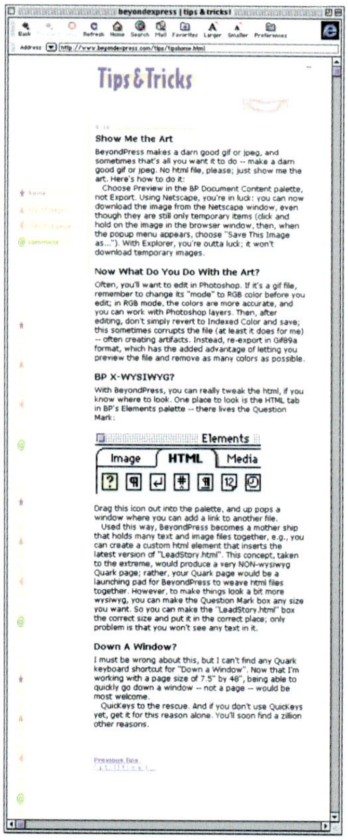

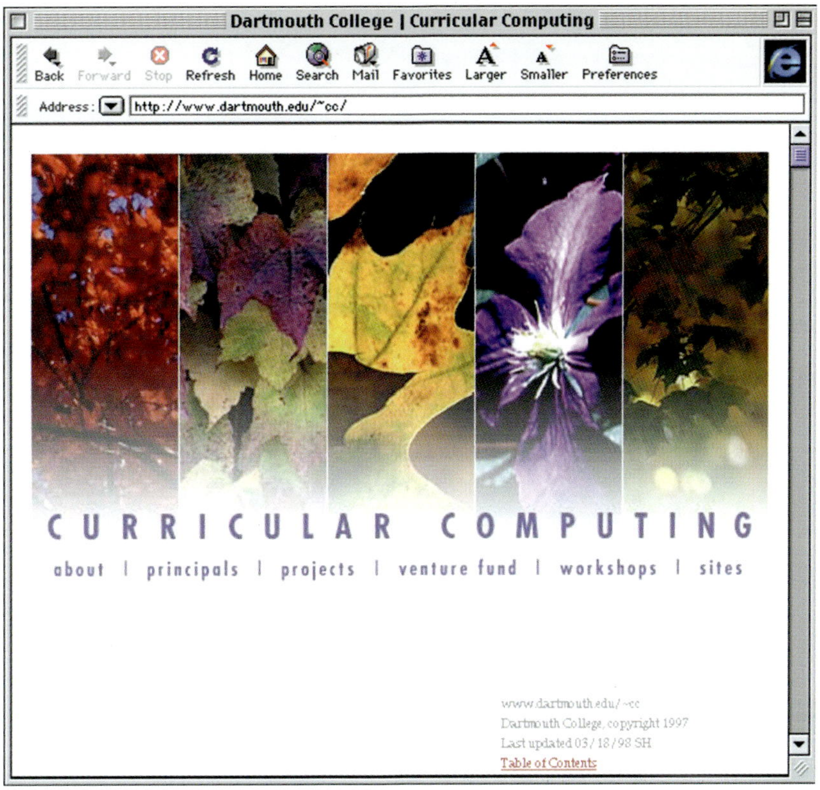

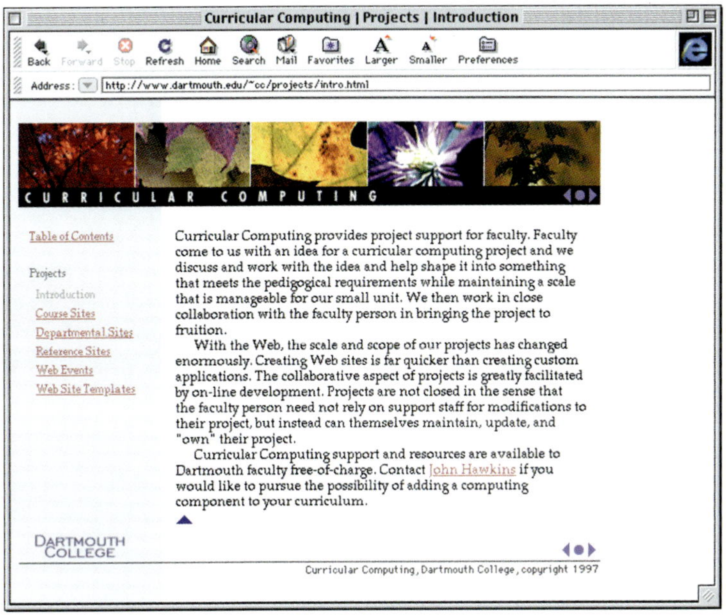

title
curricular computing
URL
http://www.dartmouth.edu/~cc/
design firm
Dartmouth College Curricular Computing
designer/illustrator/photographer/programmer
Sarah Horton
authoring platform
Mac
images courtesy of PhotoDisc, Inc. the copyright holder

Spare, elegant text drives navigation in this site. By using the illustrations for appearance only, the site is made accessible to a wide variety of users necessary at an institution of higher learning, where text browsers using antique Lynx software co-exist with modern, high-performance PCs. The navigation on the left opens up in each section to list subcategories.

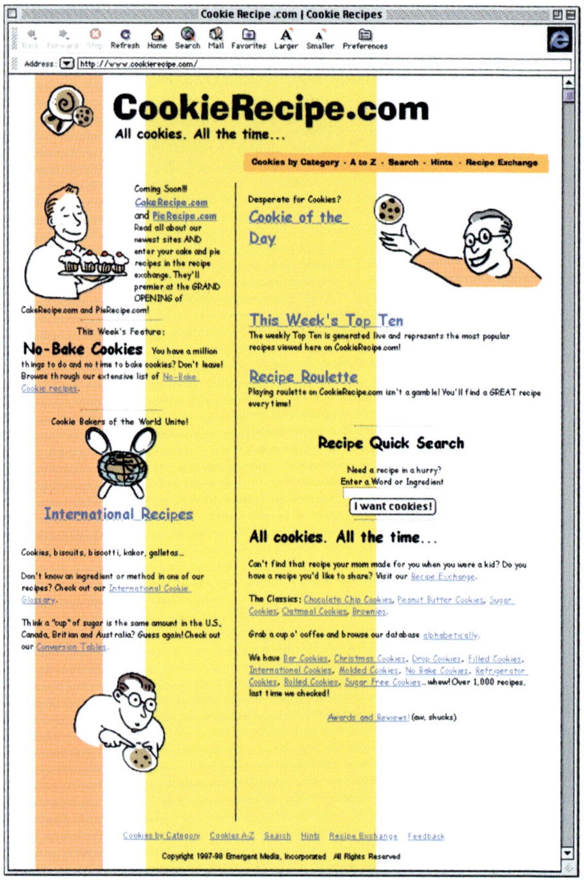

title
cookierecipe.com
URL
http://www.cookierecipe.com/
design firm
Emergent Media, Inc.
designer/illustrator
Yann Oehl
programmers
Tim Hunt, Kala Anderson, Dan Shepherd
authoring platform
PC

For a site this simple, rather than construct elaborate metaphors or navigational aids, Cookierecipe.com puts its links in the text. You can jump straight to popular recipes, or to any of the organizational pages in the site. They manage to encapsulate the entire site's scope in a single page.

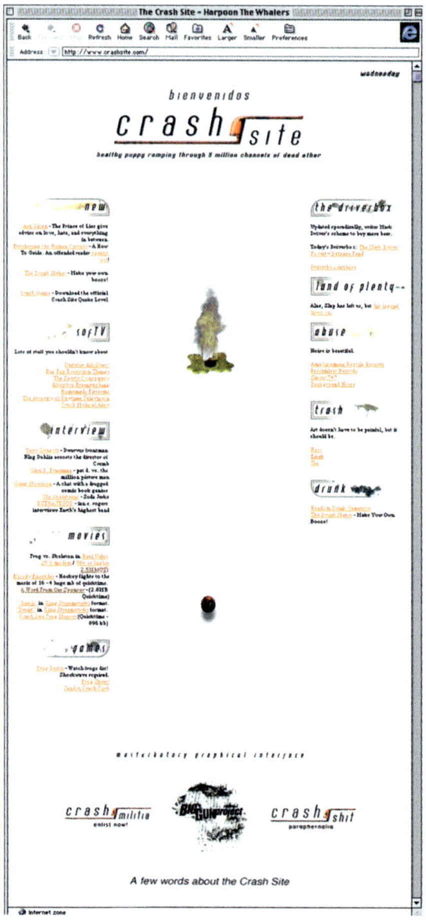

title
crash site
URL
http://www.crashsite.com/
design firm
Rvision/Big Gun Project
designers
Jim Evans, Gibran Evans
illustrator
Gibran Evans
programmers
Ian Rogers, Mark Thompson
authoring platform
Mac

Crash site somehow makes effective use of flush-right type, a long page, small type, and lots of white space—kind of a tour de force of items that designers are usually encouraged to avoid. But the simple text links divided into categories explain enough about every section and subsection to avoid deep linking. The page, though deep, loads fast because of the focus on text.

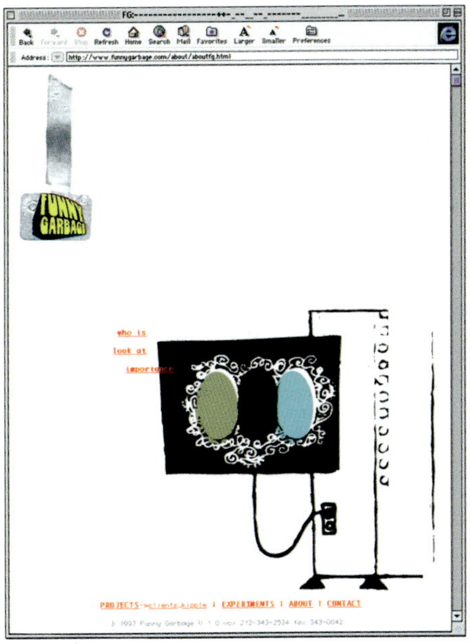

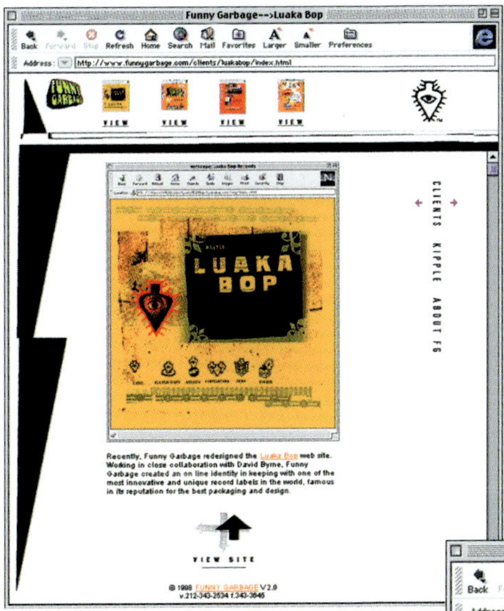

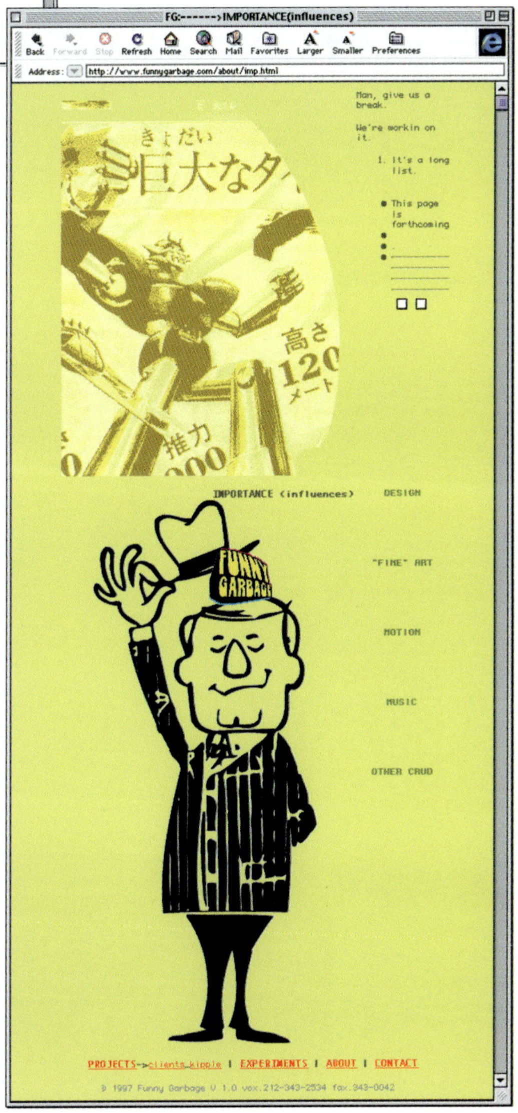

Title
funny garbage
URL
http://www.funnygarbage.com/about/aboutfg.html
Design Firm
funny garbage
Designers
peter girardi, chris capuozzo
Illustrators
Todd James, Devin Flynn
Programmers
Fred Kahl, Dan Wyszynski, Nina Ong
Producers
Fred Kahl, Kristin Ellington, Esther Robinson
Authoring Platform
Mac, PC

This site is included as an exercise in creating wonderful obscurity. Funny Garbage is so interesting and challenging that navigating it may not be easy, but it's worthwhile, as the depth of the site rewards random clicking. Links are hidden, typed in mixed case or different sizes, or even struck through. Get down to the portfolio level and the navigation becomes slightly more conventional with tiny screen captures used as a guide in a top navigation bar to view other items from the same client.

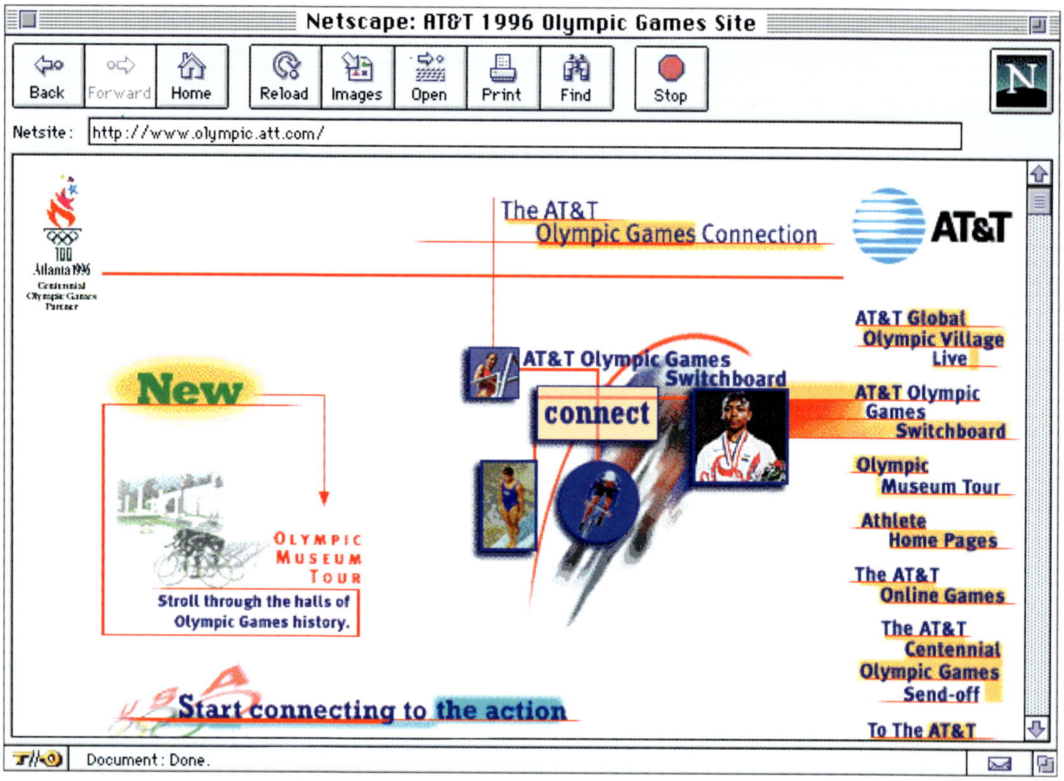

title
AT&T 1996 olympic games
URL
http://www.olympic.att.com/
design firm
Modem Media
creative director
Joe Mccambley
associate creative director
David J. Link
art directors
Tracy Long, Stefanie Trinkl
producers
Joseph Salvati, Glen White, Bob Carelli

Perhaps it's because most languages are read left to right: the prevalence of left-side navigation bars has rendered many otherwise interesting Web pages mediocre. Realizing that people would rather see the meat of a page before the navigation, the designers here shifted the links to the right.

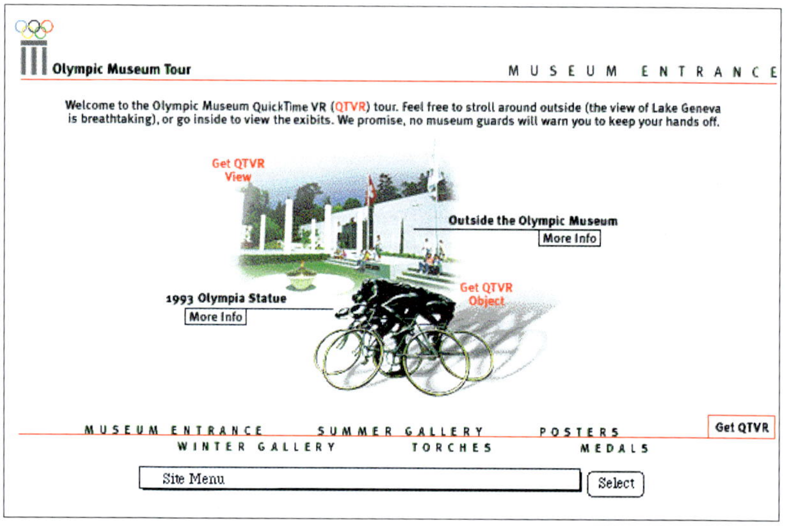

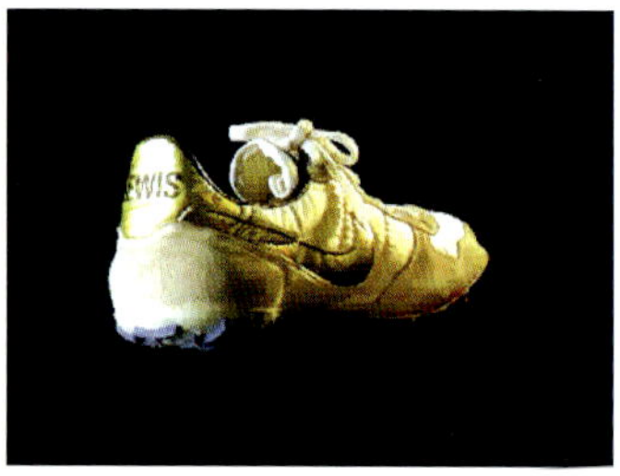

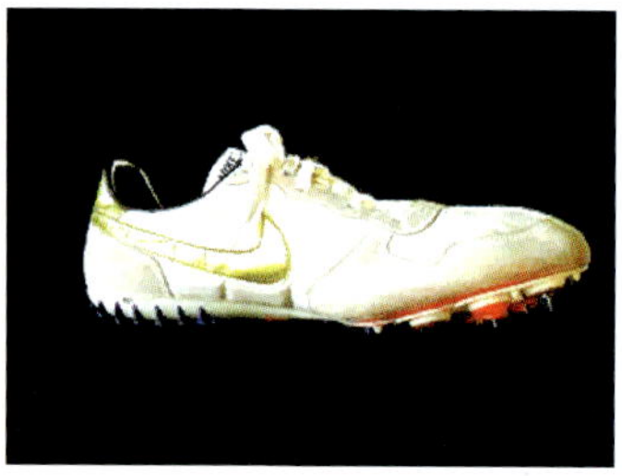

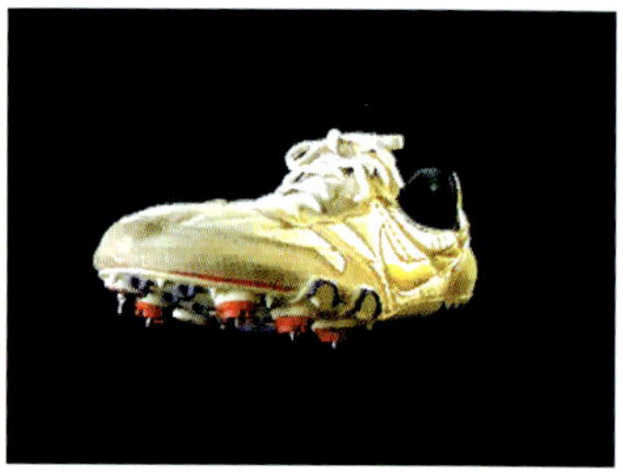

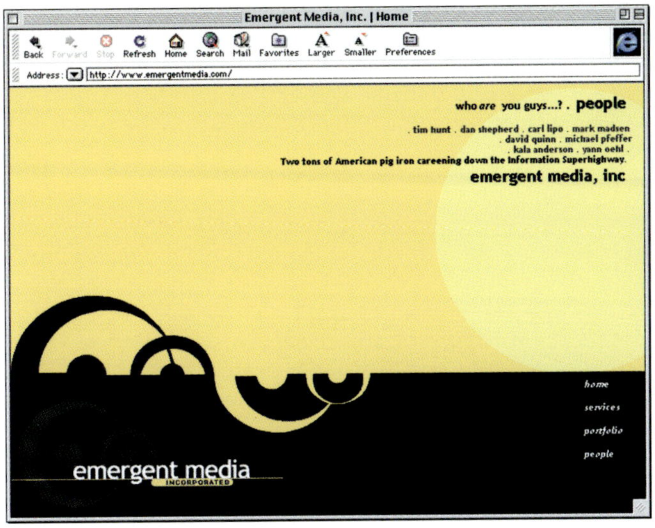

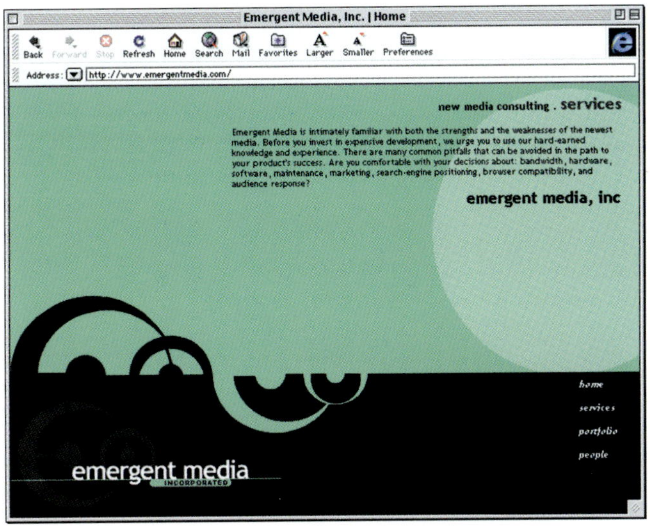

Title
Emergent Media, Inc.
URL
http://www.emergentmedia.com/
Design Firm
Emergent Media, Inc.
Designer
Yann Oehl
Programmers
Tim Hunt, Kala Anderson, Dan Shepherd
Authoring Platform
PC

A color scheme for each section emphasizes location, while a tiny number of options clearly lets you move around the site. Four items in the lower right take you to main topics; each topic uses text links in the upper right for subcategories. The section is identified by color and by somewhat larger type firmly lodged in the extreme upper right.

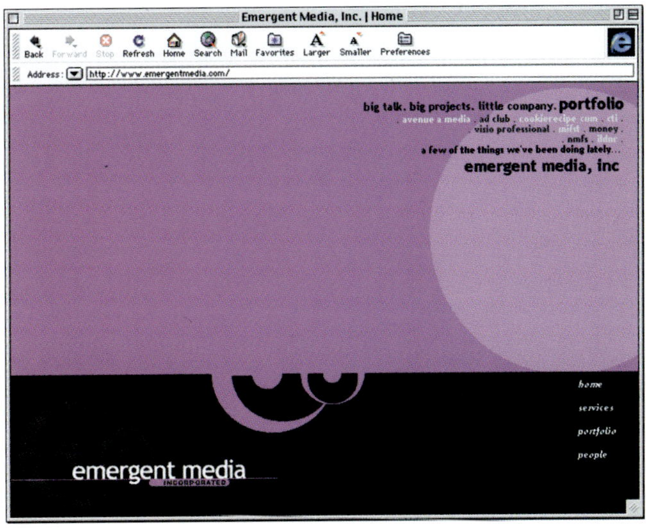

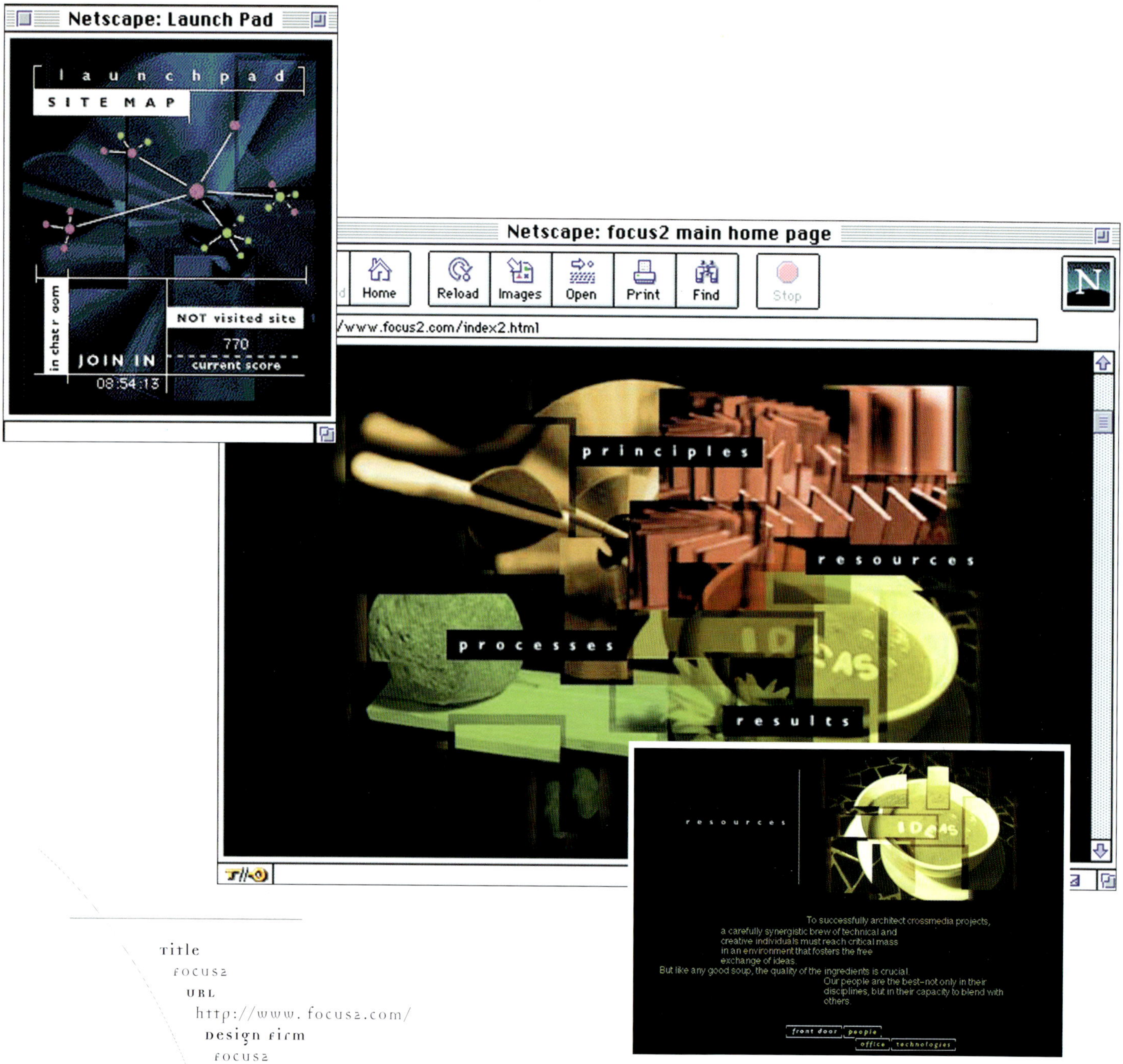

Title
Focus2
URL
http://www.focus2.com/
Design firm
Focus2
Designers
Shawn Freeman, Todd Hart,
Cort Langworthy, Brad Walton
Illustrators
Shawn Freeman, Cort Langworthy
Photographers
Dick Patrick, Jake Dean, Richard Seagraves
Programmers
David Adams, Walker Hale IV
Authoring platform
HTML, JavaScript

Two items about the Focus2 site navigation stand out among most others. The flashiest of the two is a Java-based Launch Pad that maps where the visitor has been in the site and creates a score for his or her experience through the site. Less flashy, but equally effective, is a linked textual hierarchy in the lower-right corner of many pages for easy orientation.

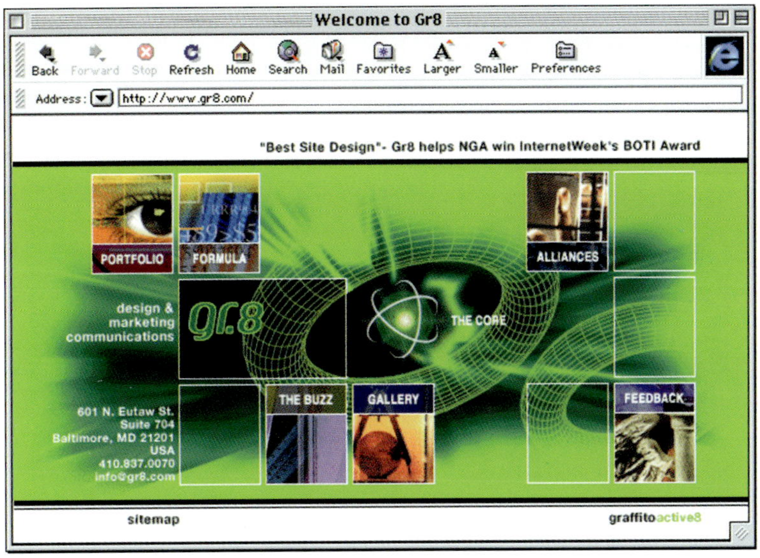

title
gr8
URL
http://www.gr8.com/
design firm
gr8
designers
Morton Jackson, Heath Flohre,
Becky Bochatey, Chuck Gates,
Matt Agro, Chuck Seeley
programmers
Chris Walsh, Heath Flohre,
Becky Bochatey
authoring platform
Mac, PC

In keeping with the futuristic appearance, the site map looks a little like the periodic table of elements, but it's really a schematic of the home-page navigation areas. The site map uses this graphical approach in the main frame, while the right panel breaks down the categories. Each subpage on the site emphasizes where you're at by highlighting the entry in the section list and by putting the section name in larger type above the section's graphic from the home page. But you can also get to any section on the site from the section list.

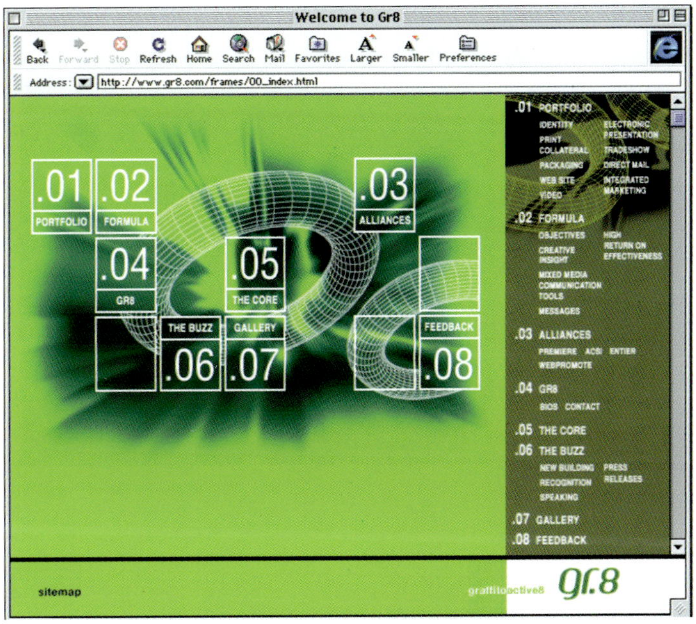

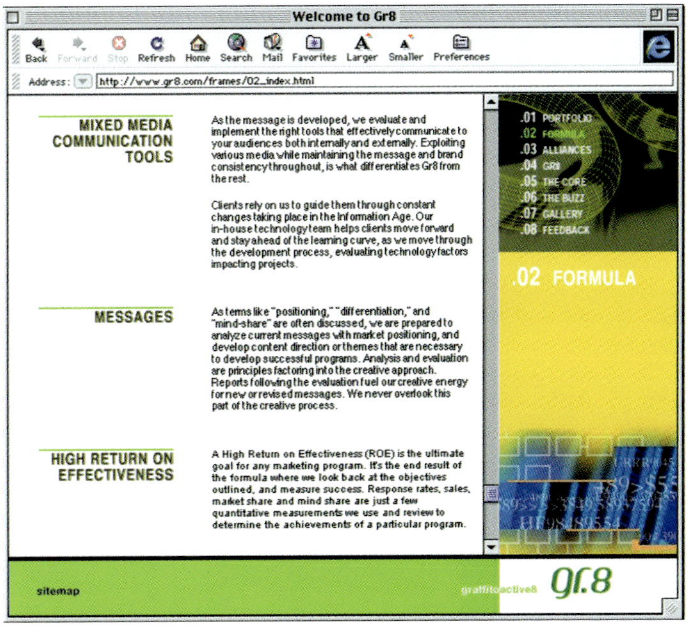

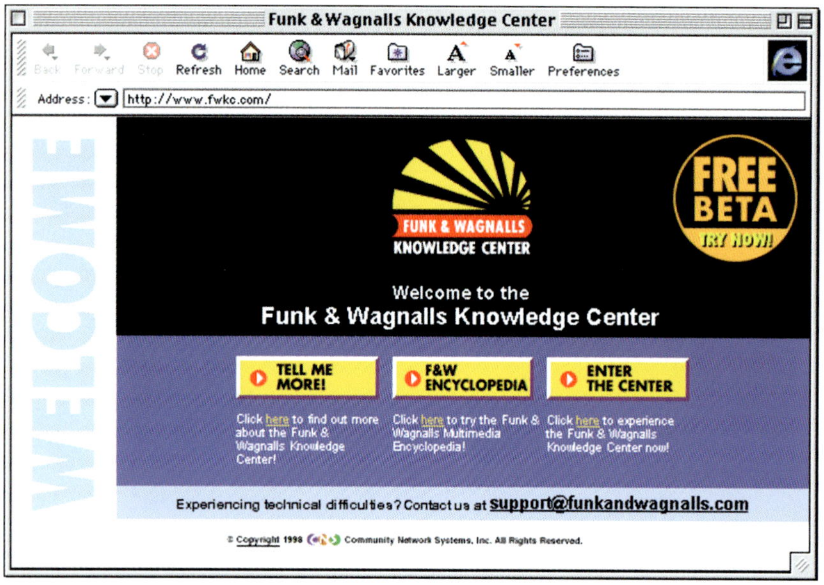

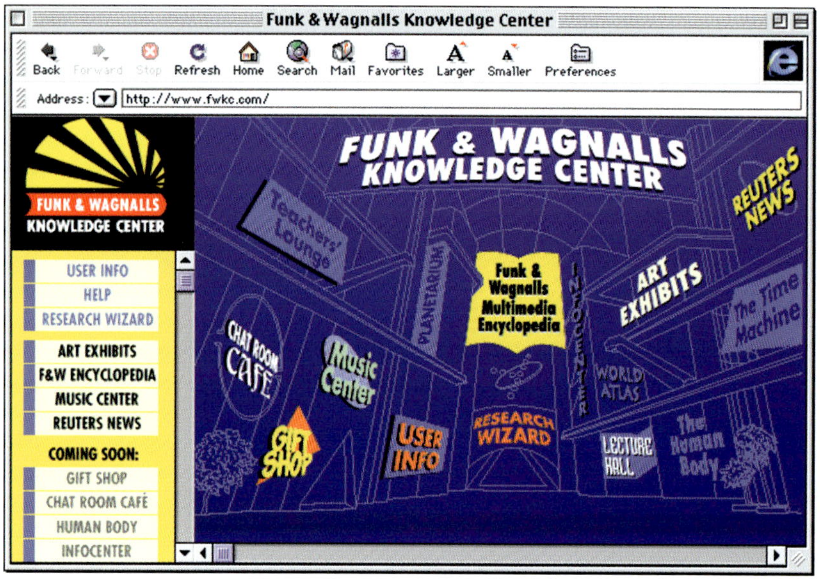

title
virtual community of tomorrow
URL
http://www.fwkc.com/
design firm
community Network systems
designers
vadim kapridov, matvey shapiro, ephraim tabackman
illustrators
vadim kapridov, alexei kazantsev
programmers
Havi goodman, yisrael Naiman, Harry cohen
project management
galen karten, kenny zwiebel
Authoring platform
Mac, pc

Funk & Wagnalls sells their product and their site, as well as making content available at the Web site, so the first few screens present an array of options, including ones that cost money. It's a big smorgasbord of options on every conceivable topic, organized both into a crisp left-side navigation bar (with future options shown, but grayed out) and a graphical version in the main screen. The actual content pages offer contextual options on the left, based on the topic chosen.

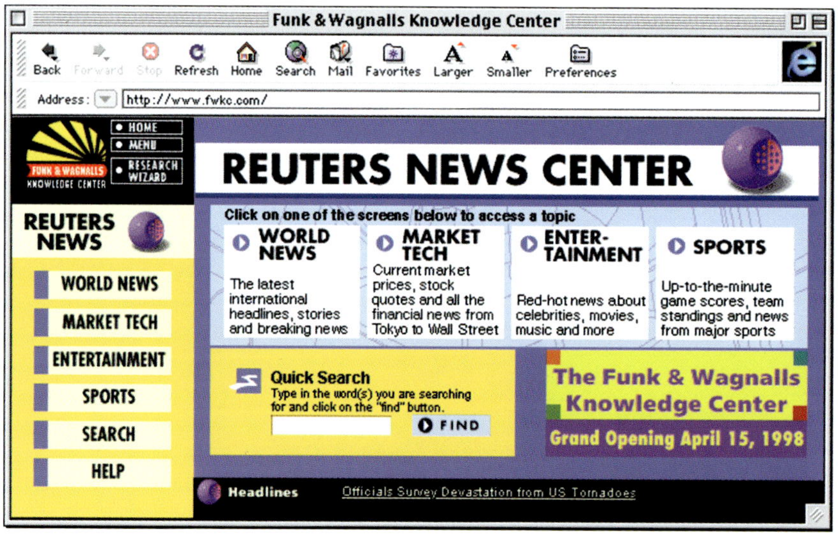

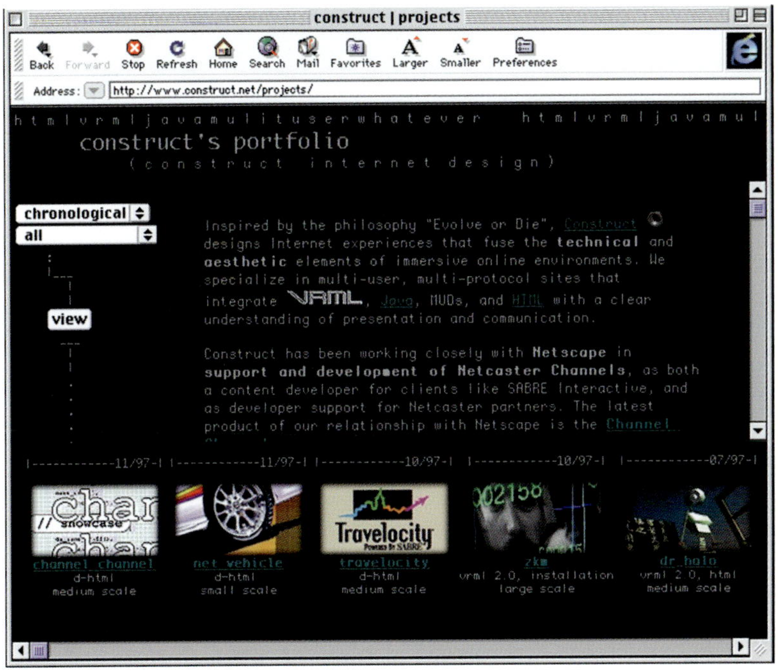

Title
construct internet design
URL
http://www.construct.net/projects/
Design firm
construct internet design
Designer/Illustrator
Annette Loudon
Programmer
cynsa bonorris
Authoring platform
Mac, SGI

An interesting use of a long, scrolling horizontal window, the site presents its portfolio as a series of ever-rightward scrolling actions. The form at the left lets you select what you are seeing in that window, and in what order.

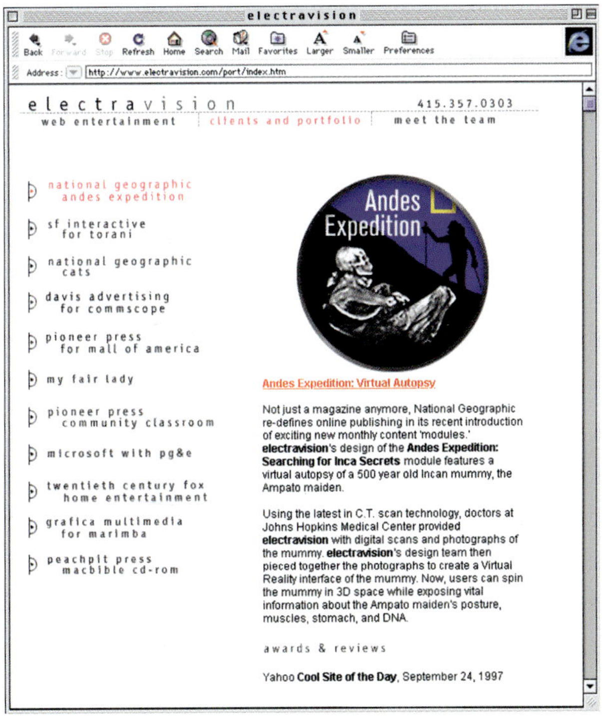

Title
electravision
URL
http://www.electravision.com/
Design firm
electravision
Designer
Rattakorn Potharam
Illustrators
Lisa Lopuck, Rattakorn Potharam
Programmer
Landon Bouma
Authoring platform
Mac, BBEdit

The site is cleanly divided into three sections; the current section is highlighted in red. Each set of subsections shows up at the left with the current location also highlighted; it's a visual two-dimensional coordination of where you're at. Every item in the subcategory is similar enough to allow equal presentation without any confusion.

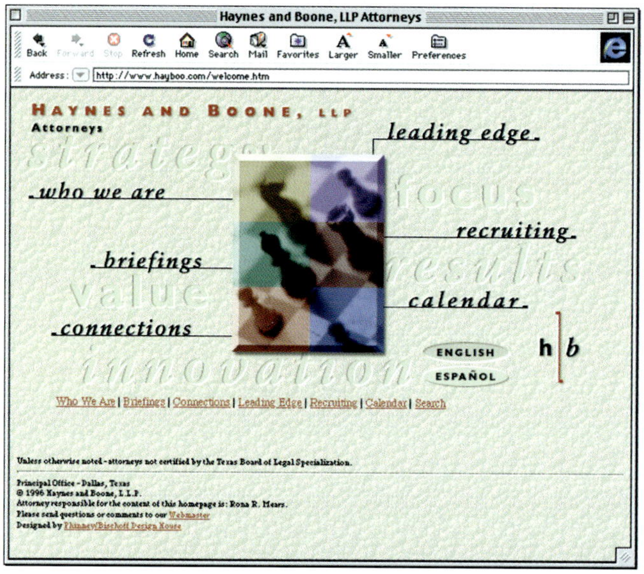

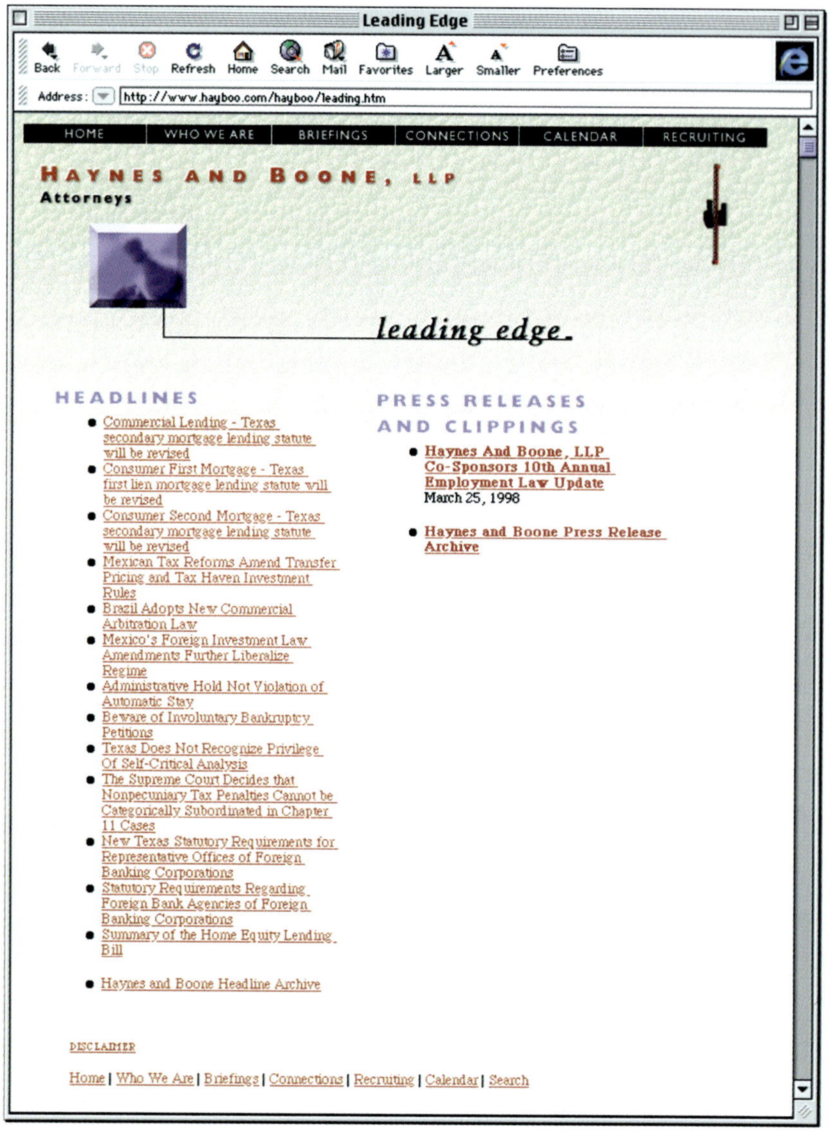

Title
Haynes and Boone web site
URL
http://www.hayboo.com/
Design firm
Phinney/Bischoff Design House, Inc.
Designers
Neil Robertson, Dean Hart
Illustrator
Dean Hart
Programmers
Glenn Fleishman, Neil Robertson
Creative directors
Karl Bischoff, Leslie Phinney
Responsible attorney
Rona Mears
Authoring platform
Mac

This information-rich site has to be careful to avoid presenting too many options at each level, but it nicely balances the number of screens you have to drill down before reaching content with the number of links on each page. All links are echoed in bottom text bars. The home page uses embossed, sandy type to present concepts, while the concrete items are black type with lines drawn to the particular piece of the graphic that represents each section. The home page allows a switch between English and Spanish through an embossed button that echoes other type on the page.

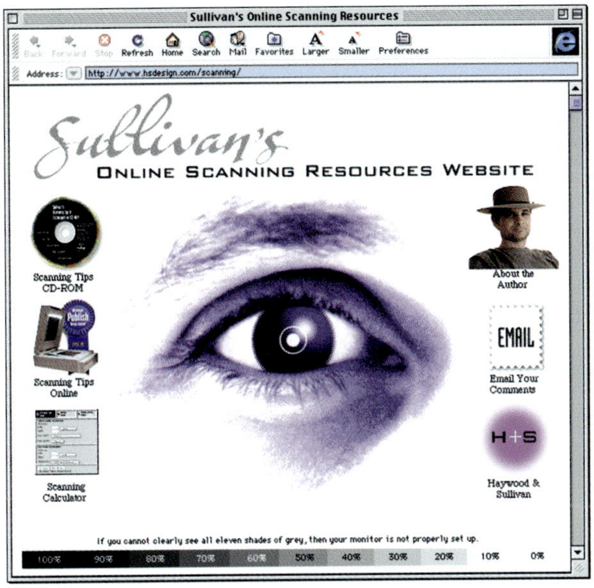

Title

Sullivan's Online Scanning Resources

URL

http://www.hsdesign.com/scanning/

Design Firm

Haywood + Sullivan, Inc.

Designer

Michael J. Sullivan

Photographer

Liz Haywood

Programmer

Michael J. Sullivan

Calligraphy

Dianna Stetson

Authoring Platform

Mac

A rare example, this site's links or items on the home page represent almost exactly what you're being taken to. The CD-ROM takes you to a CD-ROM page, the author's photo to a bio, and so on. It bypasses metaphor except for the stamp taking you to e-mail—close enough to not quibble.

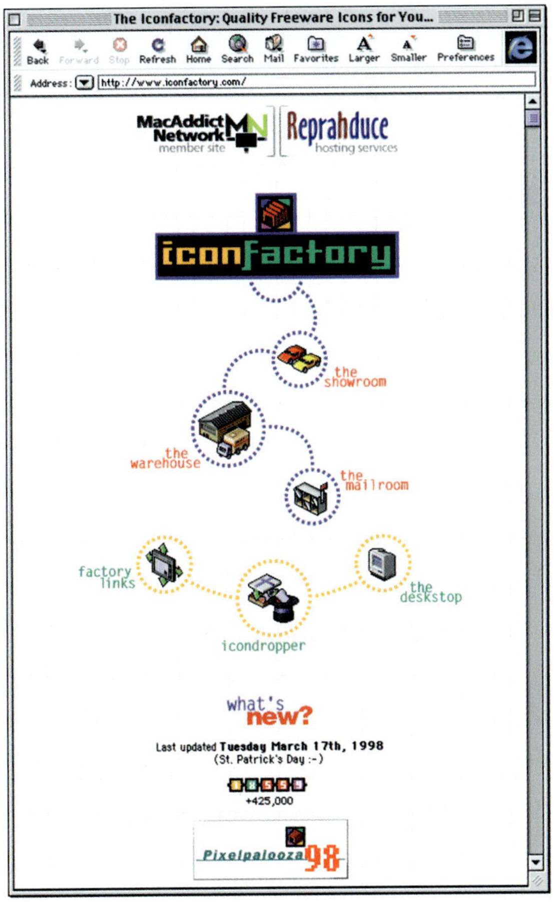

Title

The Iconfactory

URL

http://www.iconfactory.com/

Design Firm

The Iconfactory

Designers/Illustrators

Corey Marion, Talos Tsui, Gedeon Maheux

Programmer

Craig Hockenberry

Authoring Platform

Mac

The site is divided into a few primary areas, each represented by graphics that parody and parallel the icons they offer for download. Short animation series are used in each area to enhance the icons' meaning. Lines surrounding and connecting each section's icon in the two main subdivisions clearly delineate the created content from off-site links and background information.

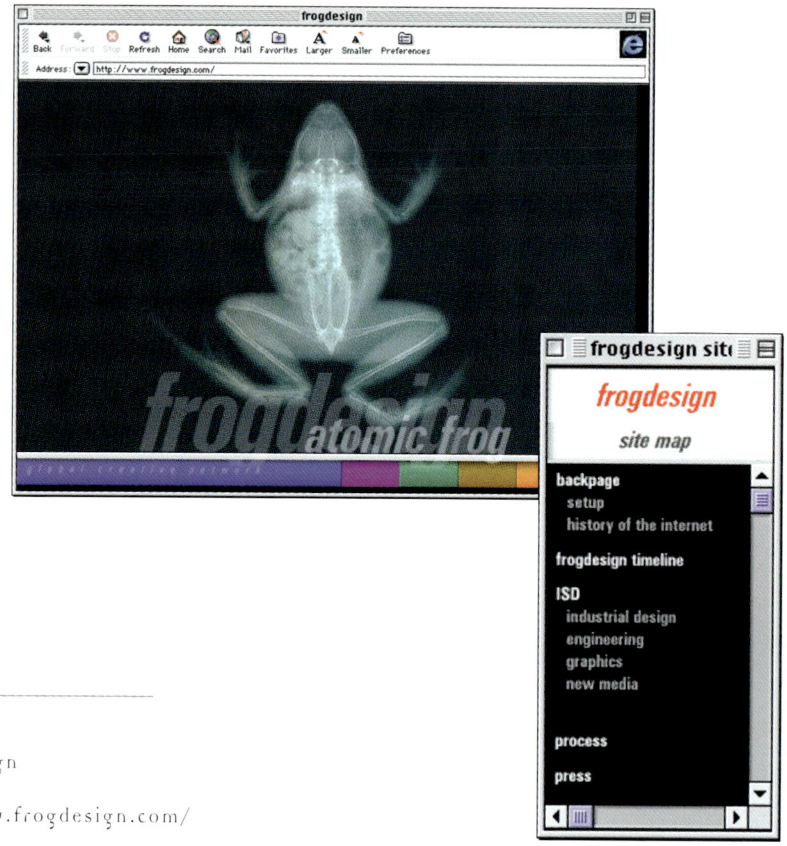

Title
frogdesign
URL
http://www.frogdesign.com/
Design firm
frogdesign
Designer/Illustrator/Programmer
frogdesign team
Authoring platform
Mac, PC

frogdesign pulls out the stops with a scrolling Shockwave presentation showing the history of the firm. A small slider at the top allows you to zoom back and forth across the years; dragging on it moves it at a variable speed. The site is built like a machine, as the company designs industrial products, like the Macintosh. Dragging the mouse over the buttons at lower right swaps in images that light up, like plastic lit from the inside. A pop-up window provides a map of the main areas of the site.

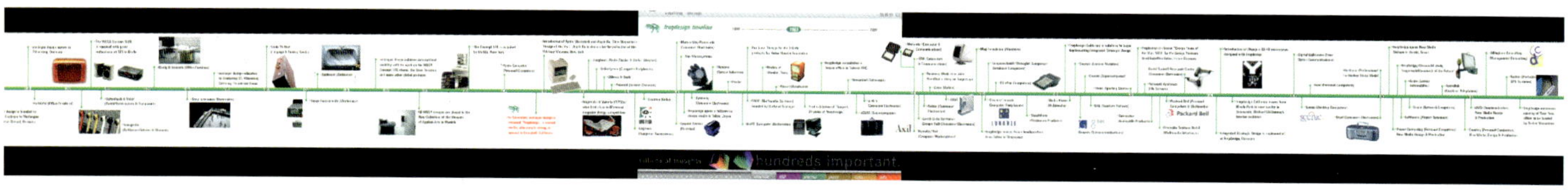

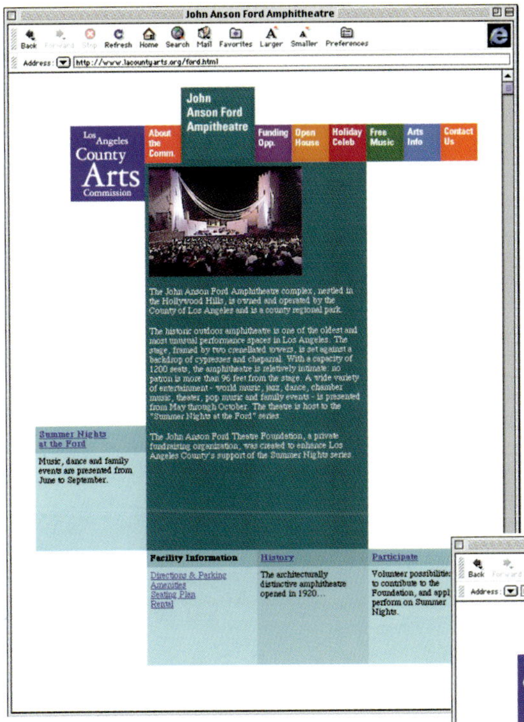

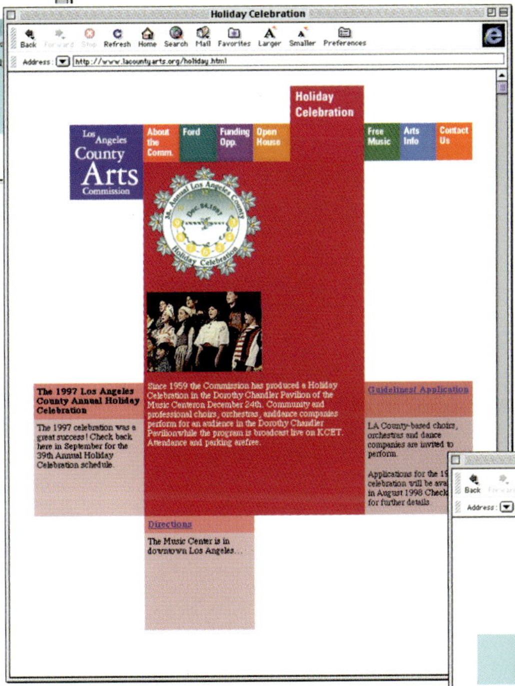

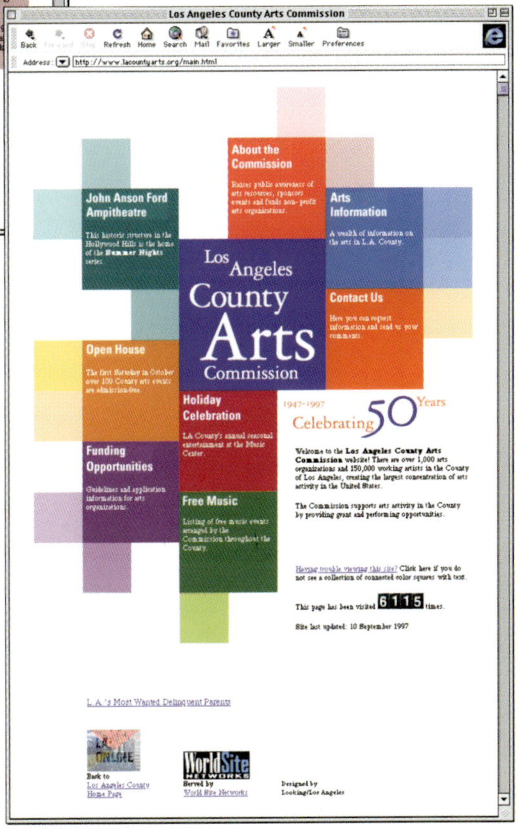

title

Los Angeles County Arts Commission

URL

http://www.lacountyarts.org/

design firm

Looking/Los Angeles

designers

Donna Fischer, David Young

programmer

David Young

authoring platform

Mac

A set of categories hovers around the central name on the home page. The importance of the categories is linked to their placement from top to bottom and in proximity to the central dark-blue box. Subsequent pages use a sort of tabbed bar at the top. They nicely don't adhere to the stricture that Web pages need to be flush with the top; nor are they strict about placement in vertical space.

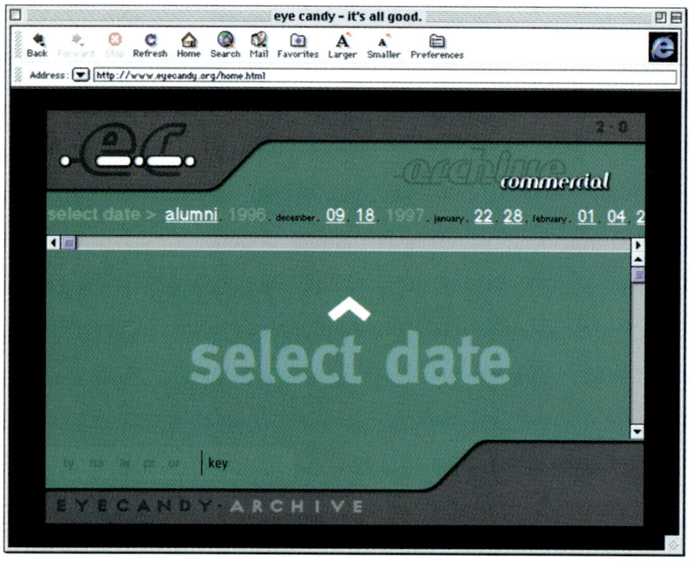

Title
eye candy
URL
http://www.eyecandy.com/
Designer/programmer
Josh Ulm
Authoring platform
Mac

Visually arresting, it's an Easter egg of a site. It's unclear why you should click on certain elements, like the Morse code (spelling *ec* for eye candy, with the dots also forming periods for *e.c.*) at the top left of the framing mechanism, but click you do. After an interstitial pause, you're presented with the standard framed screen with consistent elements; color is used to differentiate sections. An archive page uses text and vertical scrolling to retrieve older items. Clicking help brings up a small window that tells you how to configure your browser better.

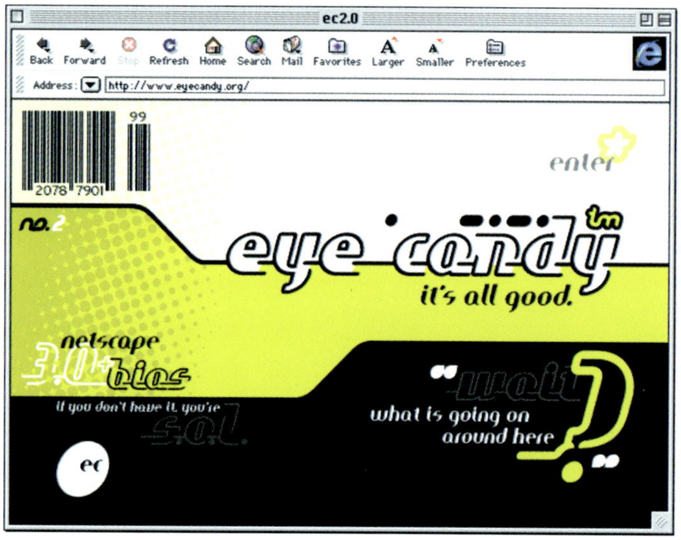

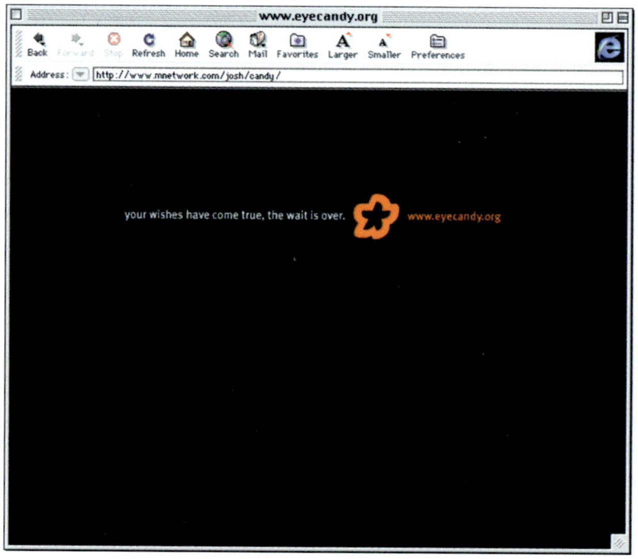

title
bianca: the alternative online community
URL
http://www.bianca.com
design firm
bianca troll productions
designer/illustrator
brady clark
programmers
chris miller, david thau
authoring platform
mac, pc, unix

Site maps are often the last place people look for directions on a Web site, but if you're in Bianca's Smut Shack (a popular shared Web environment that isn't nearly as smutty as its title suggests), the hand-drawn map is clearly the easiest way to find your way around. Pages inside the site include a small proxy map, with a small red you-are-here dot to keep you from getting lost.

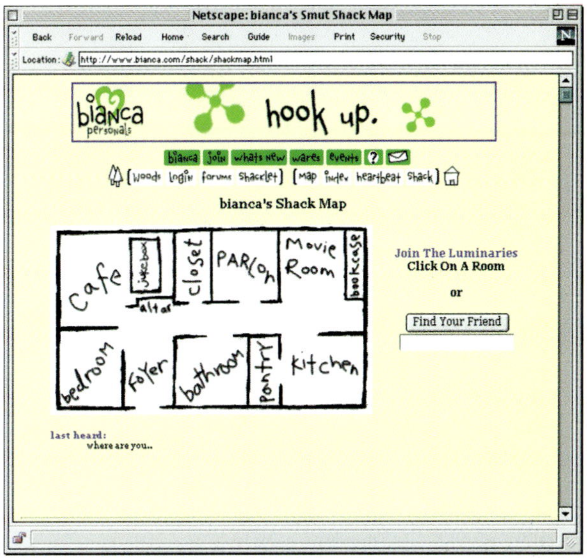

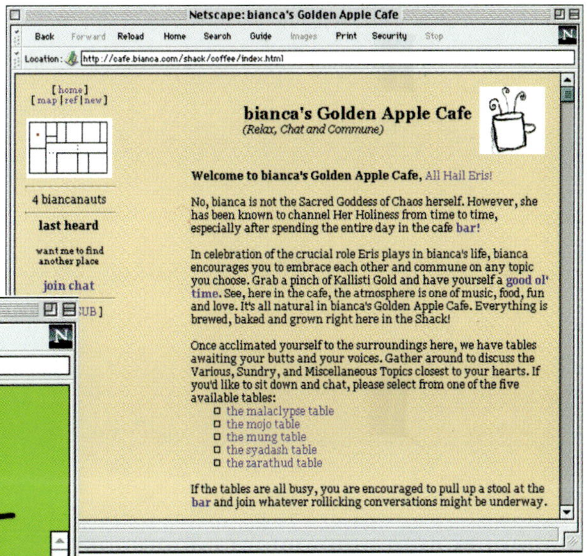

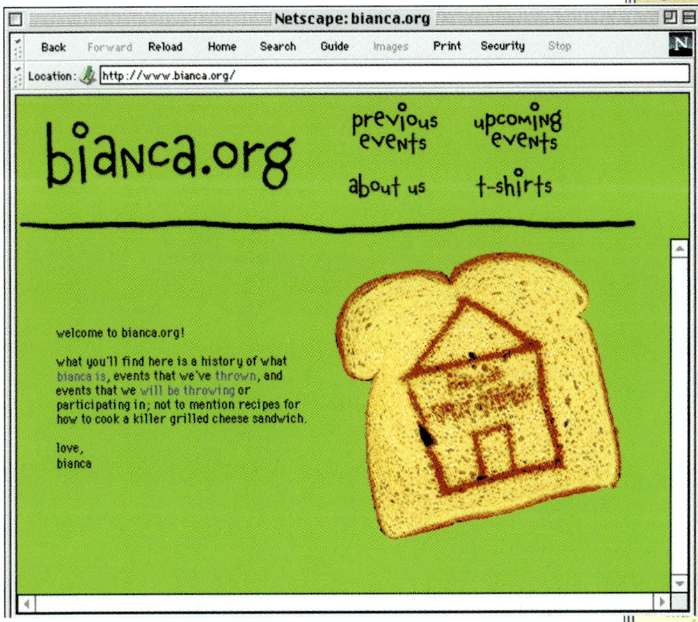

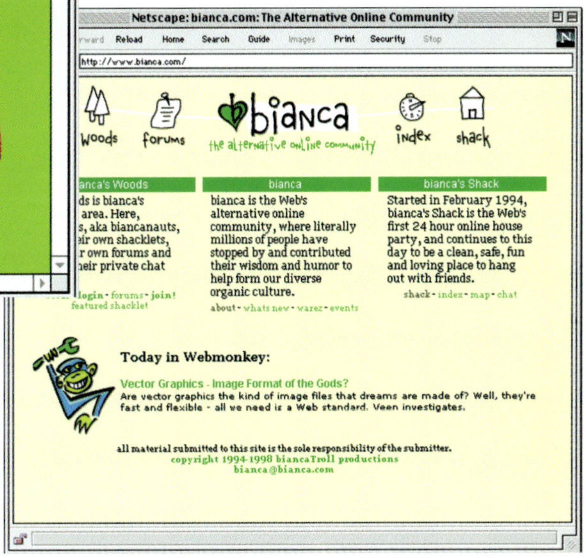

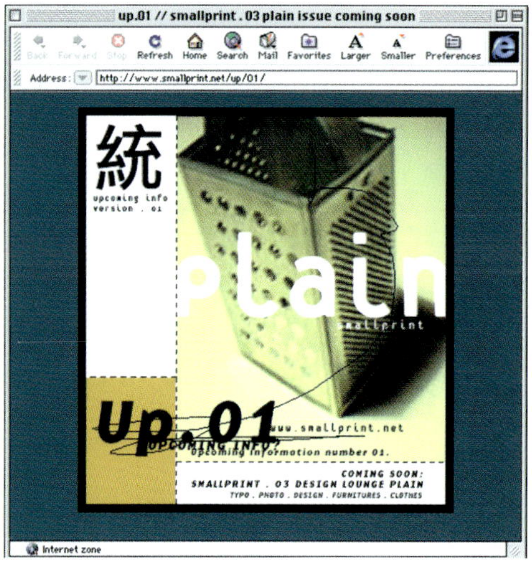

Title
smallprint
URL
http://www.smallprint.net/
Designer/Illustrator/programmer
Miika saksi
Authoring platform
pc

It is delightful to move around through the well-designed pages and interesting navigation elements of this site. The design carefully hides the fact that none of the issues of the publication Small print actually exist. What you find, instead, are links that take you cycling around from one aesthetically pleasing page to another.

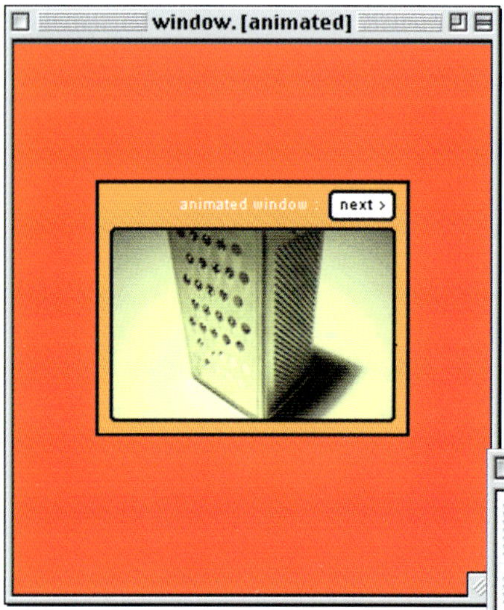

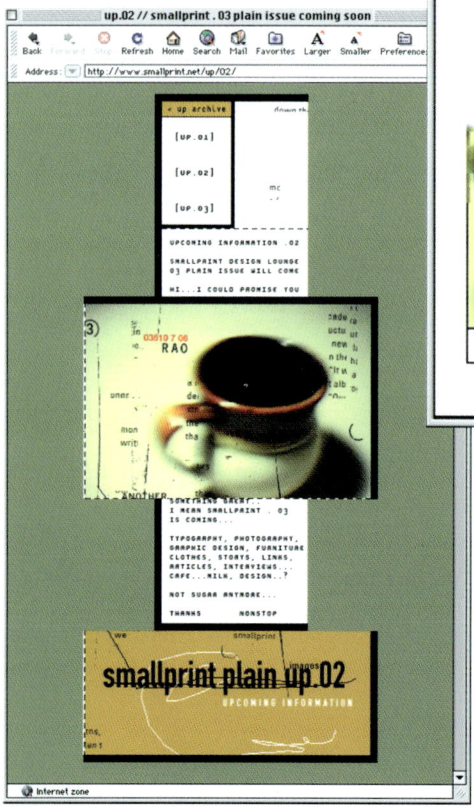

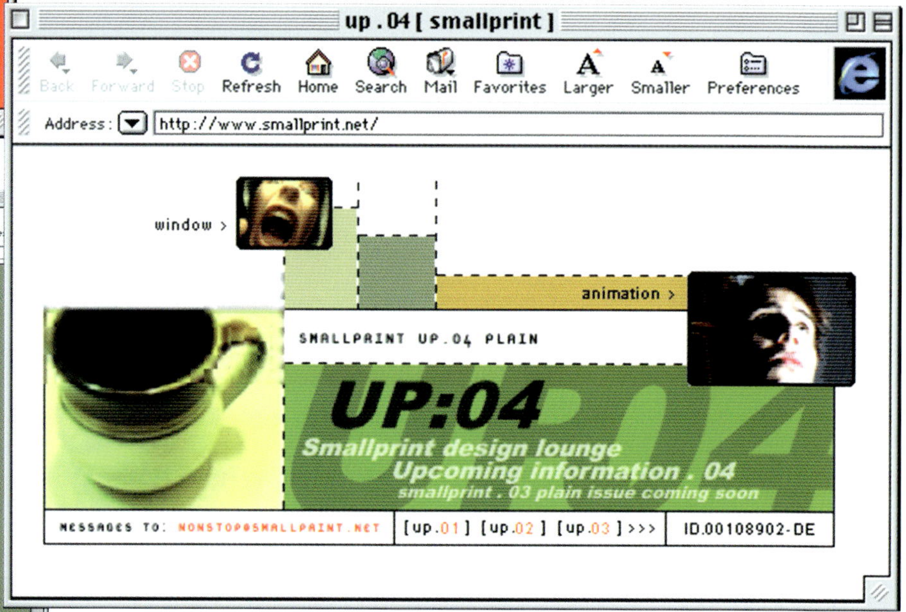

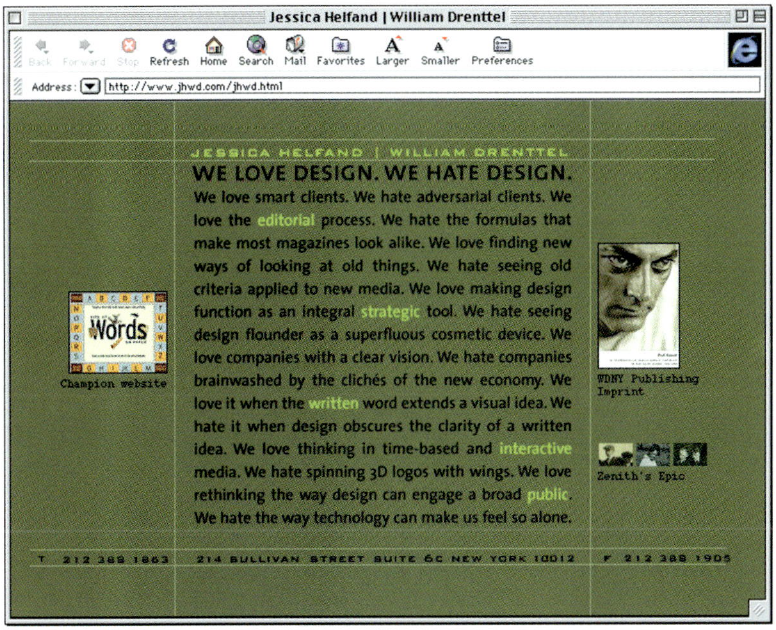

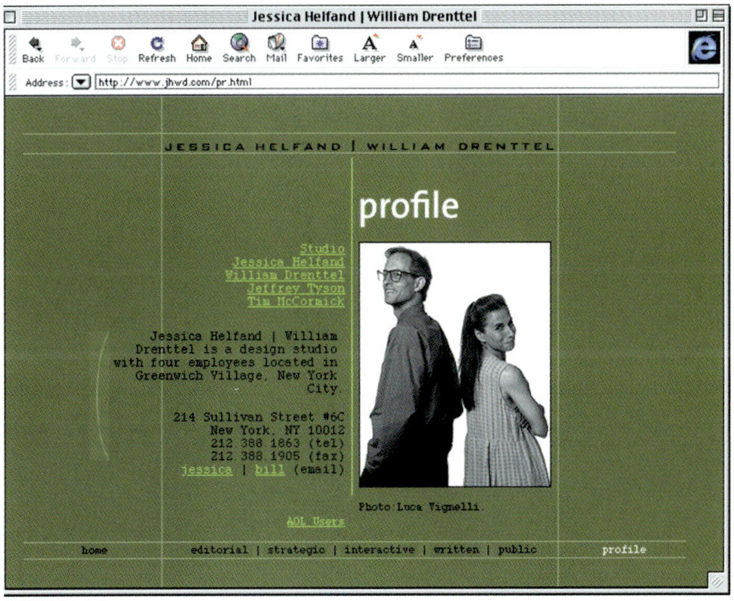

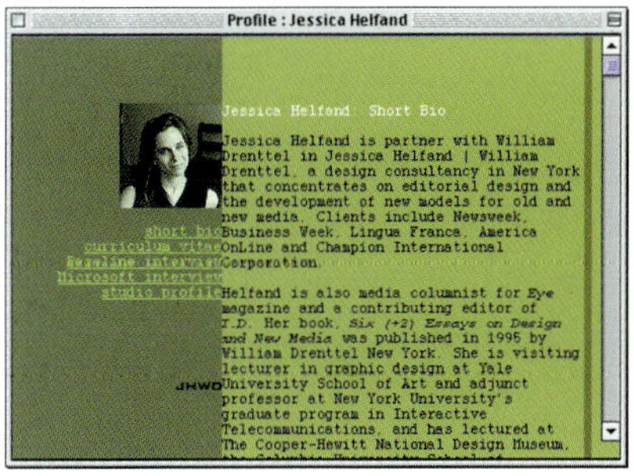

Title
Jessica Helfand | William Drenttel

URL
http://www.jhwd.com/jhwd.html

Design firm
Jessica Helfand | William Drenttel

Designers
Jessica Helfand, William Drenttel, Jeffrey Tyson

Programmers
(Java) Jeffrey Tyson, Steve Bull

Editor
Timothy McCormick

Authoring platform
Mac

These designers do something unique. They leap beyond using only isolated elements for navigation (like graphics, lists of links, and navigation bars) by embedding links into words in paragraphs of text. It's clear they are links since they share the same neon green as the text links, and it's also clear by context where they lead.

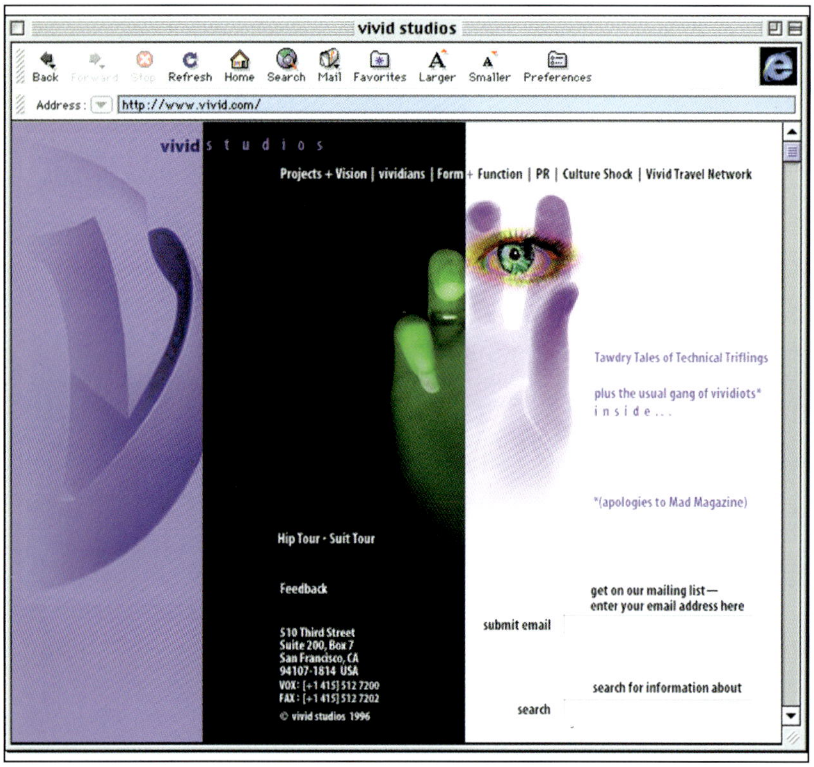

Title
vivid studios
URL
http://www.vivid.com/
design firm
vivid studios
photographers
Brian Bell, Chuck Gathard, Marsha Plat
programmers
Paul Guth, Nat Johnson
creative director
Nathan Shedroff
information designer
Drue Miller
visual designers
Jeff Davis, Nathan Shedroff, Maurice Tani
writer
Drue Miller
authoring platform
Mac, UNIX

Vivid Studios manages to have quite a few categories of links on its home page without cluttering it or confusing what goes where. The page is divided vertically into thirds, with a standard navigation bar on top that appears on subsequent pages in identical form; only the color and emphasis change to fit the background.

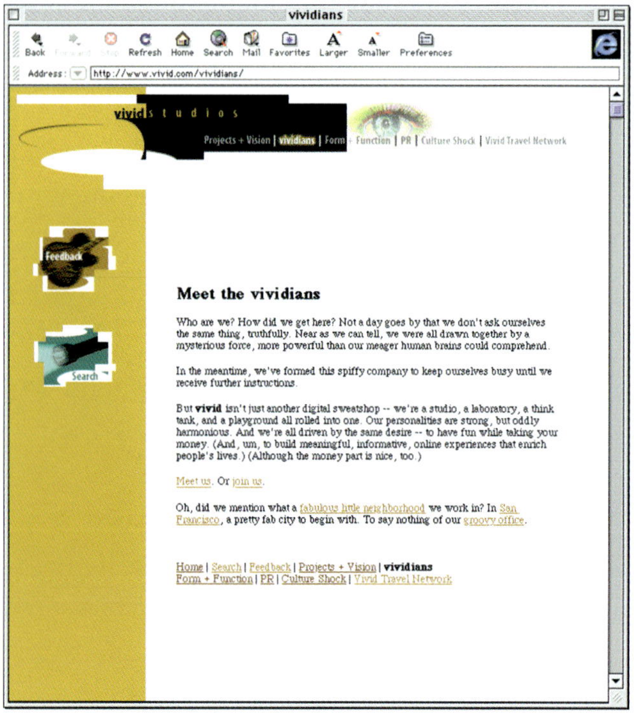

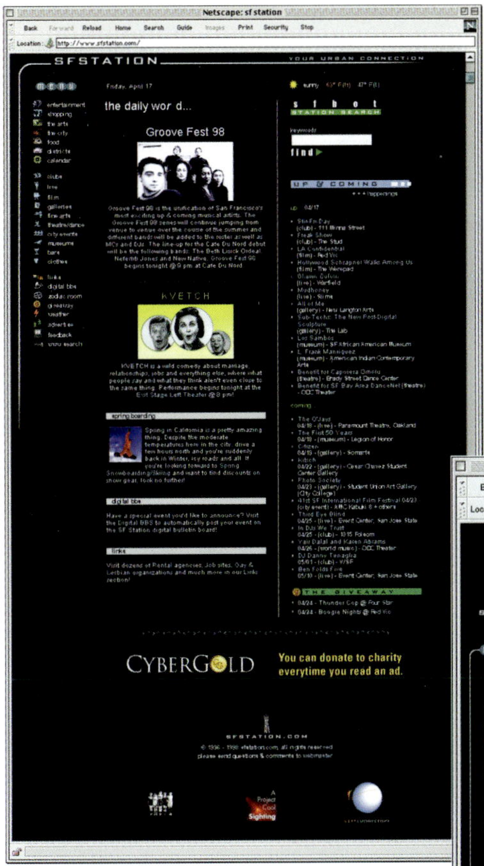

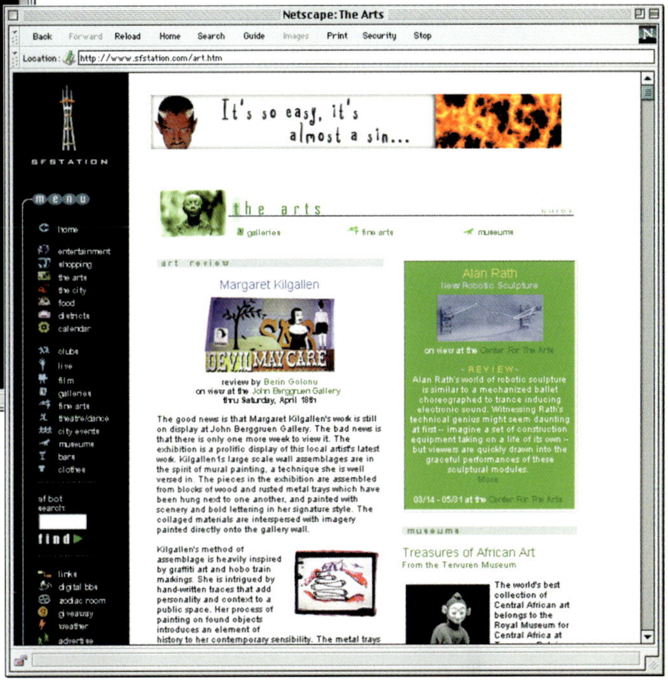

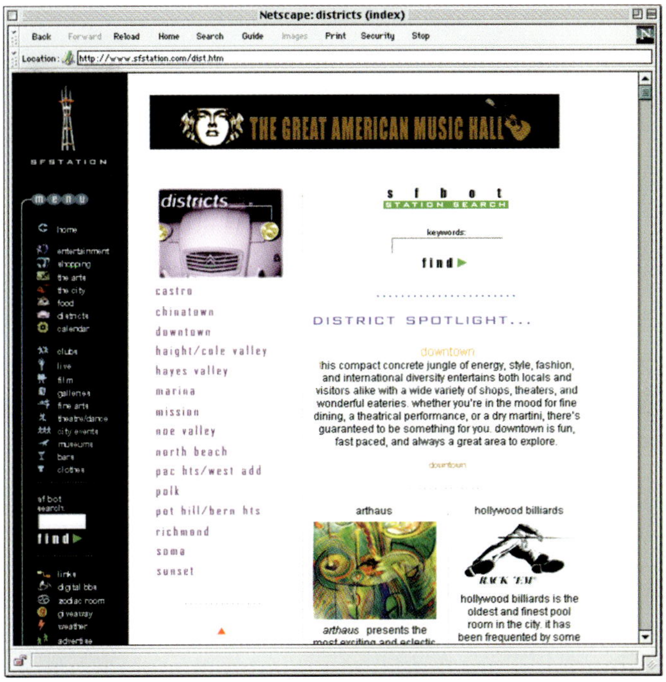

title
sfstation
URL
http://www.sfstation.com/
design firm
sfstation
designers
Mike Richards, Kyu Kyung
illustrator
Kyu Kyung
photographer
Curtis Christophersen
programmers
Vincent Archuleta, Kyu Kyung, Mike Richards
authoring platform
Mac, PC

At first glance, you might think the navigation on this site is just one step above the long link pages that designers have been trying to outgrow for the past several years. However, hidden in plain sight is a compact side navigation bar that offers twenty-five directional options using only about 20 percent of the screen space.

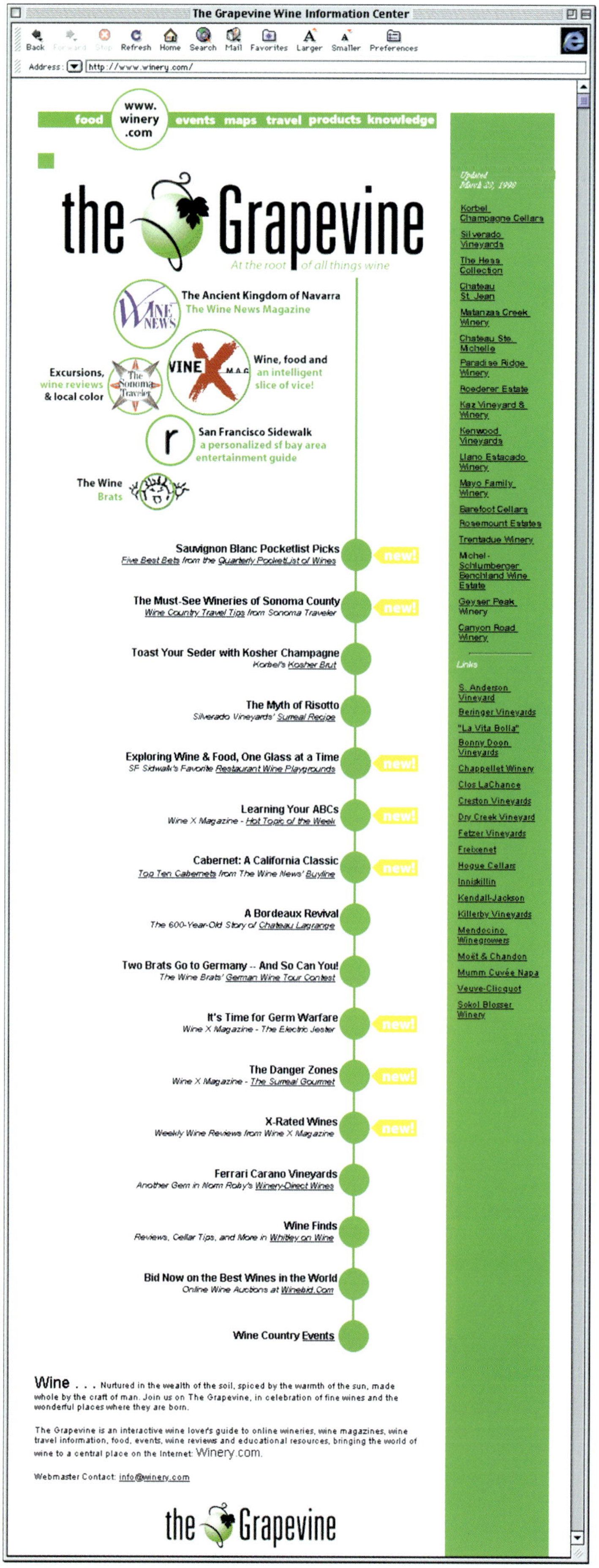

Title
winery.com
URL
http://www.winery.com/
Design firm
the grapevine
Designer/Illustrator
christopher slye
Programmer
Joe Naujokas
Authoring platform
Mac

Grapes are the form, the content, and the means of getting around. Subsequent pages may lead elsewhere, but the home page provides a cluster of options at the top followed by a long and deep list of specifics. The vertical grape line is used to call out articles, while a navigation bar at right has a similarly long list of wines and vineyards. The home page is dense, with information presented everywhere you look, but highly accessible.

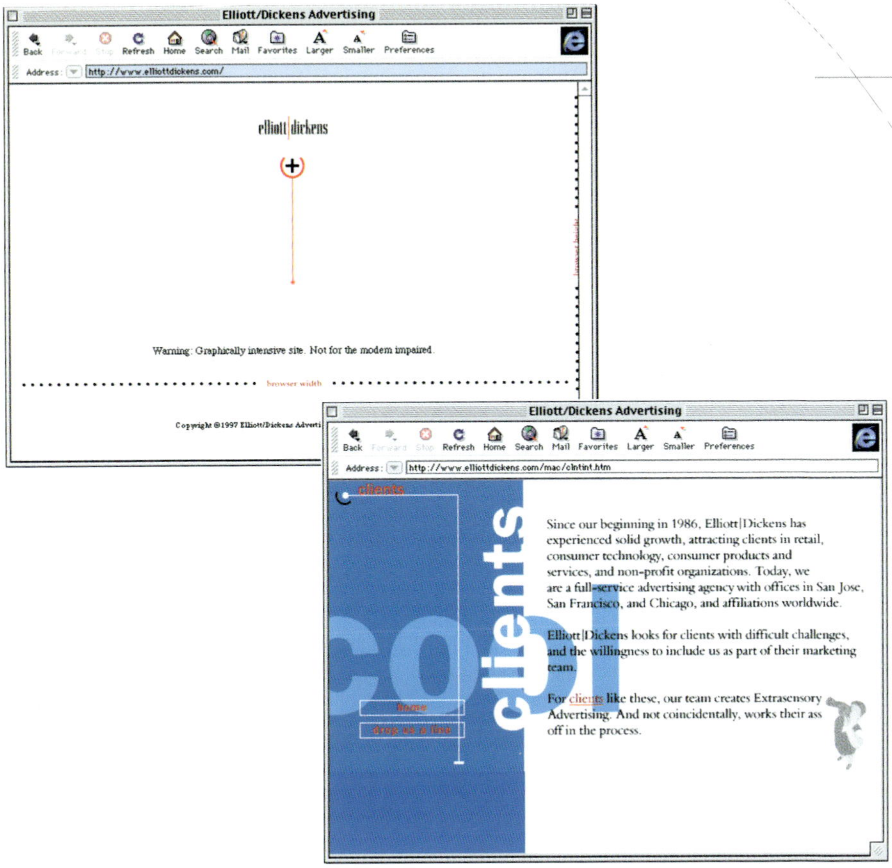

Title
elliott/dickens
URL
http://www.elliottdickens.com
Design firm
elliott/dickens
Designers
percy wang, dave cook, cardinal o'neill, chris tiernan
Photographer
jack christiansen
Producers
ted ganchiff, andy laing
Authoring platform
mac, pc

The designers take an interesting approach to navigation by advising browser height and width on the home page, and then immediately violating the horizontal direction by making pages about twice that width. They turn the horizontal scrollbar into a page flip control: when you click on the scrollbar area, you get the other half of the page instantly.

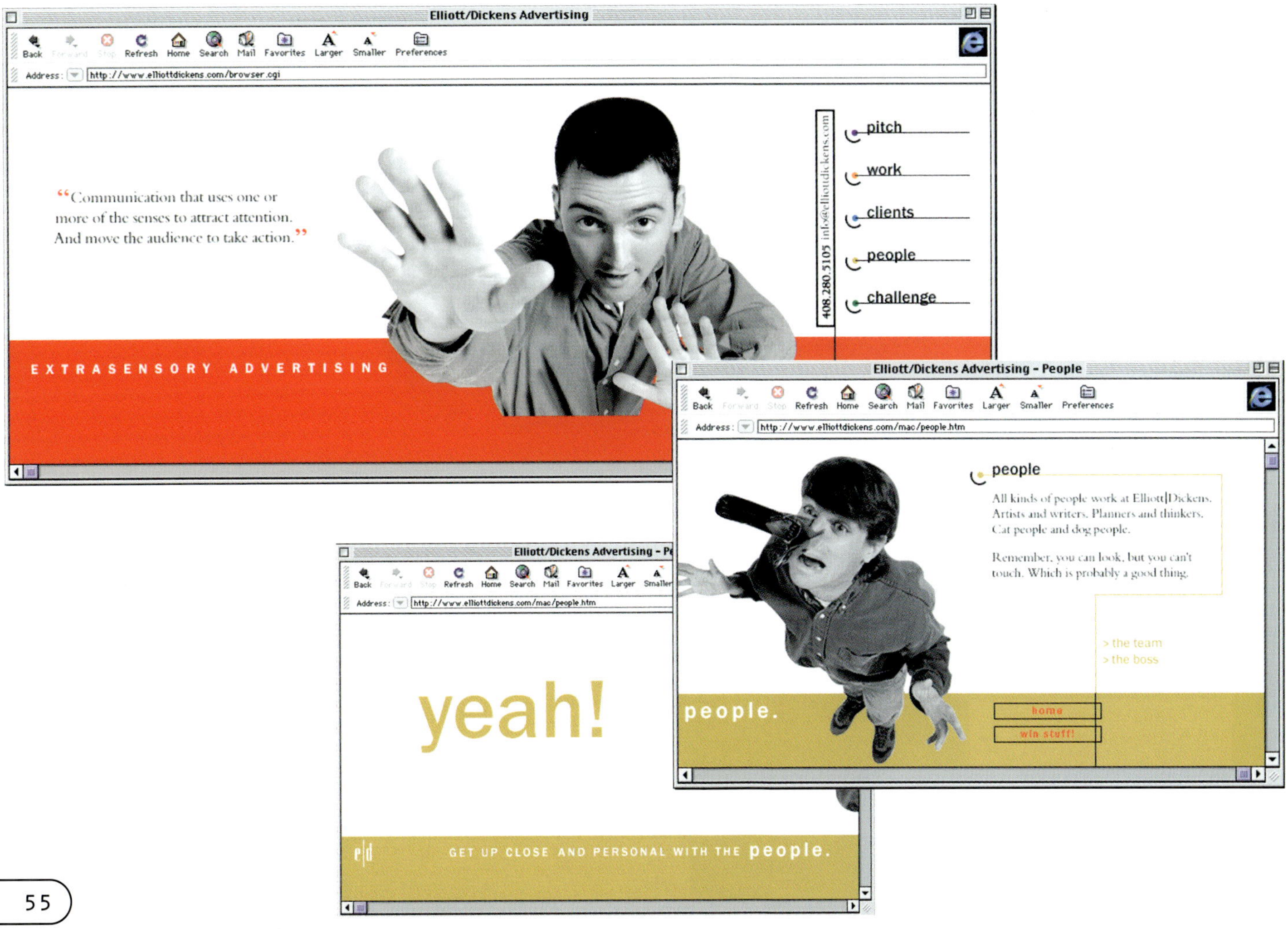

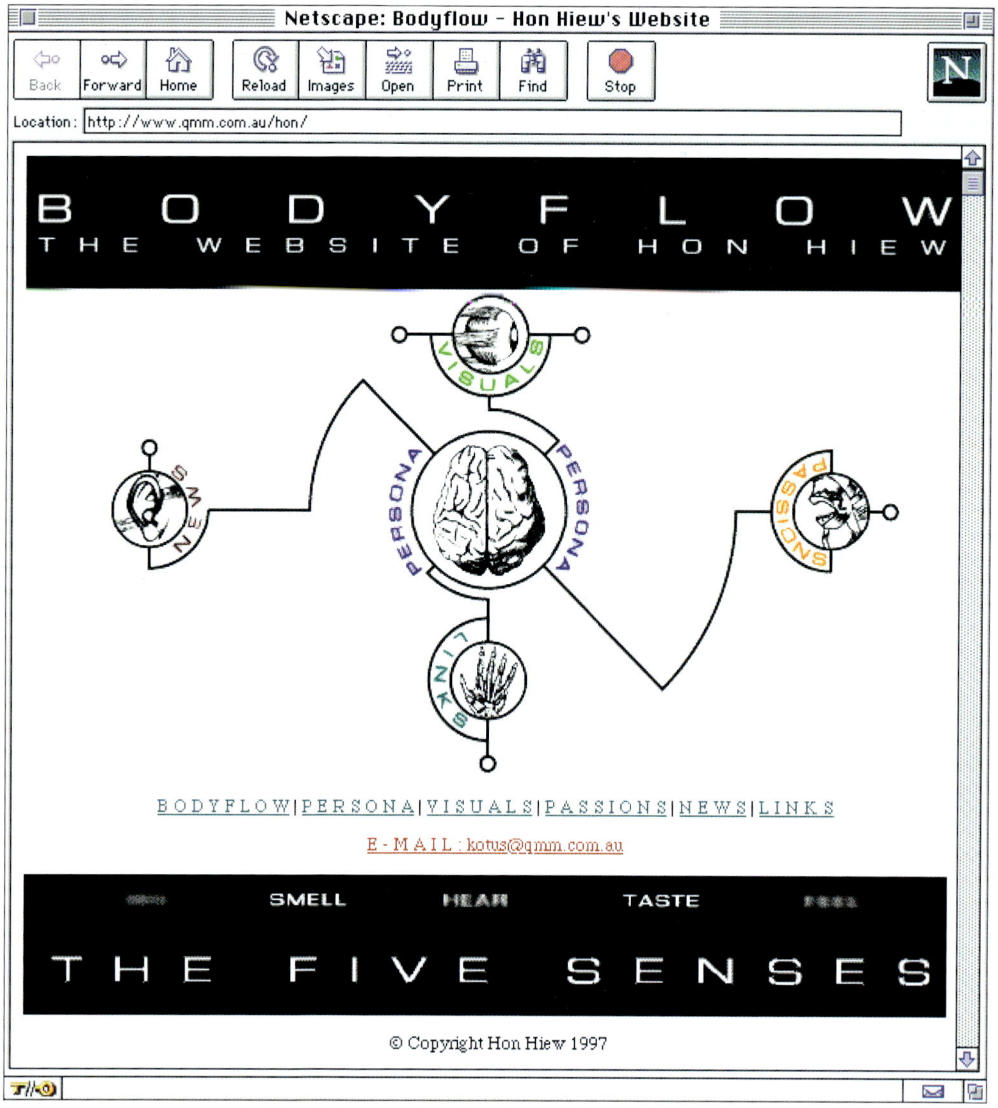

title
bodyflow portfolio
URL
http://www.qmm.com.au/hon
designer
Hon Hiew

The navigational elements here are not notable for their originality—essentially just icons with text labels—but the geometric fragments that tie them together make for a striking design. They reinforce the atmosphere of scientific cleanliness introduced by medical drawings, which add to the spirit of examination and exploration.

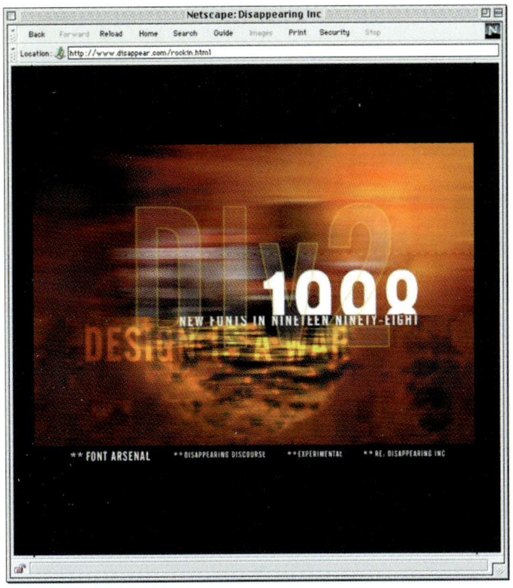

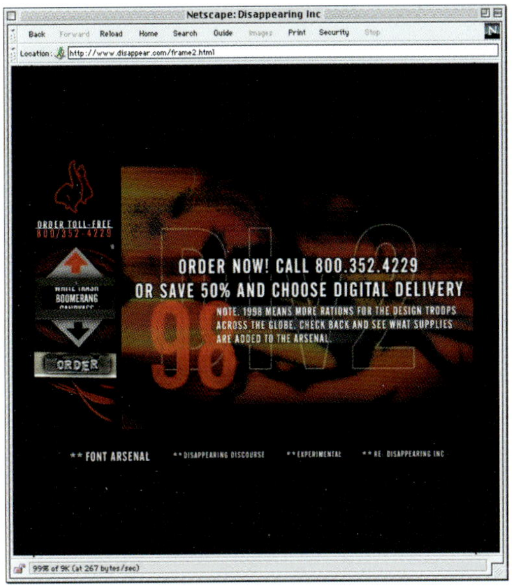

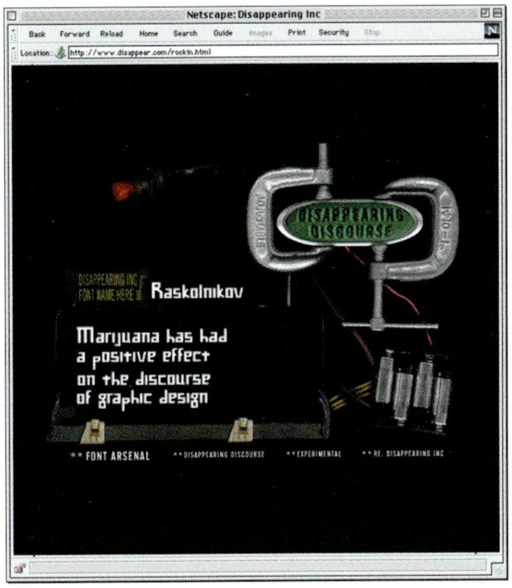

title

The Disappearing Inc Font Arsenal

URL

http://www.disappear.com/rockin.html

design firm

Disappearing Inc

designers/illustrators/photographers

Jason Lucas, Jeff Prybolsky

programmer

Al McElrath

authoring platform

Mac

Instead of cluttering the screen with a list of fonts offered by the company, the designers at Disappearing, Inc. developed this Java-based rolling gauge. With highlighted rollover effects and sound, they've added a creative element to their navigation. Other pages feature other switches and buttons to press, reinforcing the built-from-garage-scraps feel to the site.

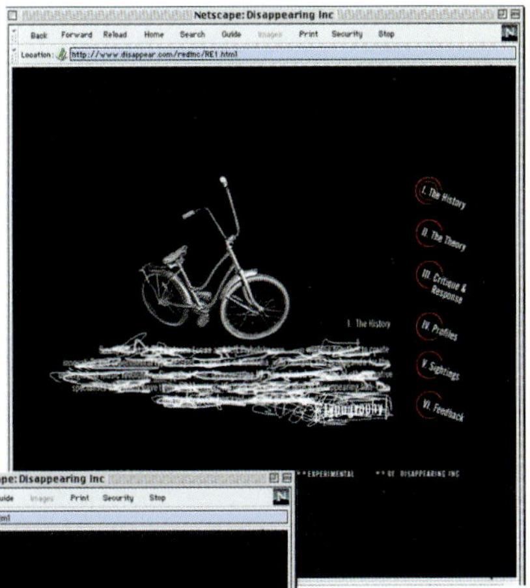

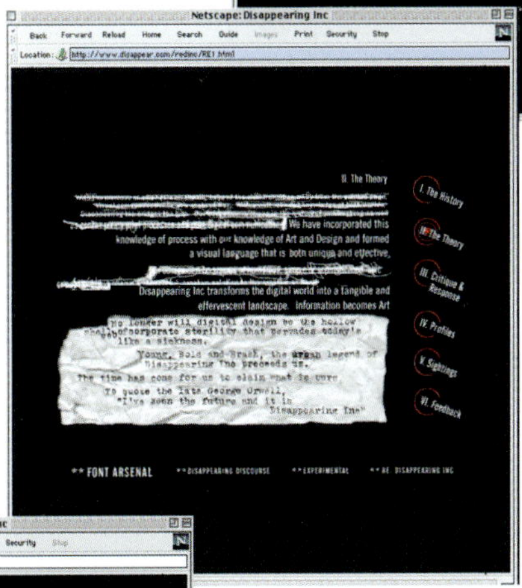

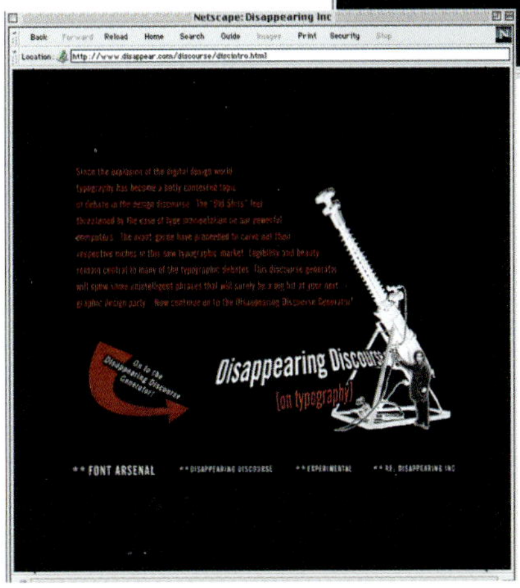

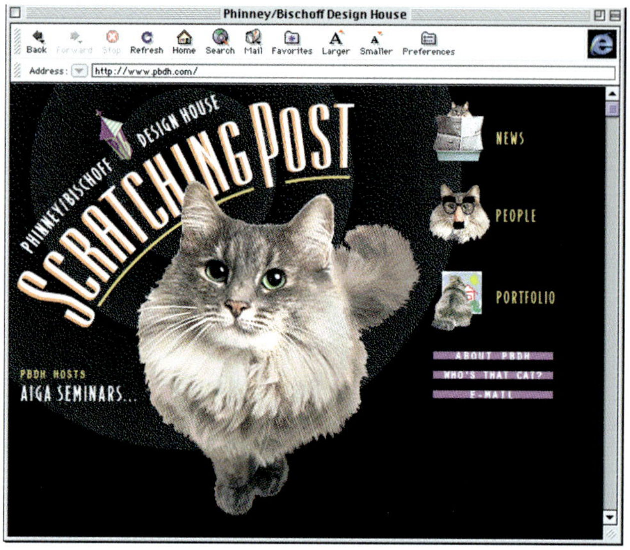

Title
phinney/bischoff design house, inc.
URL
http://www.pbdh.com/
design firm
phinney/bischoff design house, inc.
designer/illustrator
Neil Robertson
photographer
Karl Bischoff
programmers
Neil Robertson, Scotty Carreiro
creative directors
Leslie Phinney, Karl Bischoff
Authoring platform
Mac

This design firm has a few things to present to its current and potential clients, and it makes them reachable through single clicks. The cat, Ruby, is the tour guide and a recurring element. Whimsical touches (the cat reading a newspaper on a litter box) make it clear what the area in question is about (news).

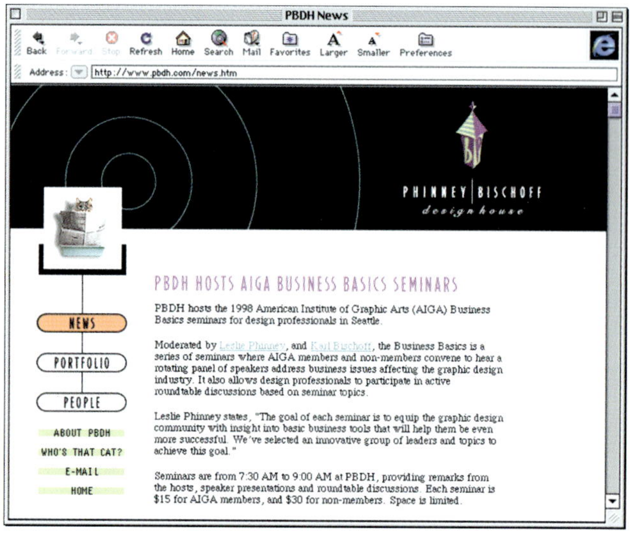

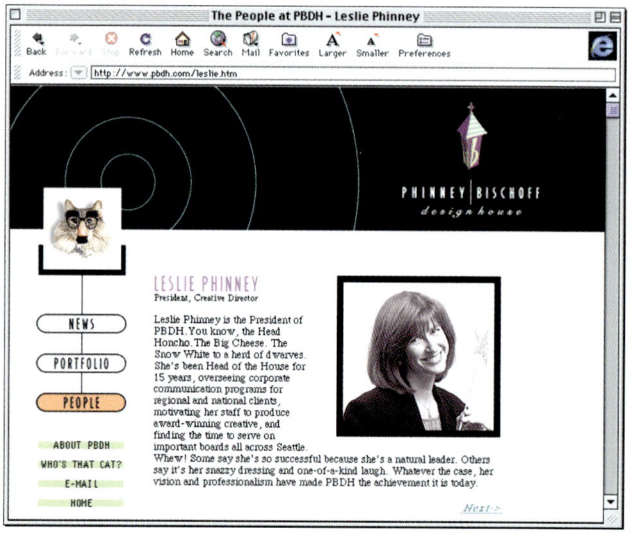

title
Bau-Da Design Lab, Inc.
URL
http://www.bauda.com/
design firm
Bau-Da Design Lab, Inc.
designer/illustrator
P.R. Brown
programmer
Eric Brown
authoring platform
Mac

Bau-Da Design Lab has overlaid scientific organization on top of its elegant site, assigning numbers and letters to different categories. The tab and numbers at the top are framed consistently, while each section loads an interstitial quote before loading the section's main page. To add to the scientific quality, braces are used to tie together navigation links.

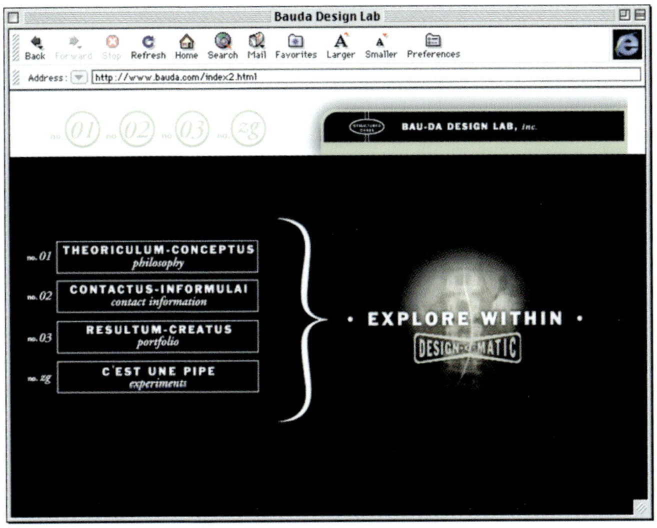

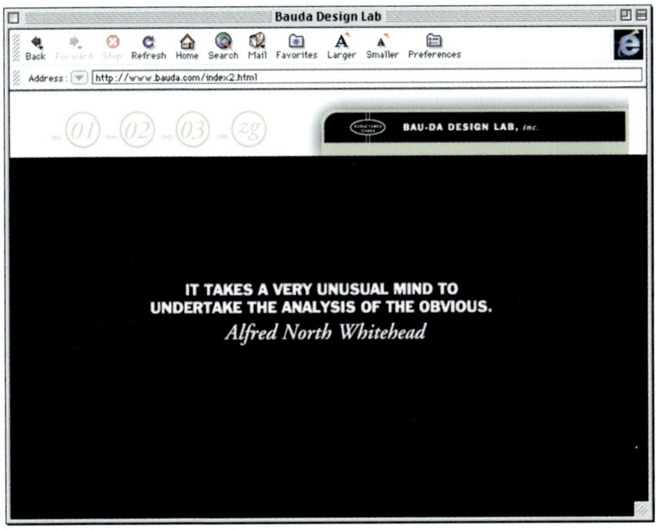

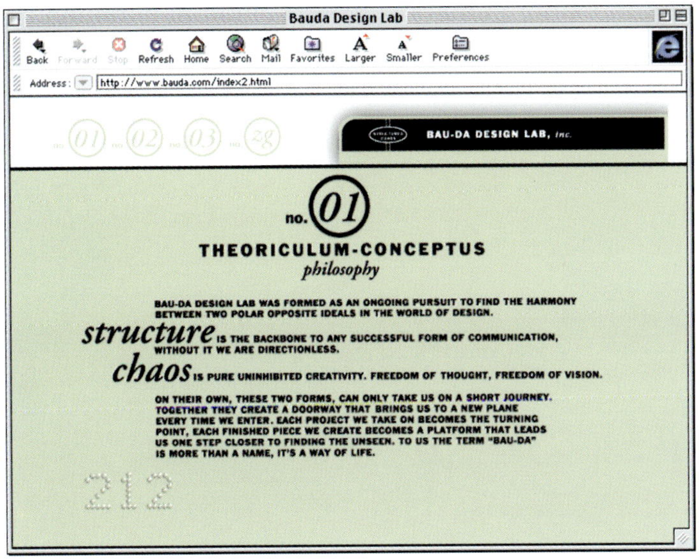

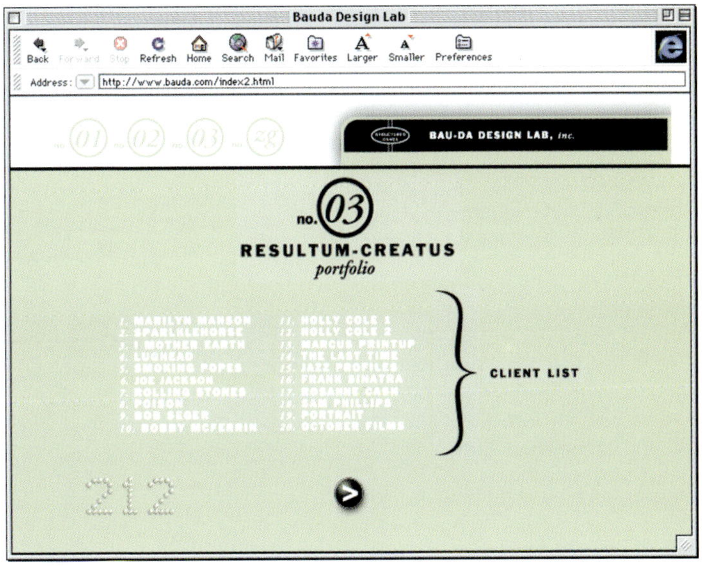

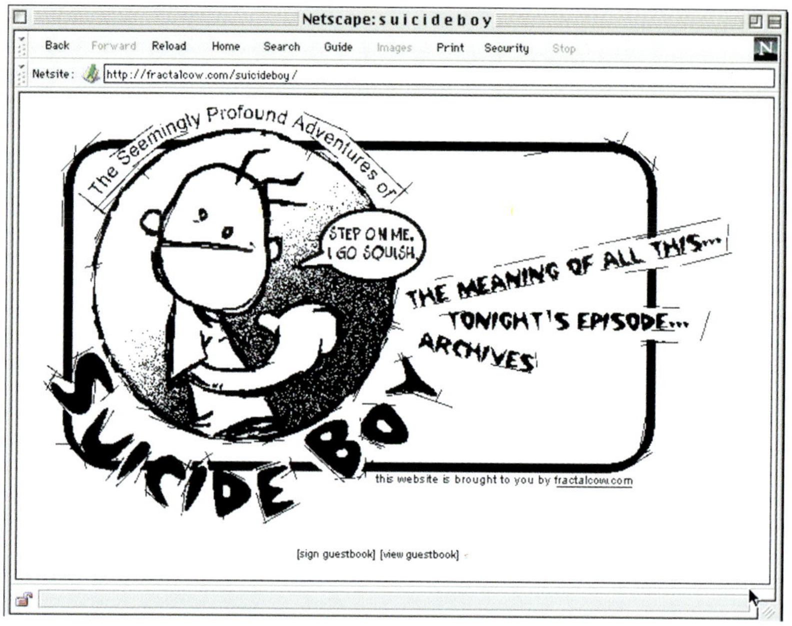

title
fractal cow studio
URL
http://www.fractalcow.com/
design firm
http://www.binary-soup.com
and fractal cow studio
designer/illustrator/
photographer/programmer
Dino Ignacio
authoring platform
PC

The comics you see in the newspaper are divided into panels to show where one thought or action ends and the next begins in a limited amount of space. Surprisingly, many comics appearing on the Web follow the same pattern, despite the increased flexibility of available screen space. Fractal Cow's comics take advantage of the medium by displaying panels as their own windows (with simple arrows to move to the next panel, but not back to the previous one—who wants to read backwards?).

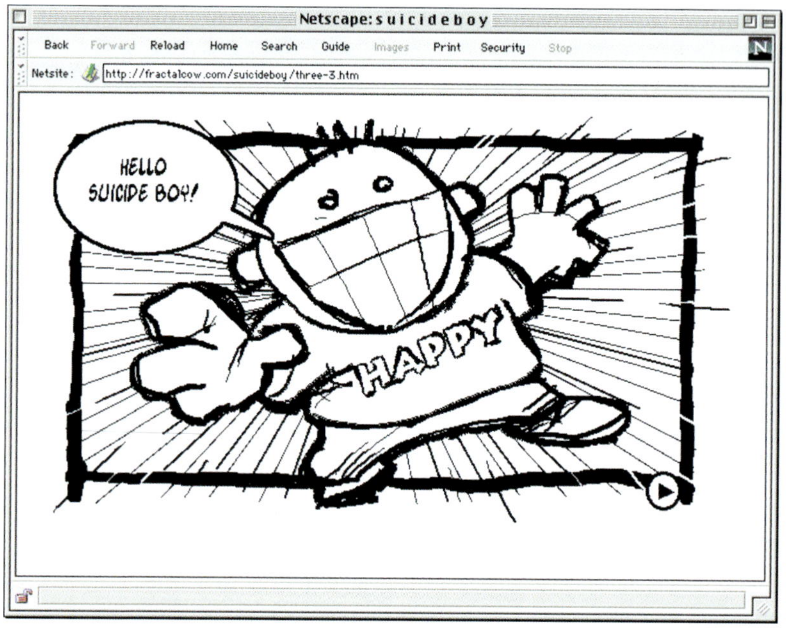

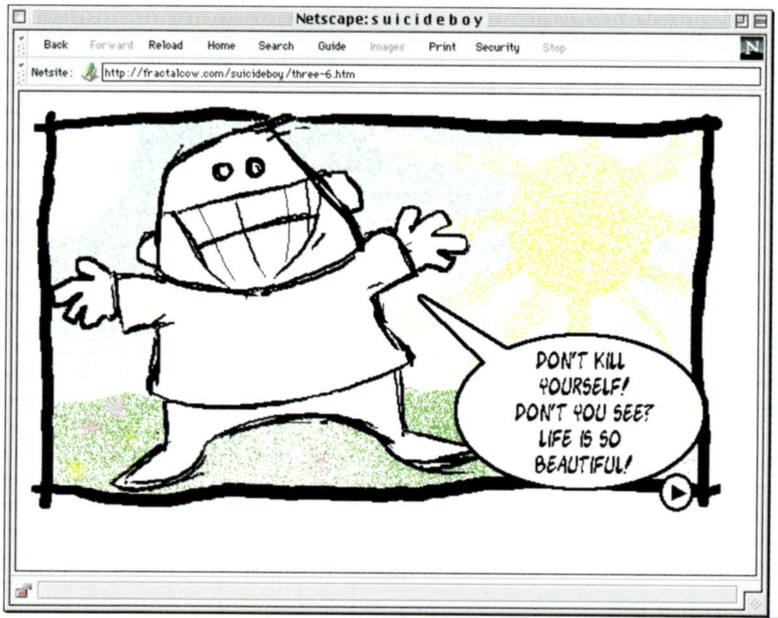

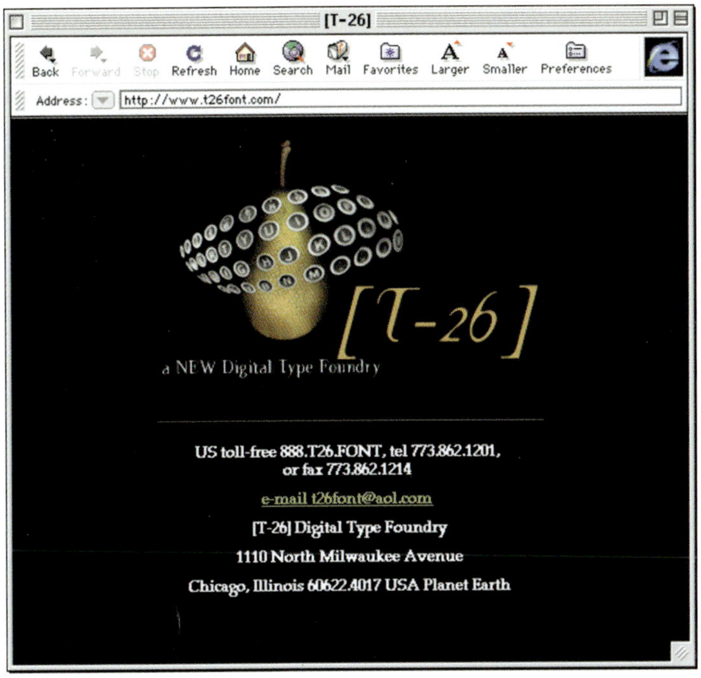

title
[T-26] Digital Type Foundry
URL
http://www.t26font.com/
design firm
Segura Inc.
designer/illustrator/programmer
Jim Marcus
photographers
Jim Marcus, Sandy Sager
authoring platform
Mac

The left-side navigation bar uses triangles to expand and collapse a site map. You can be in a section and click expand or collapse, or click on the triangle to blow out the section. Whatever section you're in has its subcategories displayed in a top frame in a more artistic fashion than the utilitarian (and useful) side bar.

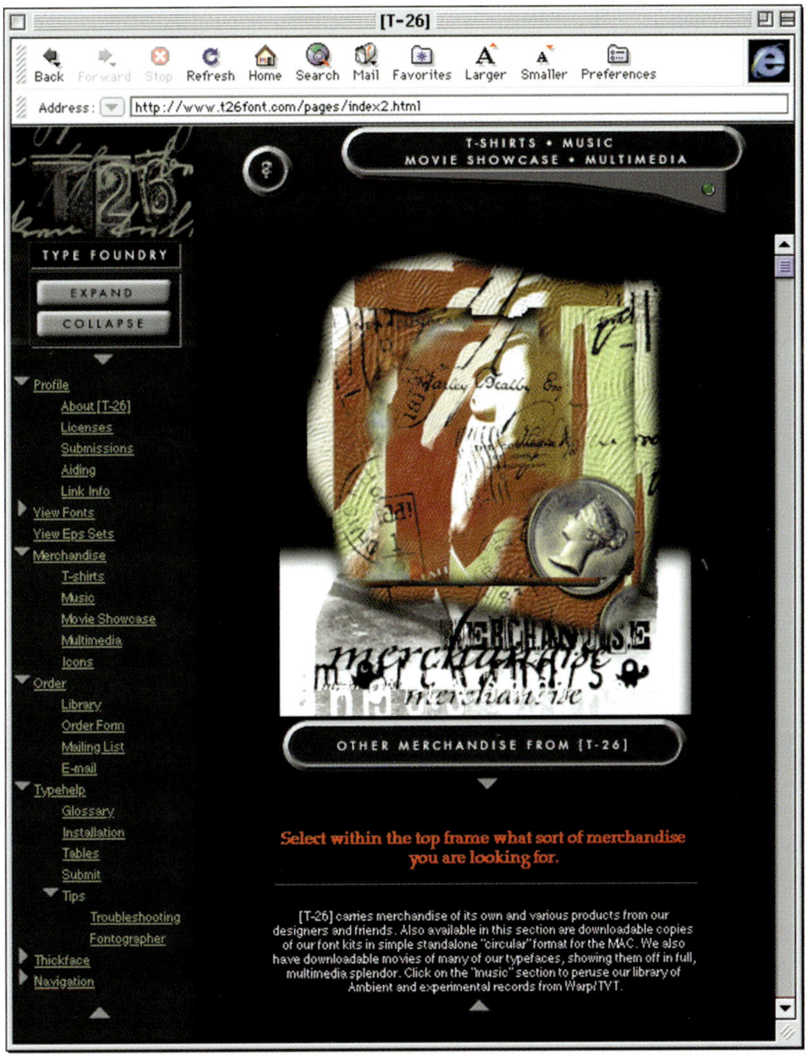

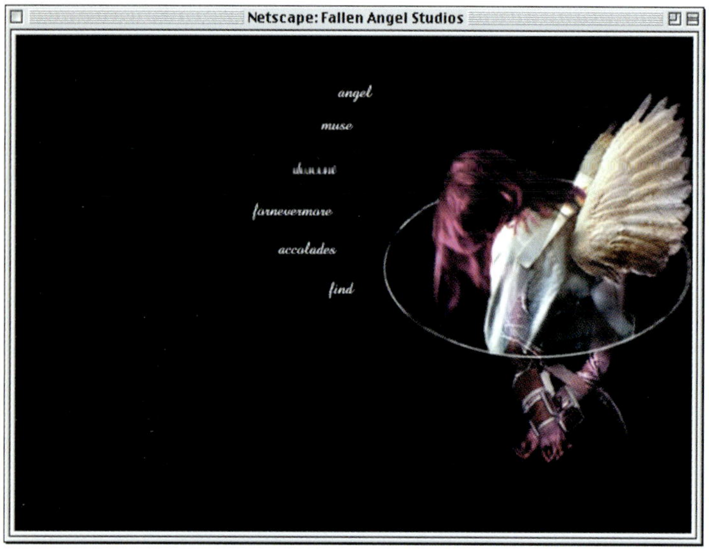

Title
fallen Angel studios
URL
http://www.fallenangelstudio.com/
Design firm
knight errant design
Designer/Illustrator/photographer
Bob Libby
Authoring platform
pc

Overall, the Web tends to be a fairly structured place; consistent navigational elements ensure that people will traverse the site without too much difficulty. For some sites, however, navigation can be as much of a page's content as the delivery vehicle. Fallen Angel's navigation depends on the subject matter and visual balance, often changing for artistic, not architectural, reasons.

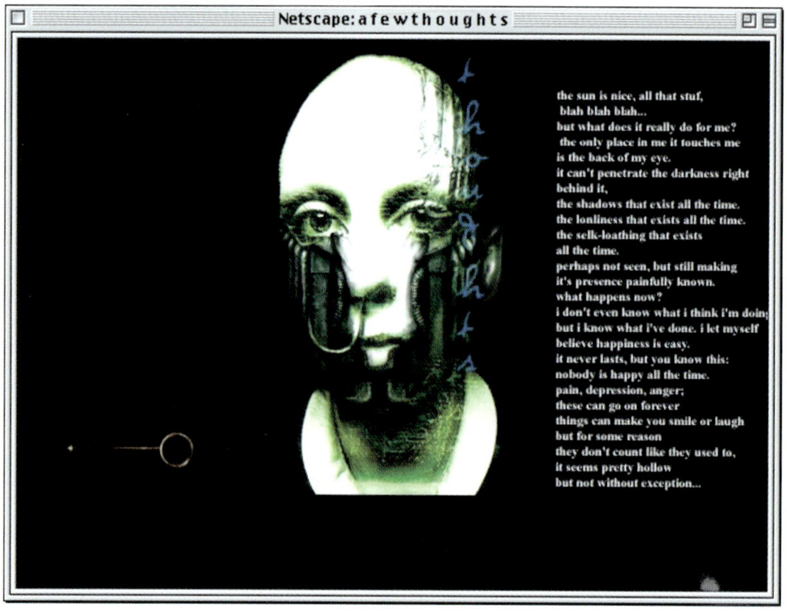

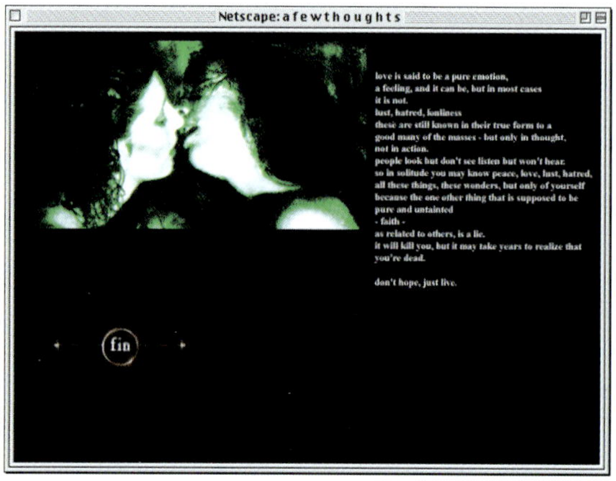

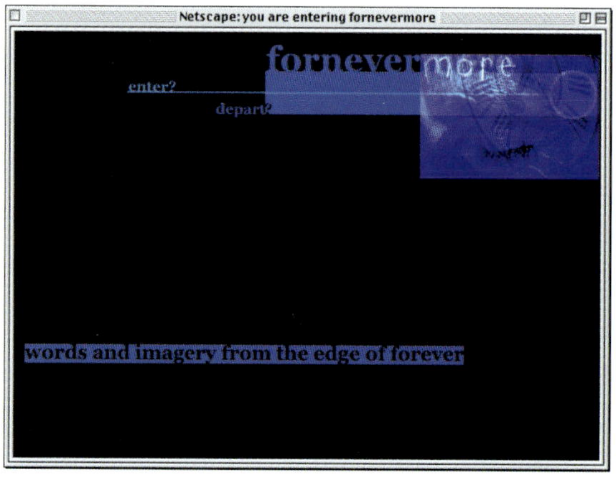

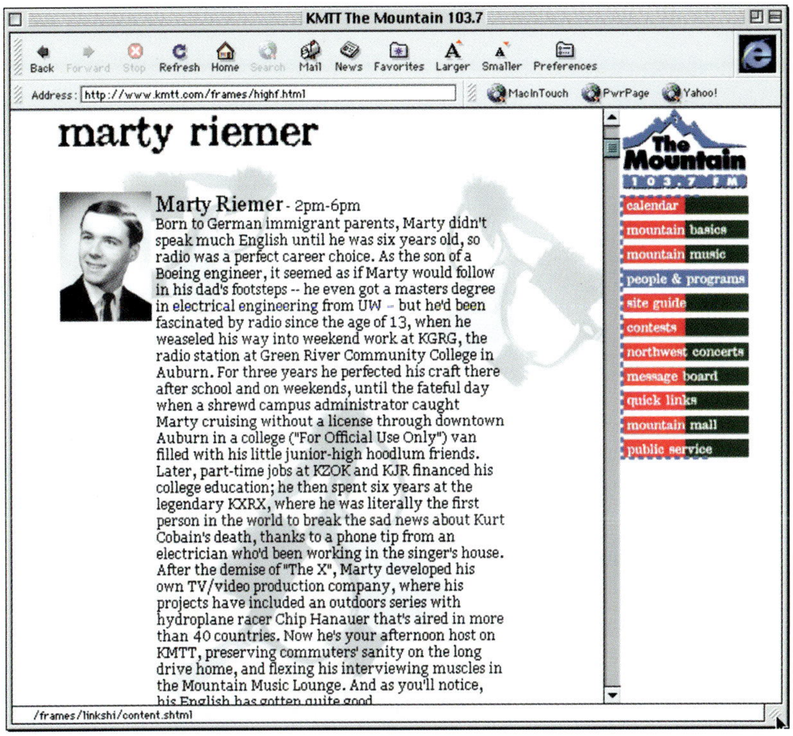

Title
KMTT-FM
URL
http://www.kmtt.com/
Design Firm
US Web
Designers
Kristin Ingalls, Mark Fromson
Programmer
Bob Cottrell
Authoring Platform
Mac, PC

Despite its surrounding hype, Java is still in its very early stages of usefulness, which is why many complex Java implementations invariably fail. This radio-station Web site uses Java in a more limited manner, providing directional headings from which subdirectory links pop up when highlighted by the cursor.

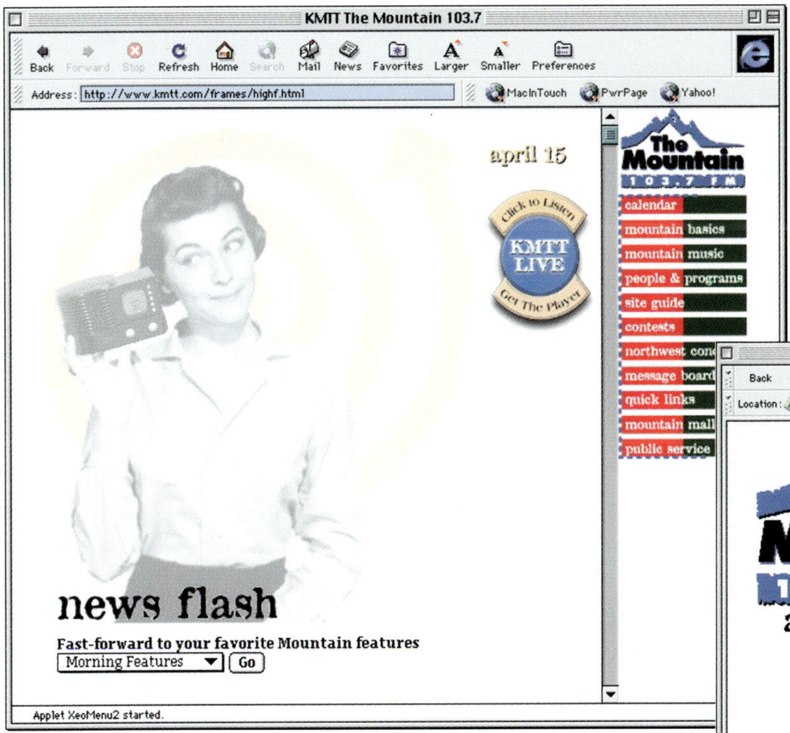

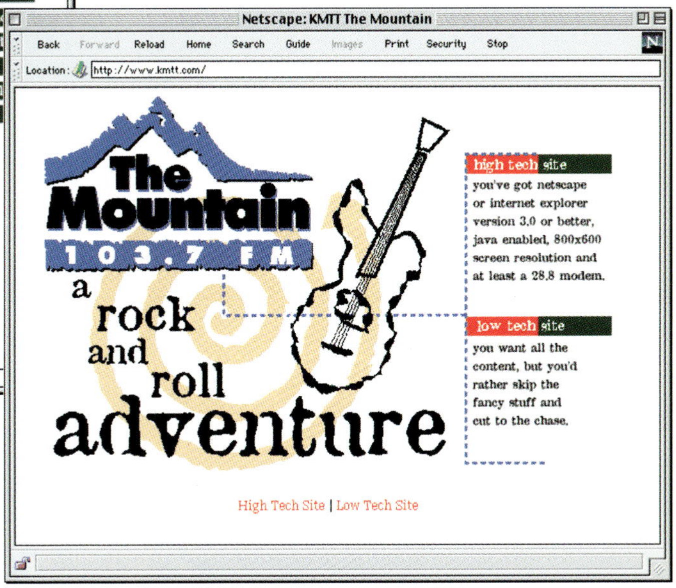

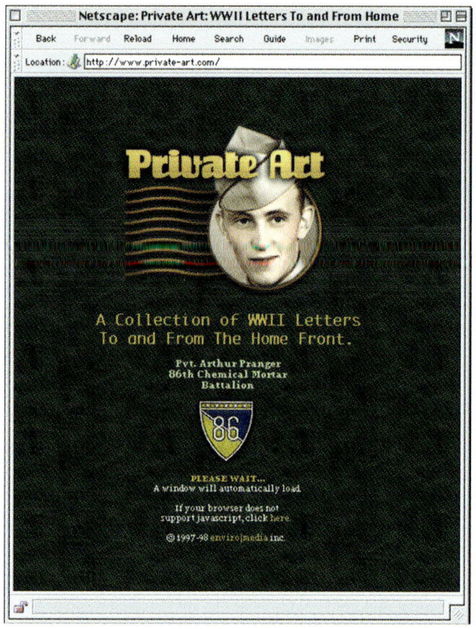

Title
private Art: WWII Letters To and From Home
URL
http://www.private-art.com/
Design firm
enviromedia, inc.
Designer/Illustrator
Rebecca pranger
programmer
Larry pranger
Authoring platform
Mac

This collection of World War II photos and remembrances features navigational elements that blend in with their surroundings. Using a frames-based layout offers flexibility; the top frame's image changes depending on where you are in the site, as do the links in the bottom frame. Because it uses frames, you never have to wait for full pages to completely reload; new material appears in its respective panel.

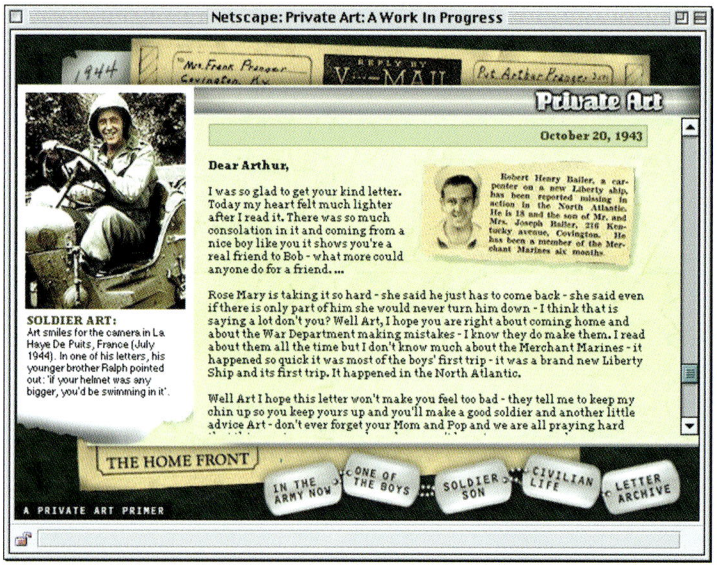

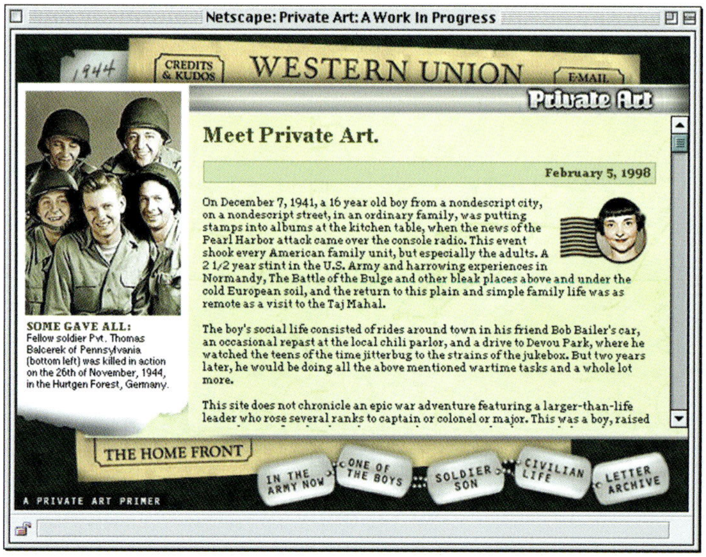

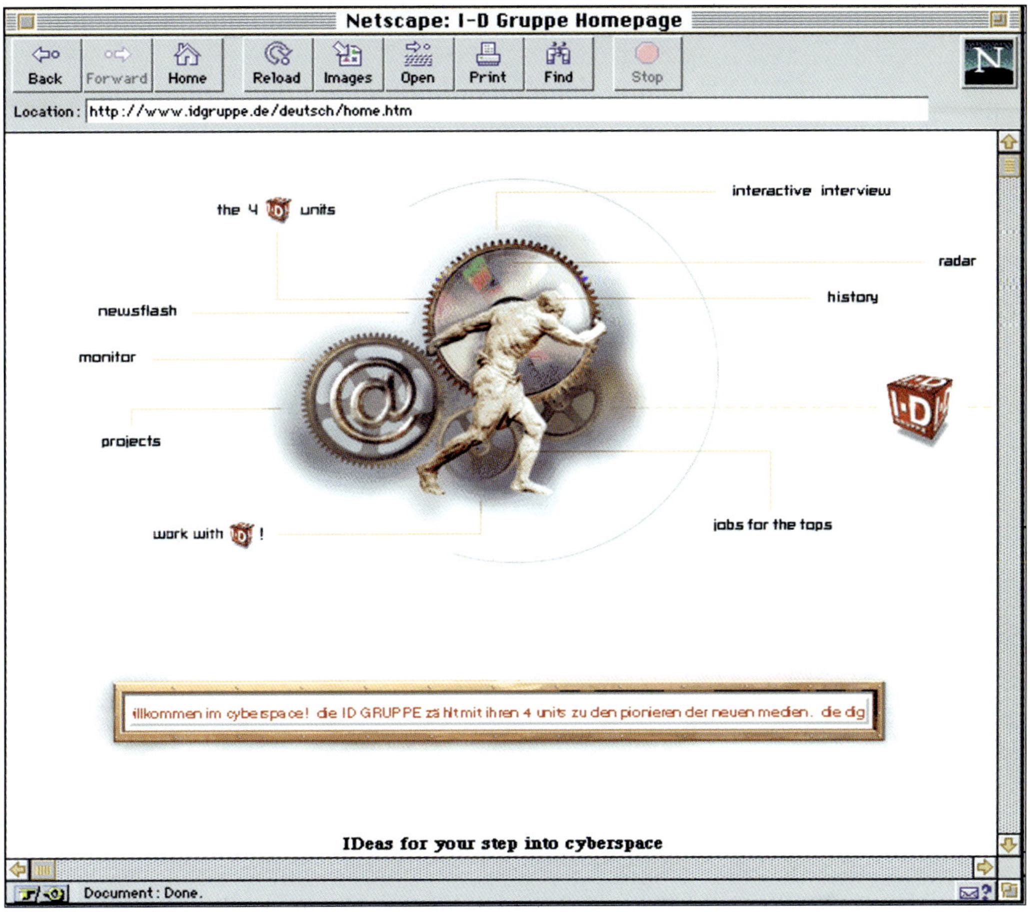

Title
ID Gruppe
URL
http://www.idgruppe.de/deutsch/home.htm
Design Firm
ID Gruppe

One of the current Web-design fads, it seems, is to attach labels to everything using lines that bend at right angles. The reason this approach works for this site is that the designers have opted to give the labels and rules enough room to breathe. Generous white space around the varying-width lines creates a visually interesting page.

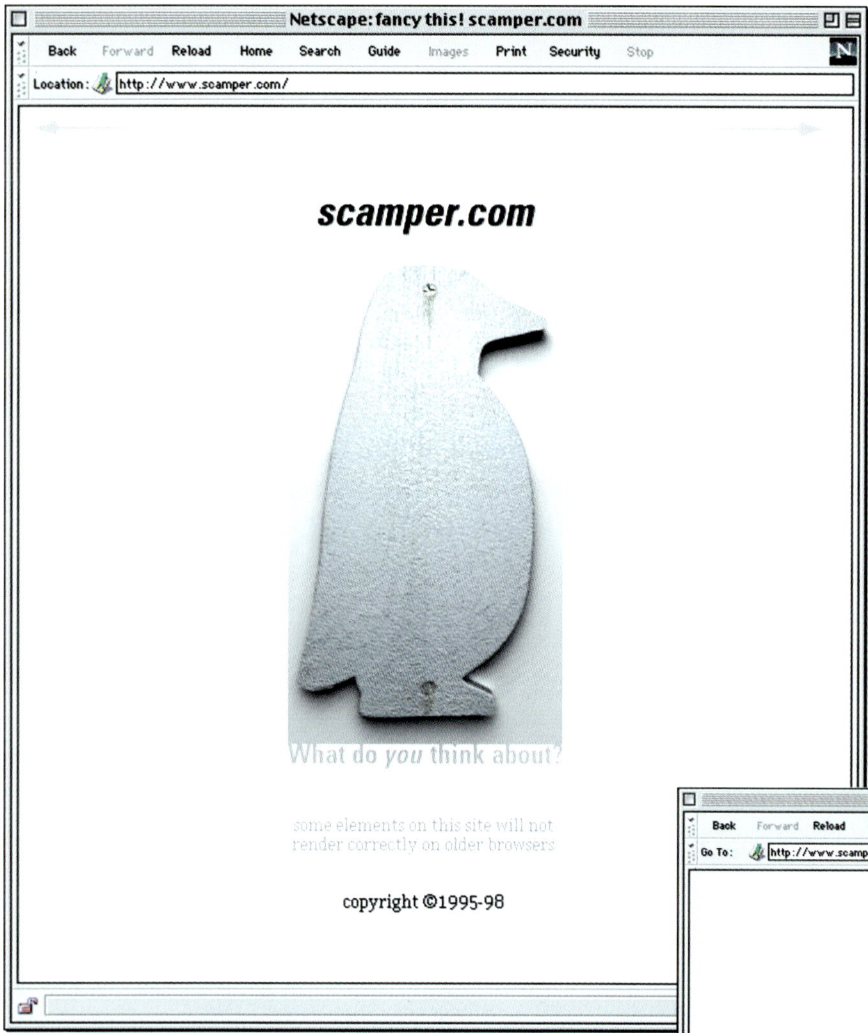

Netscape: fancy this! scamper.com
Back Forward Reload Home Search Guide Images Print Security Stop
Location: http://www.scamper.com/
scamper.com
What do you think about?
some elements on this site will not render correctly on older browsers
copyright ©1995-98

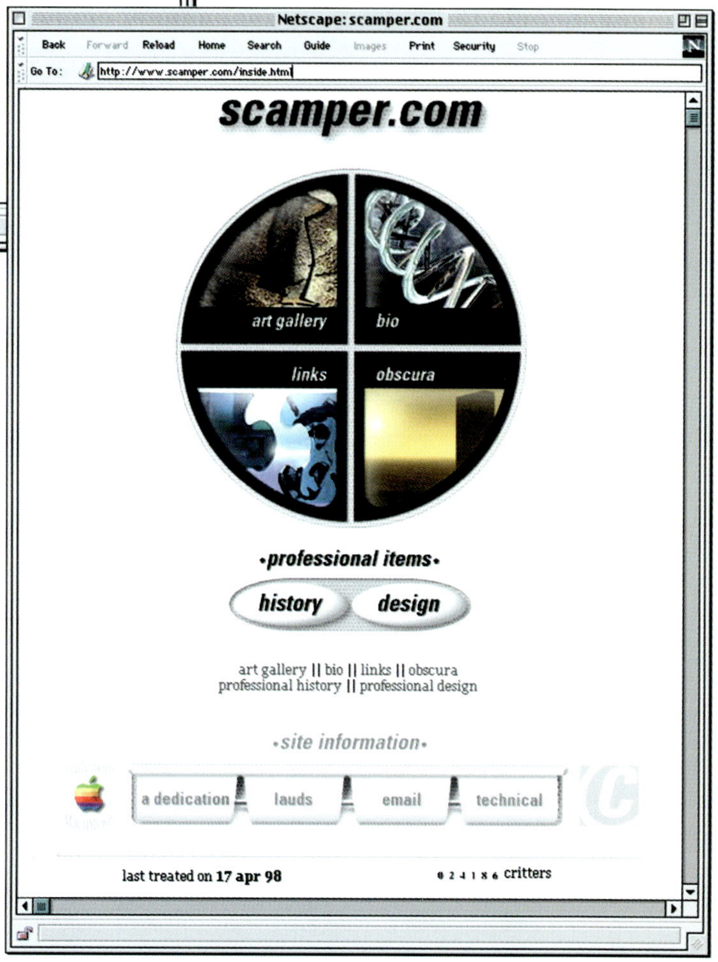

Netscape: scamper.com
Back Forward Reload Home Search Guide Images Print Security Stop
Go To: http://www.scamper.com/inside.html
scamper.com
art gallery
bio
links
obscura
•professional items•
history
design
art gallery || bio || links || obscura
professional history || professional design
•site information•
a dedication
lauds
email
technical
last treated on 17 apr 98
critters

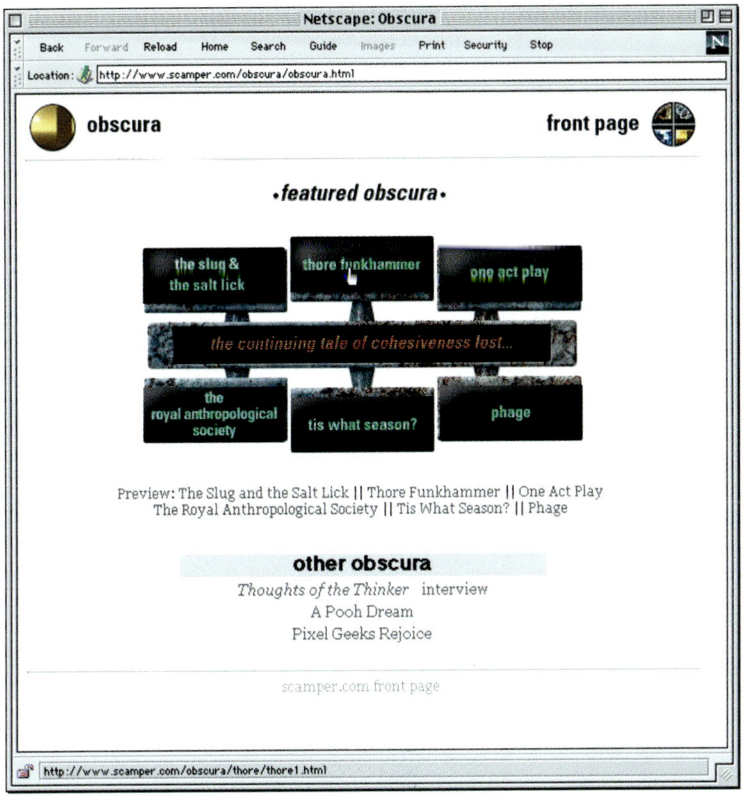

Title
scamper
URL
http://www.scamper.com/inside.html
Design Firm
scamper.com
Designer/programmer
Jeff Robinson
Authoring platform
Mac

Initially, the navigation here appears rather standard. With the exception of some nice JavaScript rollover effects on the main graphics, the page is pretty straightforward. But its standard appearance is a testament to the fact that there are three levels of information being presented (the main buttons, professional items, and site details). That's twelve possible directions on a page whose clean design suggests 6.

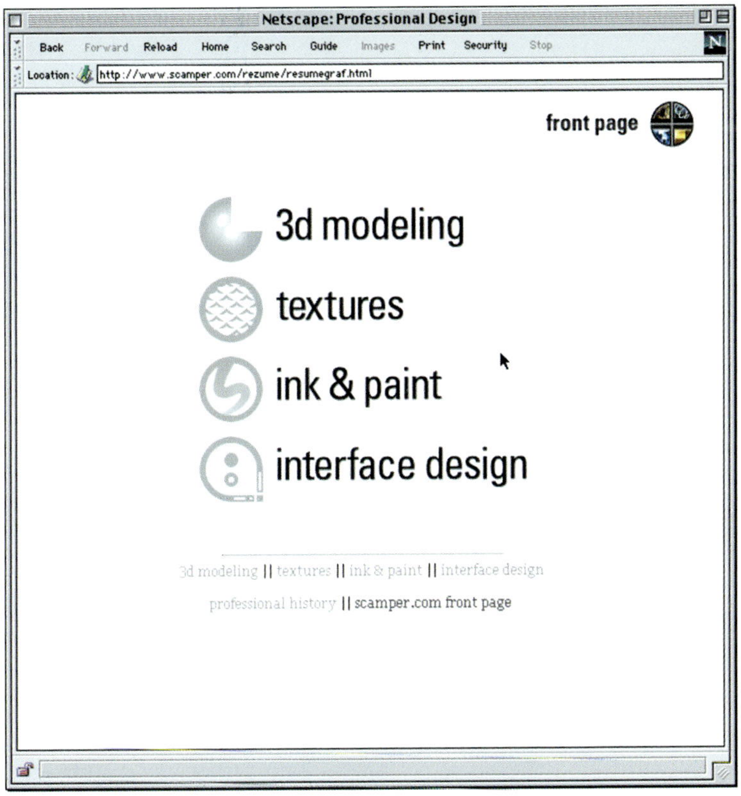

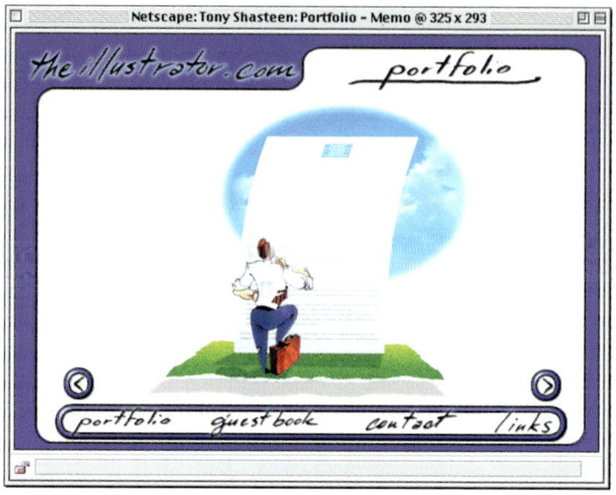

Title
The Illustrator
URL
http://www.theillustrator.com/
Design Firm
Tony Shasteen Illustration & Design
Designer/Illustrator
Tony Shasteen
Programmers
Digital Positions:
David Taylor-Klaus, Beth Cooper
Authoring Platform
Mac

Web navigation is more than just providing viewers with options that lead deeper into a site. It's also a matter of control: how to direct a viewer's experience while he's exploring a site to ensure that he finds the information he's looking for? At this site, nearly all of the elements, except for the logo drawing and gallery examples, are navigational elements—clicking on the arrow buttons moves forward and backward in succession, rather than presenting a varied palette of options.

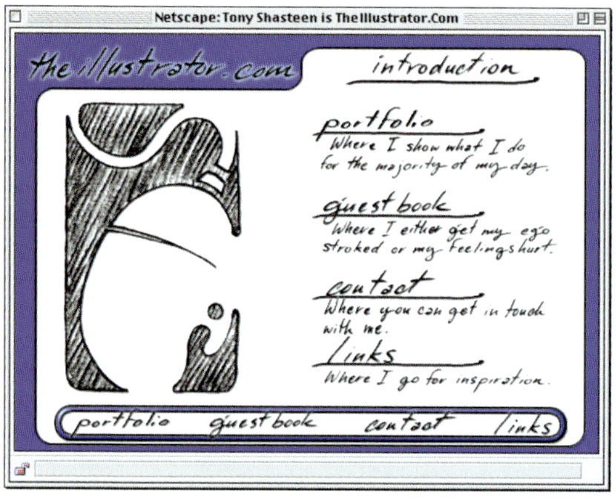

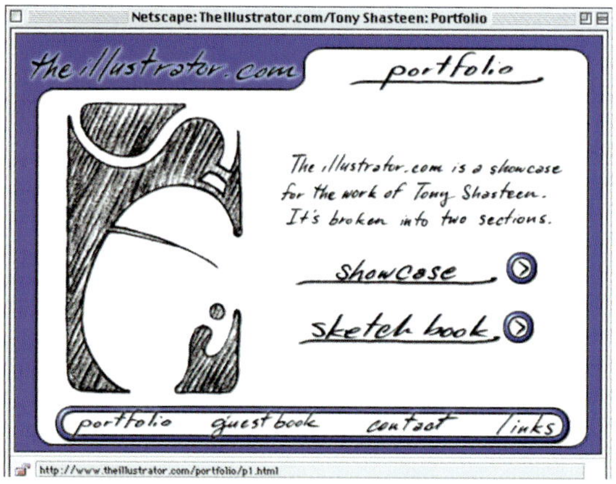

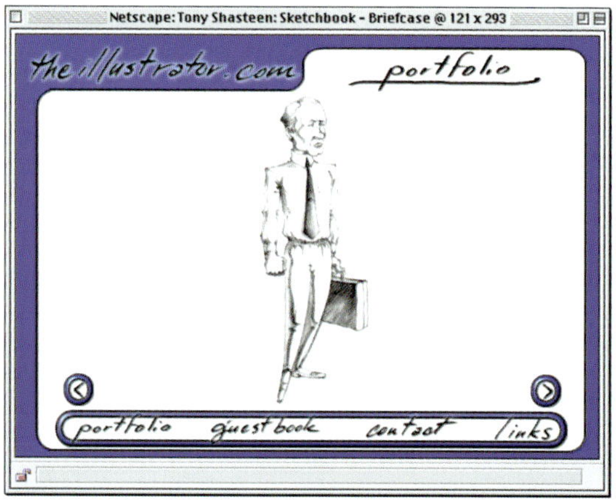

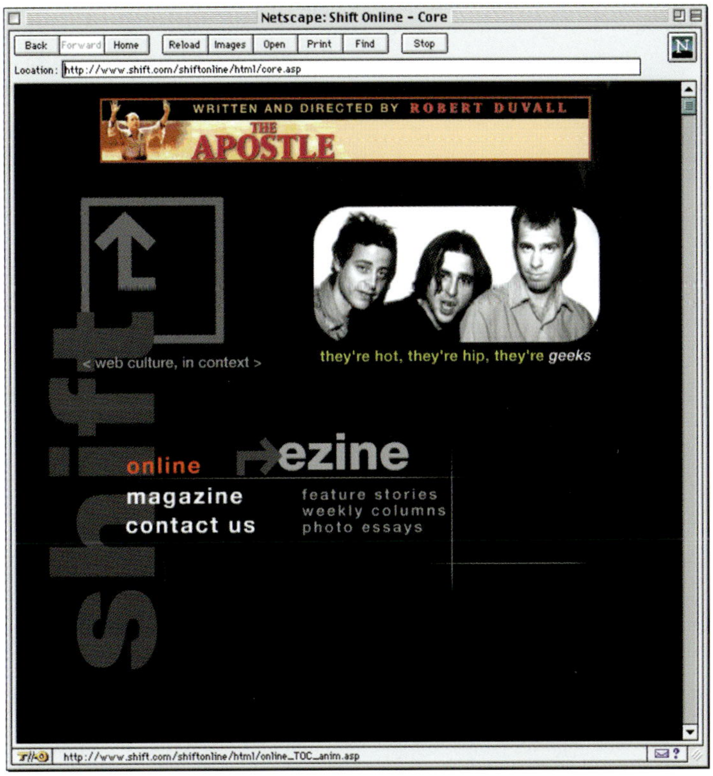

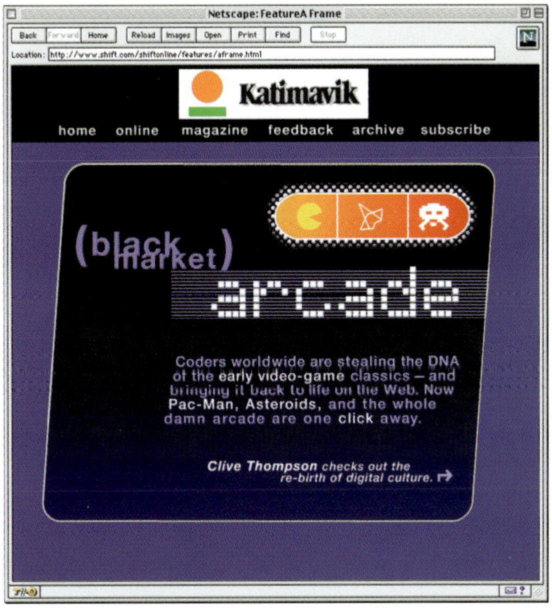

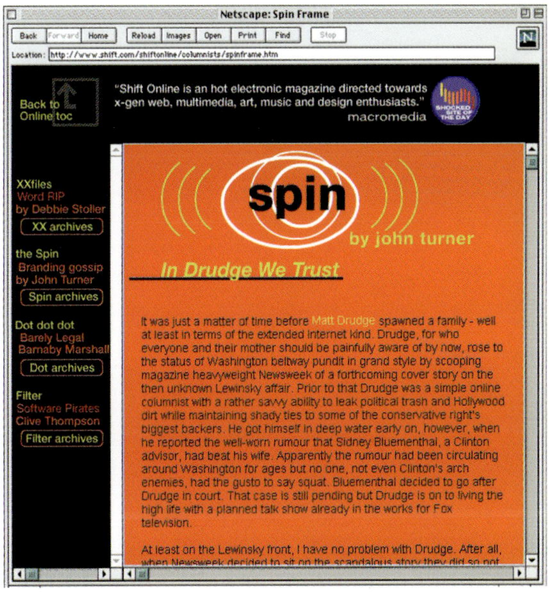

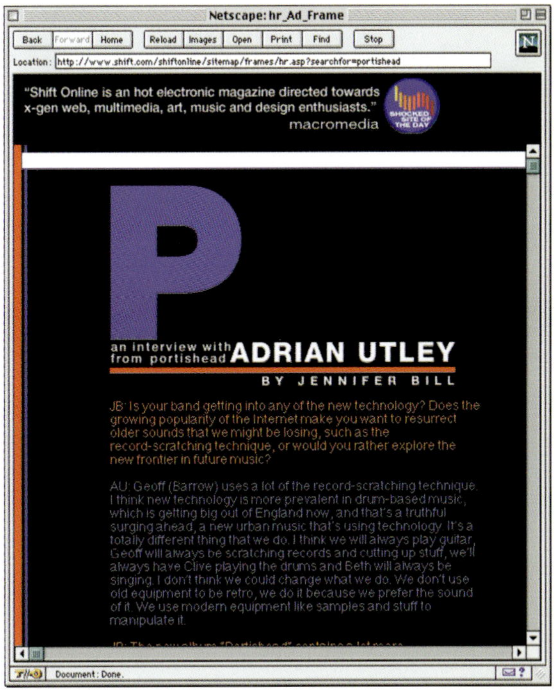

title
shift online
URL
http://www.shift.com/shiftonline/html/core.asp
designers
Barnaby Marshall, Dave Sylvestre
programmer
Al Baghal
authoring platform
Mac

If you're skeptical that a little interactivity on a Web site can make a difference, check out Shift. Except for a few sparse illustrations, the site is entirely text ... but text that moves! Employing Macromedia Flash technology, the section titles pop up more information on what can be found inside. Because the site uses text so heavily, getting around is straightforward and speedy.

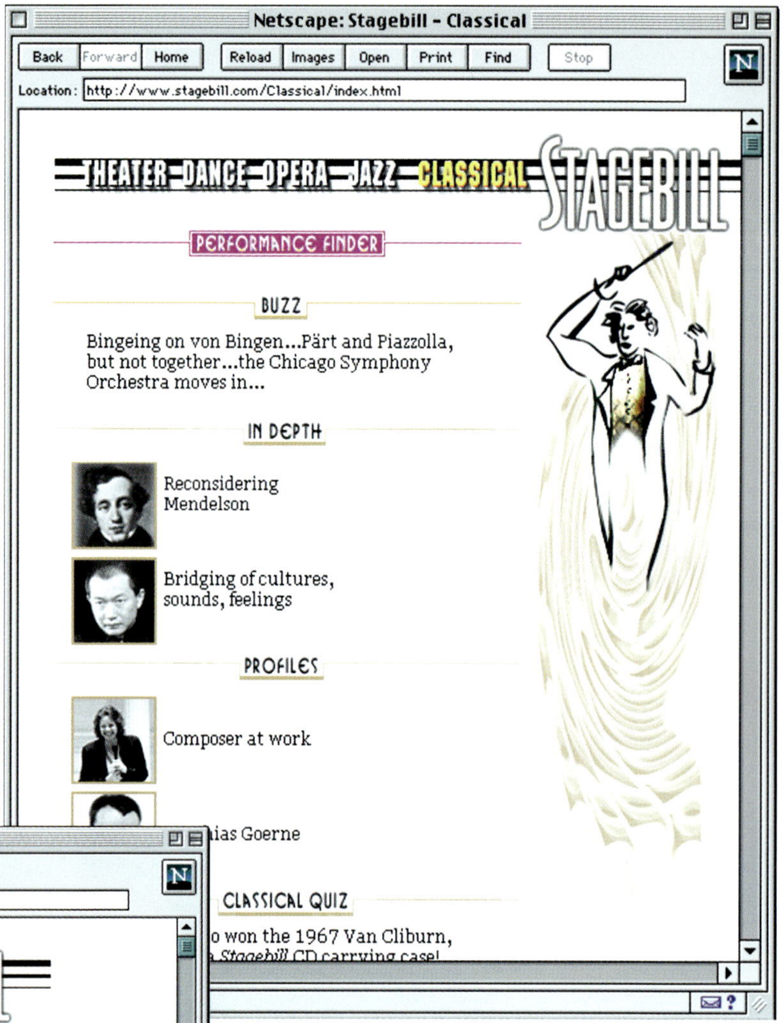
Netscape: Stagebill - Classical
Back
Forward
Home
Reload
Images
Open
Print
Find
Stop
Location: http://www.stagebill.com/Classical/index.html
THEATER DANCE OPERA JAZZ CLASSICAL
STAGEBILL
PERFORMANCE FINDER
BUZZ
Bingeing on von Bingen...Pärt and Piazzolla, but not together...the Chicago Symphony Orchestra moves in...
IN DEPTH
Reconsidering Mendelson
Bridging of cultures, sounds, feelings
PROFILES
Composer at work
CLASSICAL QUIZ

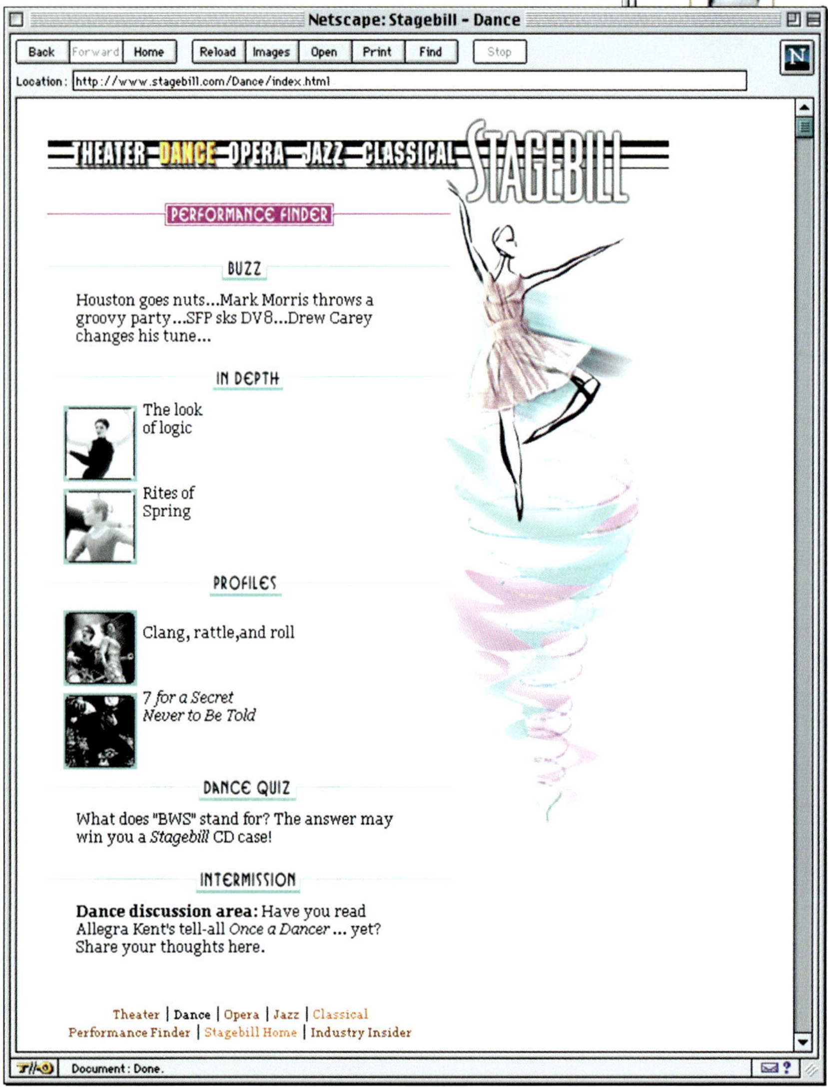
Netscape: Stagebill - Dance
Back
Forward
Home
Reload
Images
Open
Print
Find
Stop
Location: http://www.stagebill.com/Dance/index.html
THEATER DANCE OPERA JAZZ CLASSICAL
STAGEBILL
PERFORMANCE FINDER
BUZZ
Houston goes nuts...Mark Morris throws a groovy party...SFP sks DV8...Drew Carey changes his tune...
IN DEPTH
The look of logic
Rites of Spring
PROFILES
Clang, rattle,and roll
7 for a Secret Never to Be Told
DANCE QUIZ
What does "BWS" stand for? The answer may win you a Stagebill CD case!
INTERMISSION
Dance discussion area: Have you read Allegra Kent's tell-all Once a Dancer... yet? Share your thoughts here.
Theater | Dance | Opera | Jazz | Classical
Performance Finder | Stagebill Home | Industry Insider
Document: Done.

Title
stagebill
URL
http://www.stagebill.com/
Design Firm
T3 Media
Designers/Illustrators/Programmers
Chris Bryant, Michael Diamant
Producer
Shira Kalish

The designers of this site have done a good job of enlivening the pages while keeping the overall design clean and professional. JavaScript rollovers highlight the section your cursor points at, with a little razzle-dazzle added to the site's logo on subsequent pages. Inside, each main section is split into subsections, where the navigation appears within the contents of the page, rather than awkwardly grouped in a corner or side of the screen.

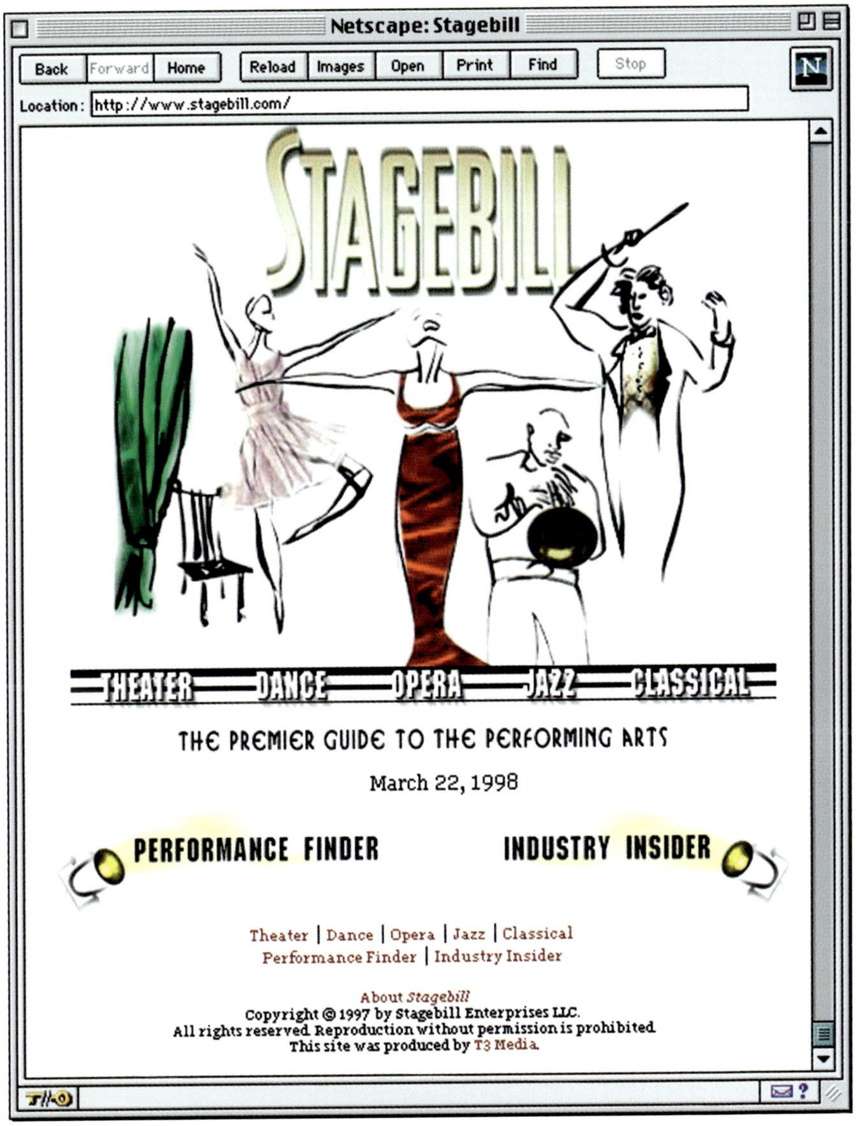

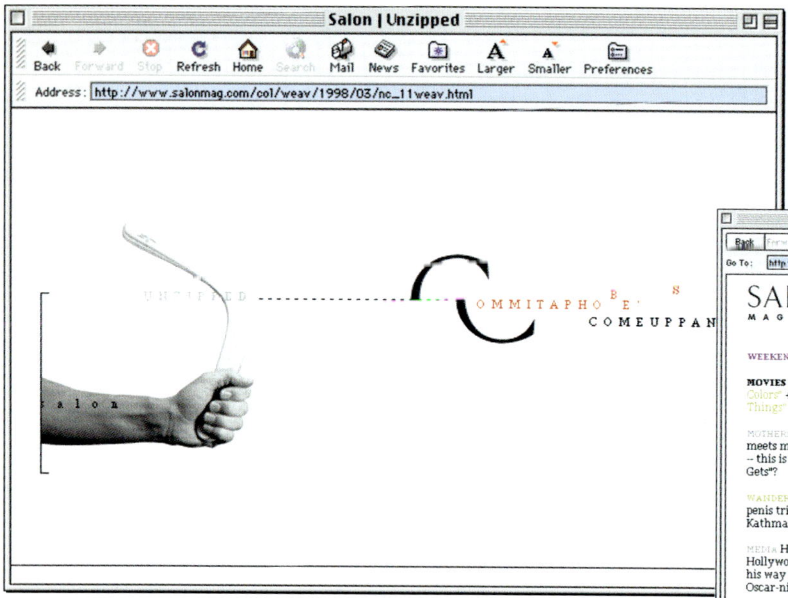

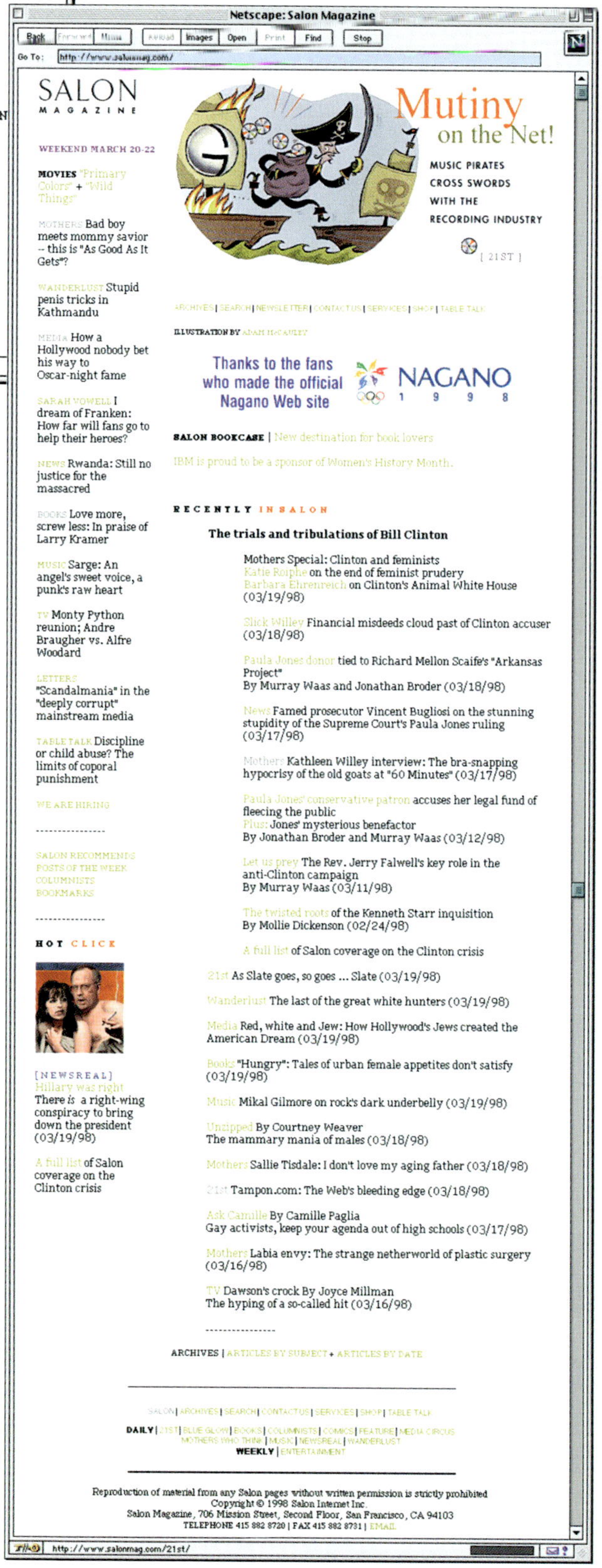

Title
salon Magazine
URL
http://www.salonmagazine.com/
Design firm
salon Magazine
Designers
Mignon Khargie ("commitaphobe's comeuppance," "girl, in Landscape"); Karen Templer ("Mutiny on the Net")
Illustrator
Adam Mcauly ("Mutiny on the Net")
Writer
Jonathan Lemen ("girl, in Landscape")
Authoring platform
Mac

Online magazines, especially ones whose content changes daily, need to not only highlight new material, but also provide a method of accessing older material that's still available (unlike print publications, which require that you visit the main office for back-issues). At Salon's main page, columns and smaller features appear along the left-hand side of the page, while recent articles and special features can be found below the main illustration. It's not only convenient, but also extremely flexible for the staff that has to frequently rotate new content.

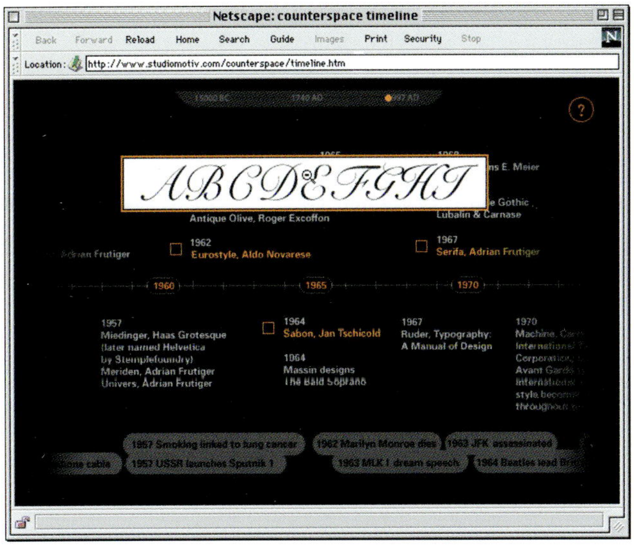

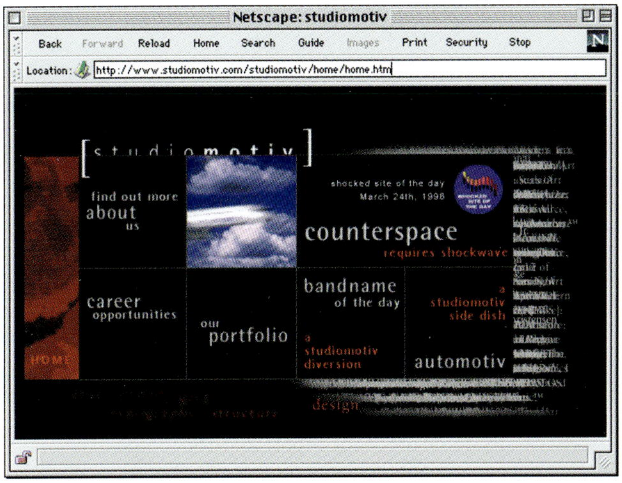

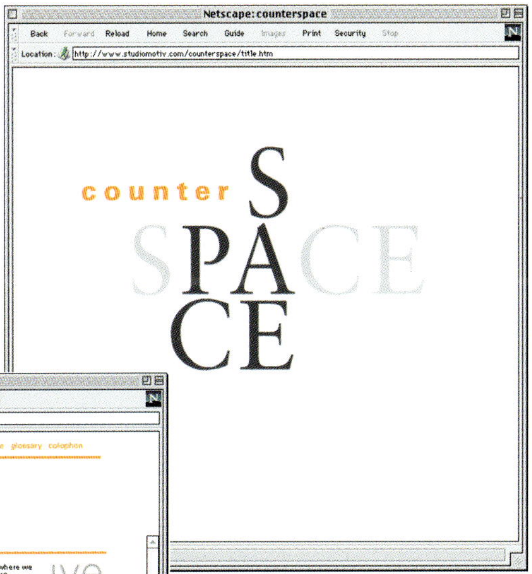

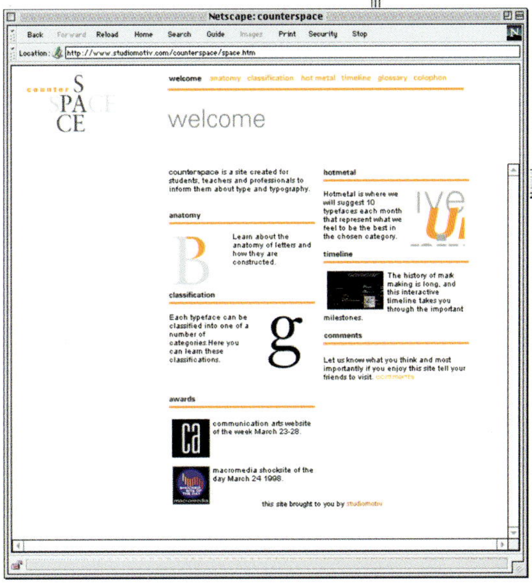

title
studiomotiv
URL
http://www.studiomotiv.com/studiomotiv/home/home.htm
design firm
studiomotiv
designers
Brett Collins, Ed Stull, Robert Abbott
illustrator
Brett Collins
programmers
Bill Litfin, Paul Rothrock
authoring platform
PC

Some designs require that the site navigation exist as its own entity, a floating palette here or a list of links there; other designs invite the navigation to be the design, as seen here. Using Macromedia Flash on the Counter Space area of the site, even straightforward text links at the top of the page emerge from a white mist.

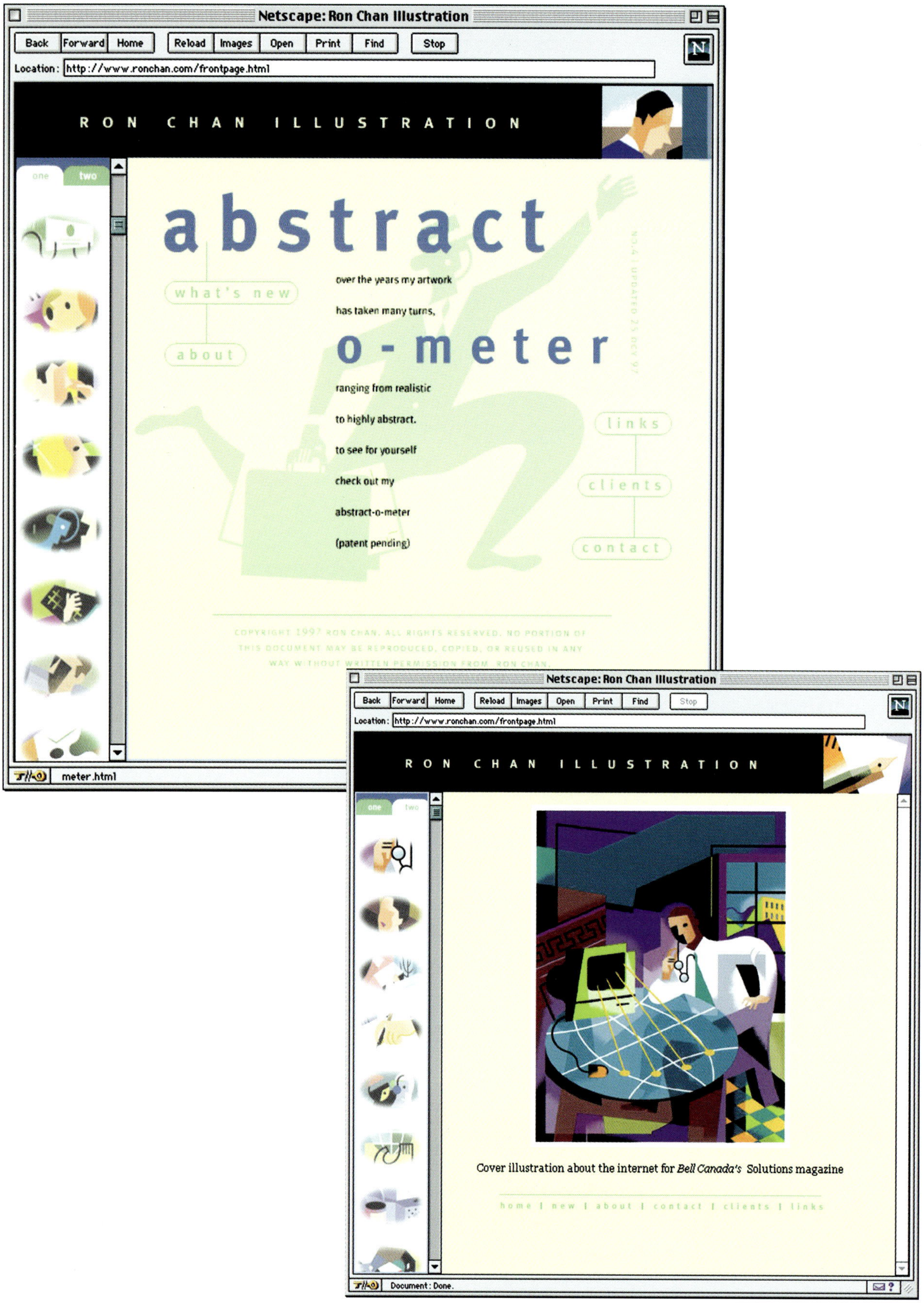
Netscape: Ron Chan Illustration
Back Forward Home Reload Images Open Print Find Stop
Location: http://www.ronchan.com/frontpage.html
RON CHAN ILLUSTRATION
one two
abstract
what's new
about
over the years my artwork
has taken many turns,
o-meter
ranging from realistic
to highly abstract.
to see for yourself
check out my
abstract-o-meter
(patent pending)
links
clients
contact
meter.html
Netscape: Ron Chan Illustration
Back Forward Home Reload Images Open Print Find Stop
Location: http://www.ronchan.com/frontpage.html
RON CHAN ILLUSTRATION
one two
Cover illustration about the internet for Bell Canada's Solutions magazine
home | new | about | contact | clients | links
Document: Done.

Title
Ron chan: portfolio
URL
http://www.ronchan.com/
Designer/Illustrator/Programmer
Ron chan
Authoring platform
Mac

The Web has become a useful medium for artists to open up their portfolios to prospective clients. Using a simple frame layout, illustrator Ron Chan offers small vignettes containing pieces of his artwork in place of full thumbnails to tempt the viewer; clicking a sample brings up the artwork in the main frame. Clicking one of the tabs in the left panel brings up another set of artworks, minimizing the need to scroll down several screens to see the rest of what's being offered.

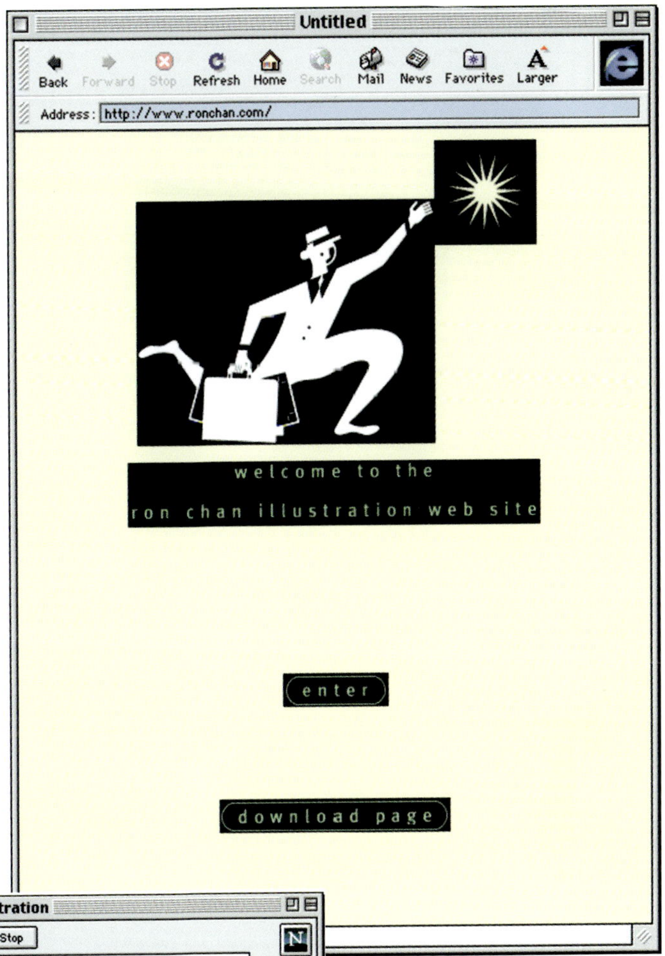

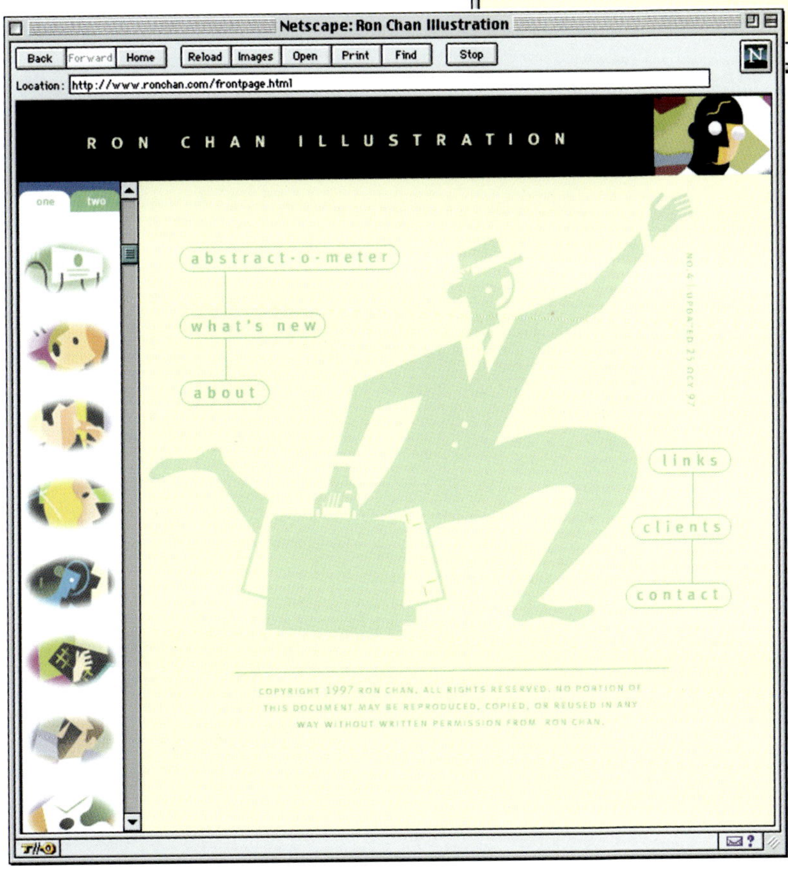

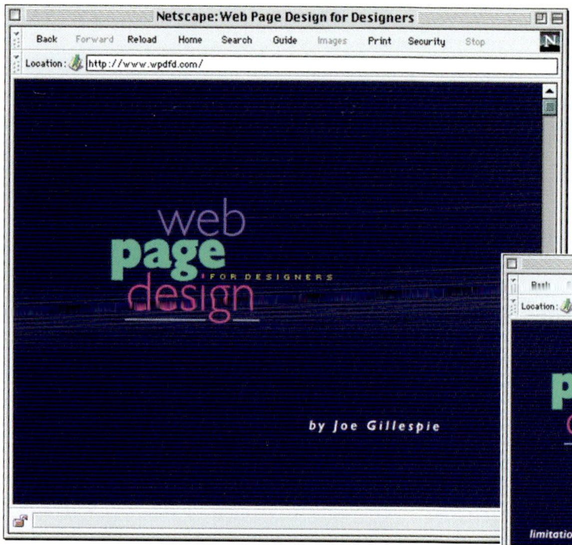

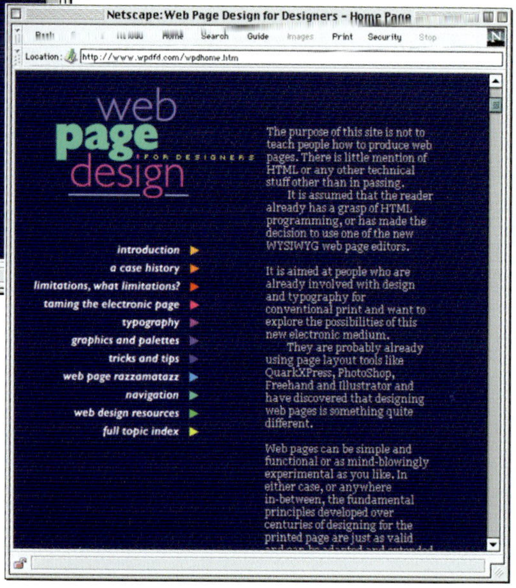

Title
web page design for designers
URL
http://www.wpdfd.com/
Design firm
pixel productions UK
Designer/illustrator/photographer/programmer
Joe Gillespie
Authoring platform
Mac

This sharply designed site doesn't even attempt to force-feed an over-engineered navigation system. The links leading to the rest of the site are listed along the left side, and enhanced with JavaScript rollovers and multiple colors. Once inside, getting to other areas of the site requires a trip back to the contents page, but everything loads so quickly that this approach wins out over cluttering up every page.

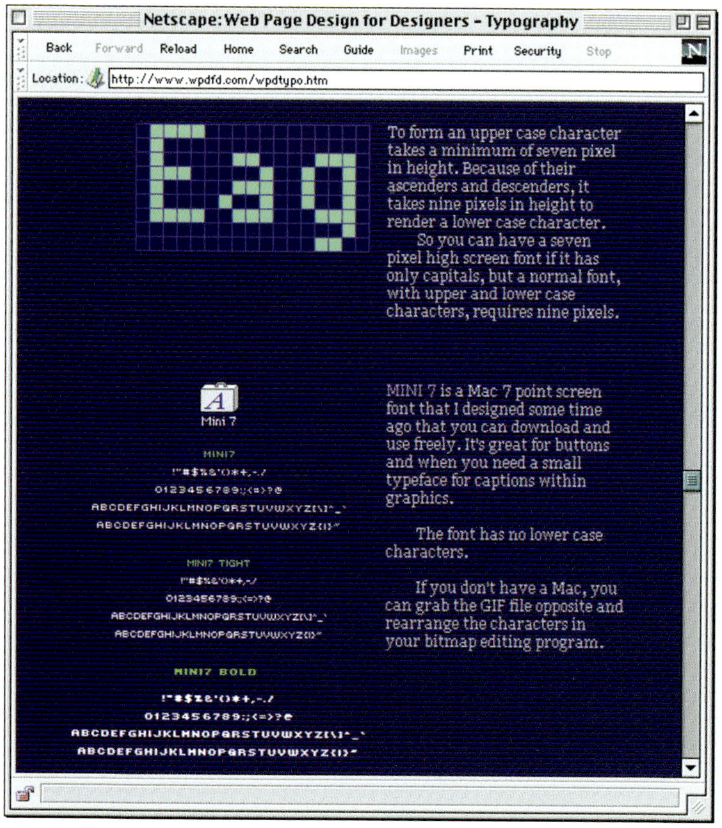

title
Thunder Lizard productions
URL
http://www.thunderlizard.com/
design firm
The Davis Group
designer/illustrator/programmer
Brett Davis
authoring platform
Mac

This is a good example of what to do when a small, simple set of Web pages evolves into a deeper, multi-layered site. The navigation moves in two directions here, with side buttons pointing to specific events and top buttons leading toward more general information. Wrapping the buttons on the fringes of the page frees up the middle for the site's content. The JavaScript techniques here are also well done, with three-stage buttons (instead of simple rollovers) at the top that actually press in before jumping to the appropriate page.

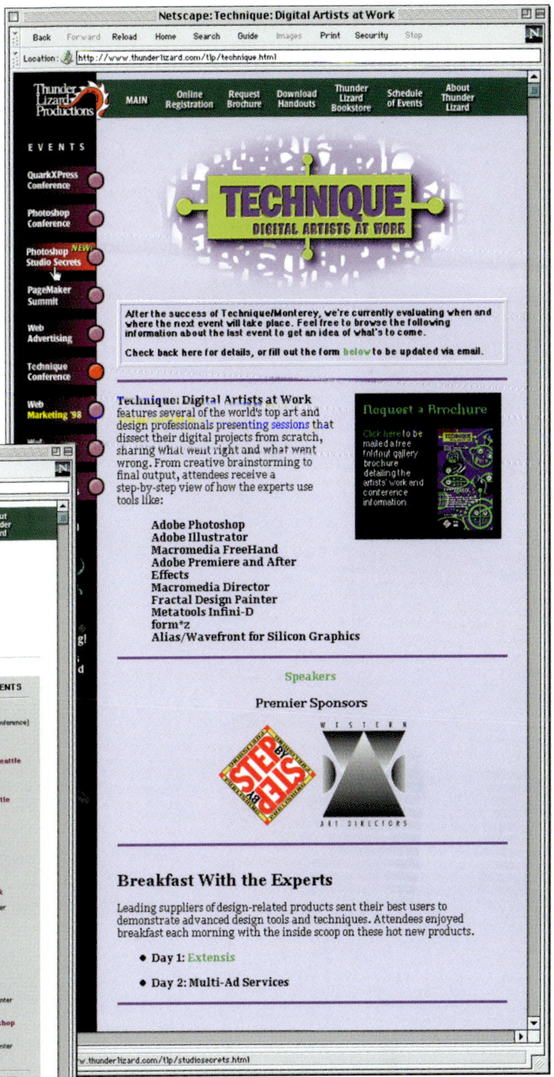

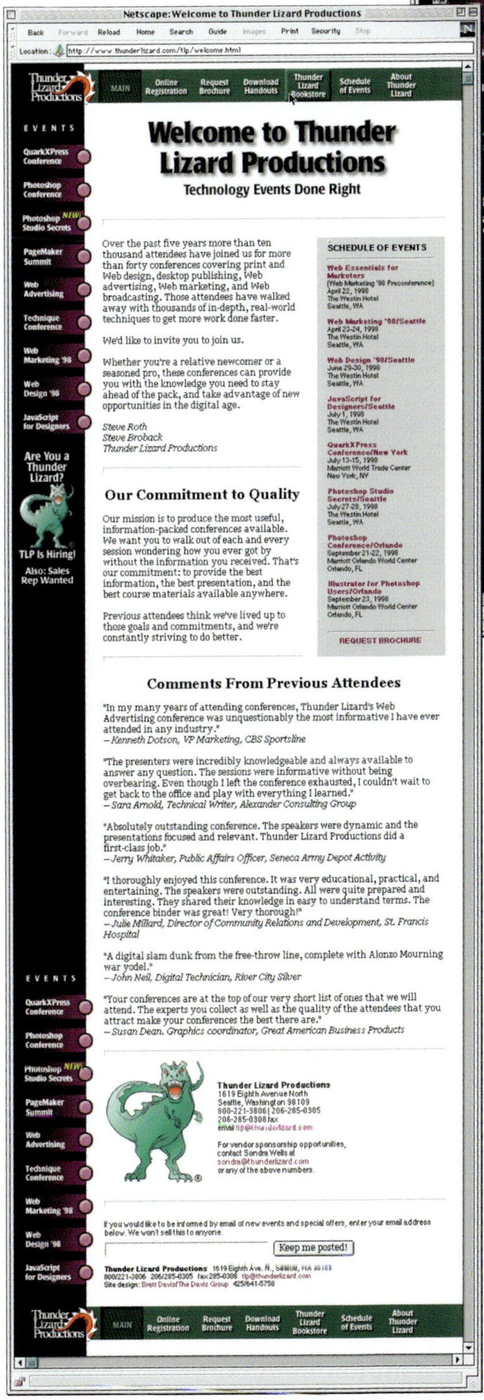

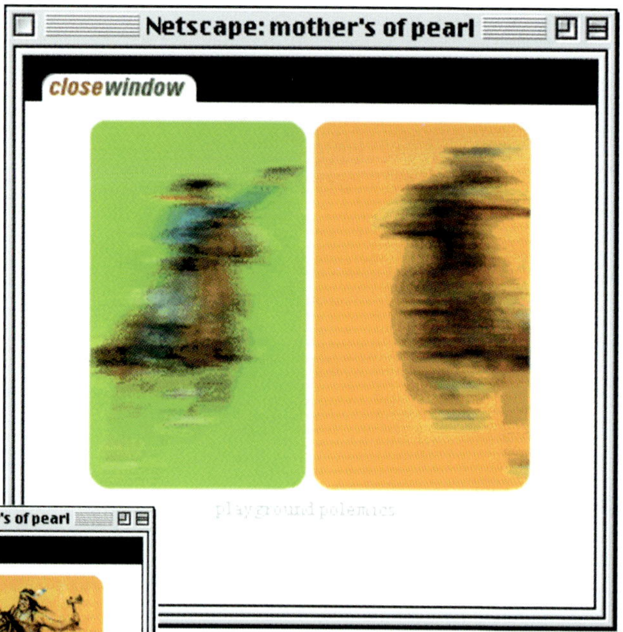

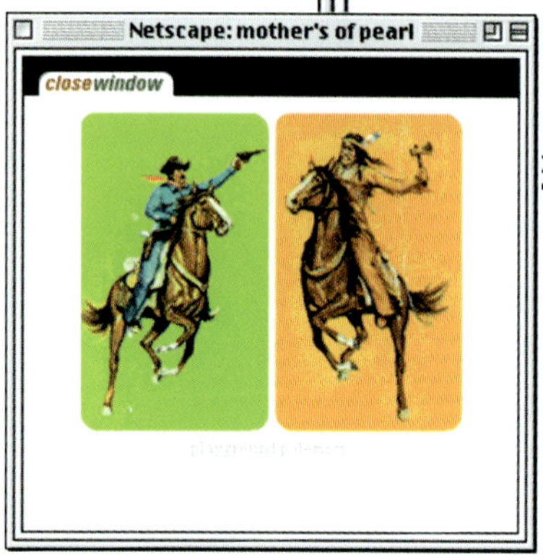

title
volumeone
URL
http://www.volumeone.com/spring.html
Designer/programmer
Matt Owens
Authoring platform
Mac

Your window to the Web world, alas, is a simple rectangle, but there's no reason you have to be content with just one window. Clicking on the small puzzle-piece icons on the main page brings up a new, presized window containing artwork.

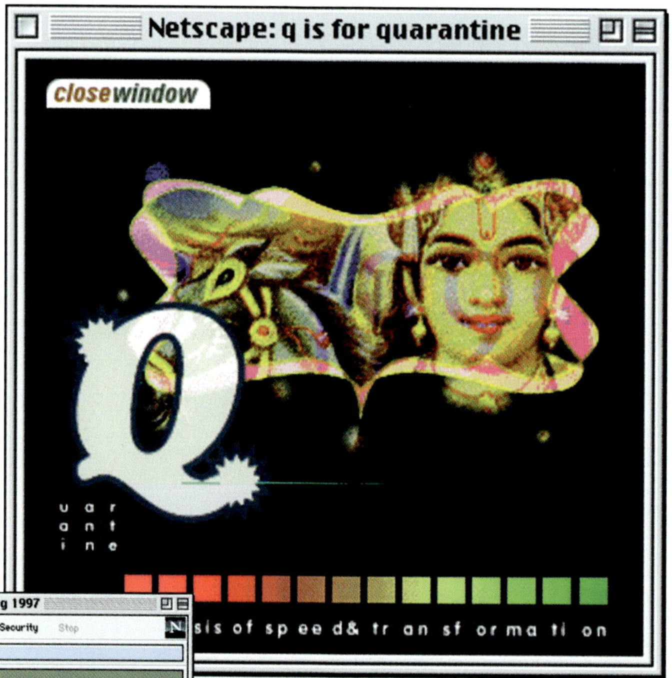

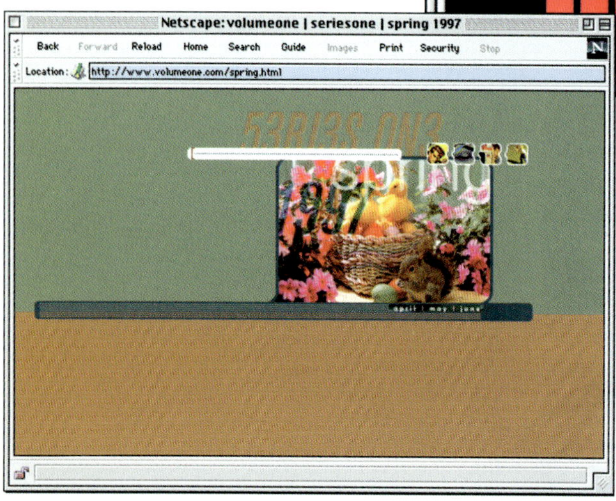

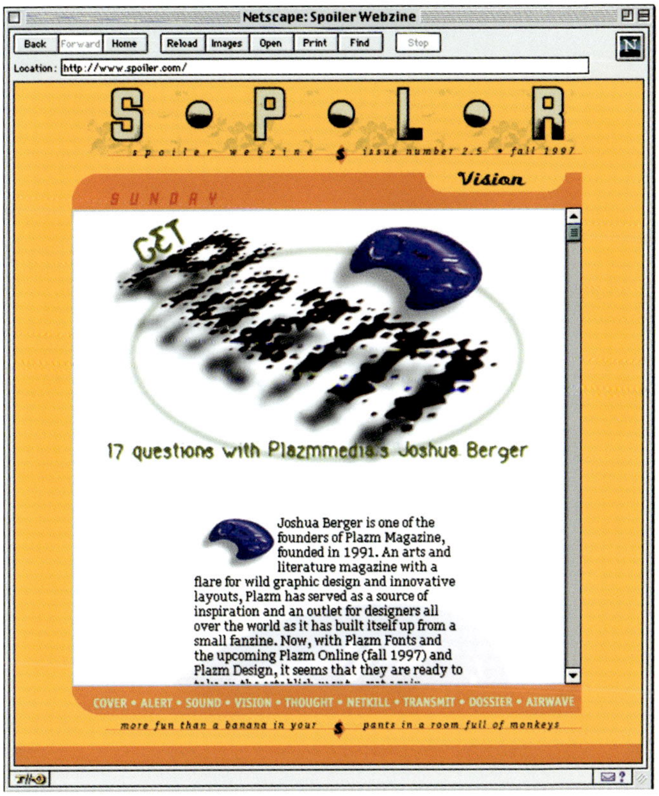

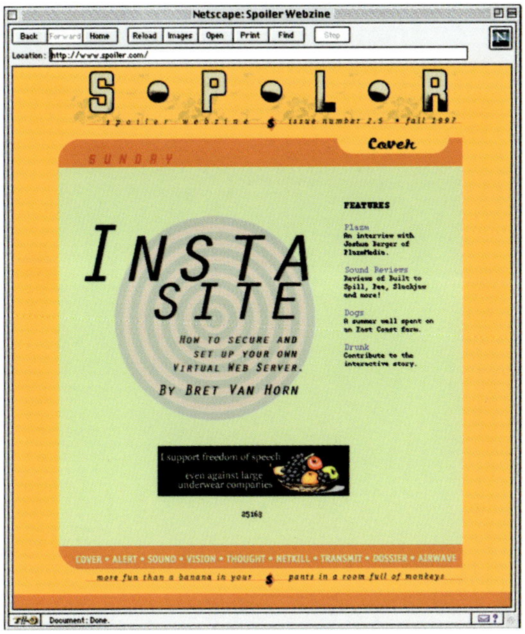

Title
spoiler webzine
URL
http://www.spoiler.com/
Design firm
Spoiler Media
Designer/programmer
Bret Van Horn
Authoring platform
Mac, Unix

When people new to the Web start exploring, they're often bothered by things that online veterans have learned to completely ignore. Many Web browser programs, when they load a new page, tend to flash—fill quickly with white or gray before loading a new page. Spoiler gets around this problem, and also centralizes its navigation system, by loading all of its content in a center frame, surrounded by unchanging outer frames. Although appearing more like a television, the site tends to feel solid, instead of transitive.

title
The James Gang
URL
http://www.jamesgang.com/
design firm
The James Gang: Art + Technology
designers
Franke James, MFA; Bill James
illustrator/photographer
Franke James, MFA
programmer
Bill James
models
Bonnae (Ford Models)
authoring platform
Mac

Placing the central navigation in a top frame is a straightforward method of providing direction throughout a site without sacrificing much screen space, and assures that the visitor will always have a visible way to move about, even when scrolling on long pages. What's nice here is that the designer has added simple JavaScript rollovers to the navigation, replacing the words not with buttons or glowing letters or other direct variation, but with color patterns and image cuts from each section. Simple word links become more texture for the site as a whole.

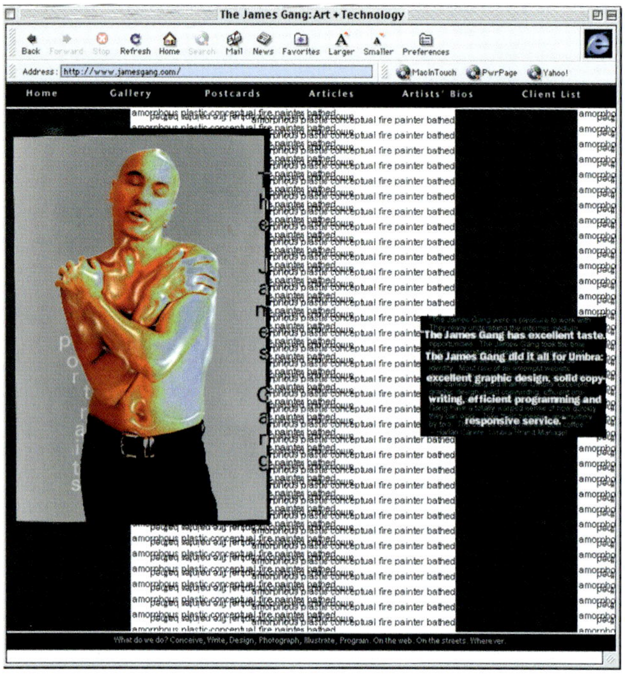

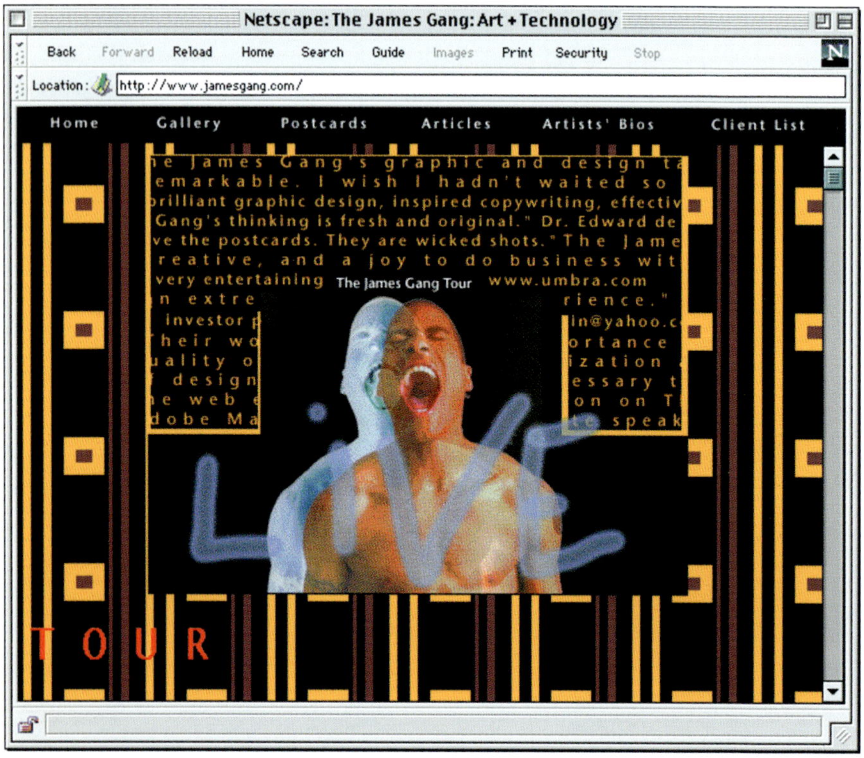

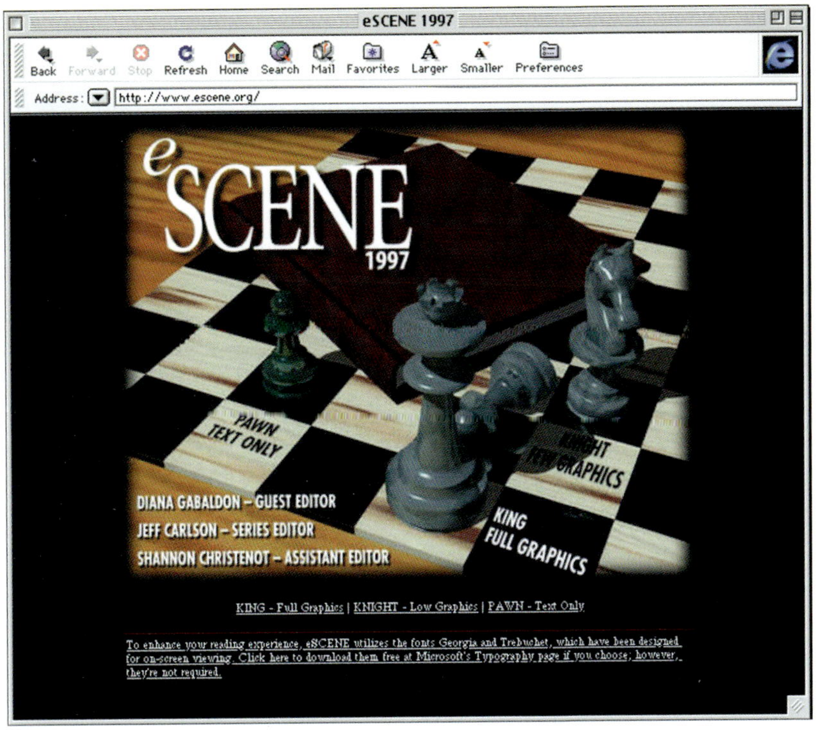

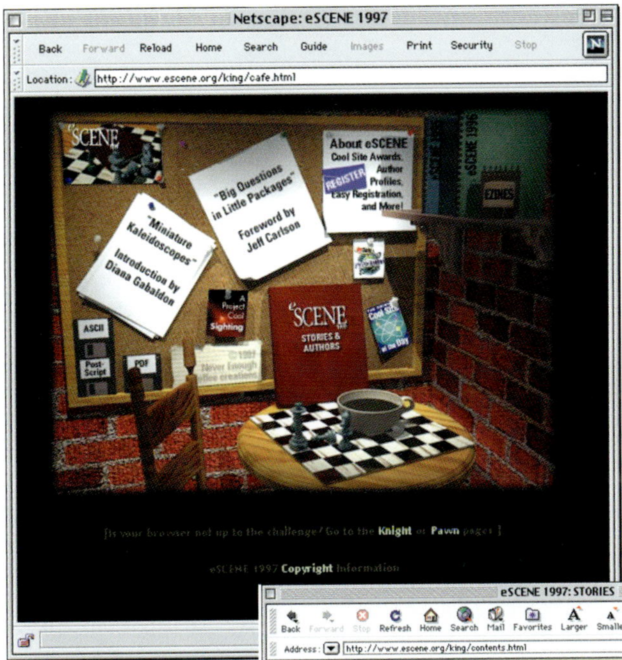

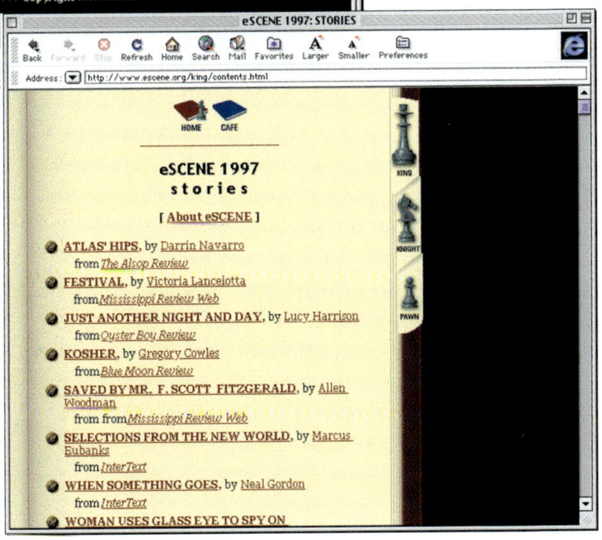

Title
eSCENE
URL
http://www.escene.org/
Design firm
Never Enough Coffee creations
Designer/illustrator/programmer
Jeff Carlson
Authoring platform
Mac

eSCENE avoids both the least-common-denominator approach to design, and the text-only alternative by providing a total of three separate navigation paths. An opening splash screen is loaded in wireframe using the LOWSRC tag that allows an alternative low-resolution image to be loaded first; a high-resolution JPEG follows. A café page for navigation uses a concrete objects, like floppy disks, to navigate to different types of resources and documents.

title
BoxTop Software, Inc.
URL
http://www.boxtopsoft.com/
design firm
MWB Interactive/invisible, ink
designer
Ed Sultan, invisible, ink.
illustrators
Daniel Thomas, MWB Interactive; Ed Sultan, invisible, ink; Travis Anton, BoxTop Software, Inc.
photographer
Travis Anton, BoxTop Software, Inc.
programmers
HTML—Ed Sultan, invisible, ink/Travis Anton, BoxTop Software, Inc.; CGI—Danny Lowe, BoxTop Software, Inc./Travis Anton, BoxTop Software, Inc.; Java—Open Cube Technologies
producer/writer
Travis Anton, BoxTop Software, Inc.
authoring platform
Mac

Each product is separately color coded and associated with a funky, fantastic machine on this site. Arriving at a product page shows you a highlighted and enlarged version of the machine graphic along with a horizontal banner with the product's color. The side navigation panel is contextual by product; the bottom text navigation bar shows departments, just as they do in text on the upper right on the home page.

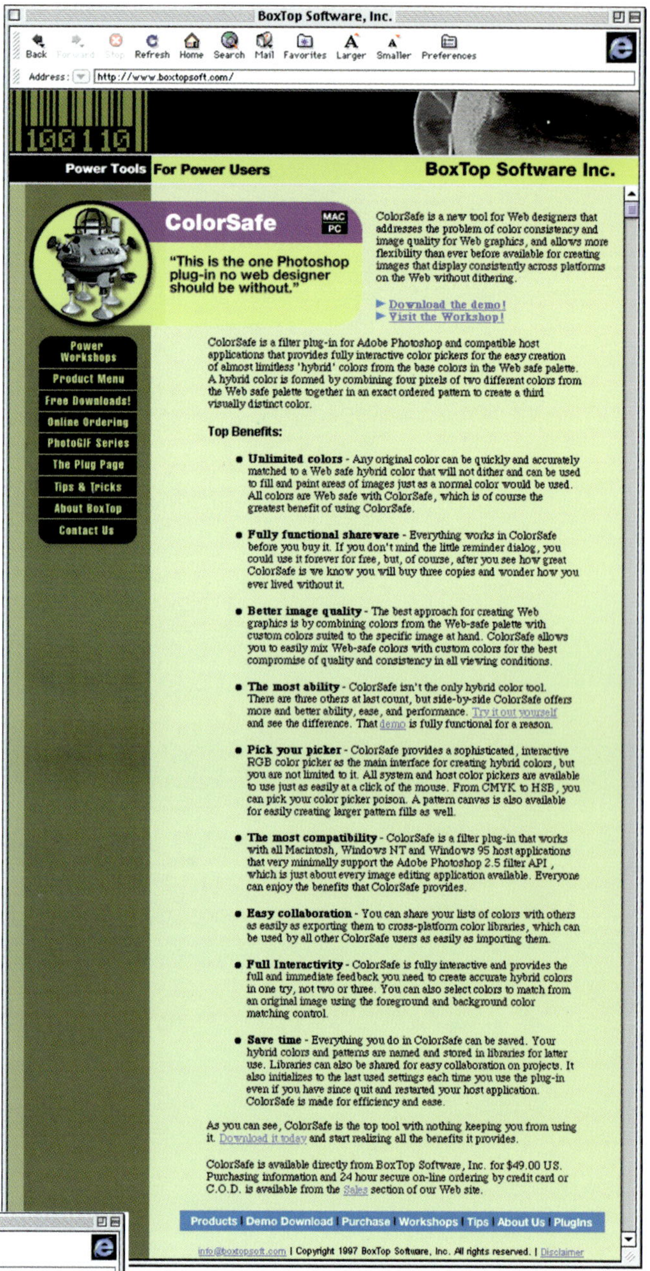

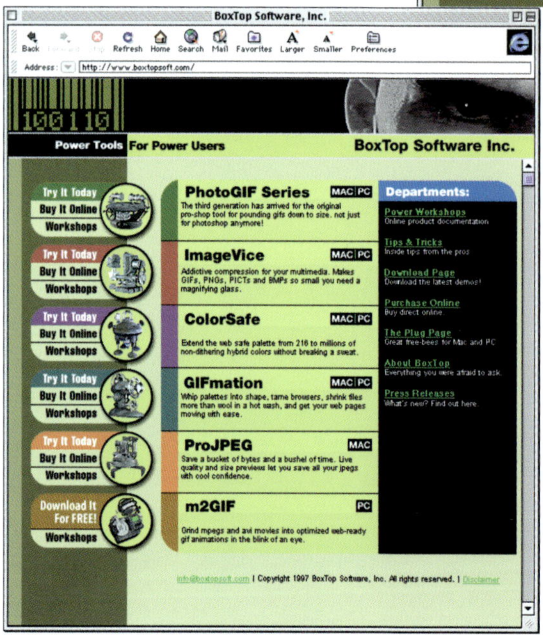

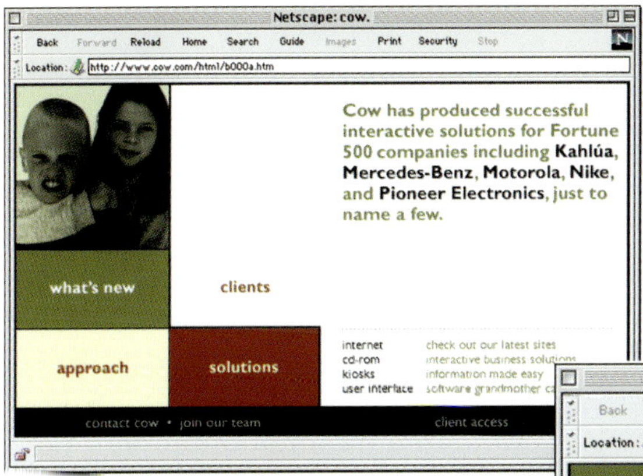

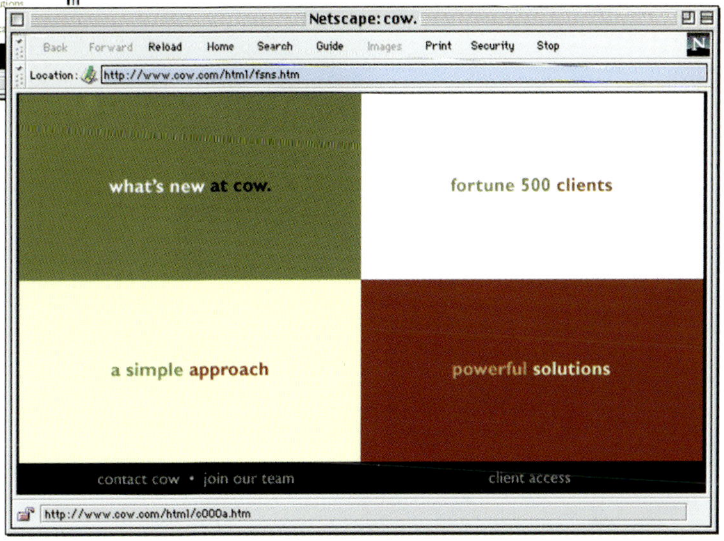

Title
cow. interactive communication
URL
http://www.cow.com/
Design Firm
cow. interactive communication
Designers
Bryan Powell, Tex Otto
Programmers
Jonathan Santos, Thierry Benichou
Account Director
Drew Sievers
Creative Directors
Bryan Dorsey, Mateo Neri
Technical Director
Jonathan Santos
Content Manager
Steven Lovy
Backend Engineer
Tammy McKean
Copywriters
Bryan Dorsey, Steven Lovy, Tom Pope, Brian Higa

This just may be the best example of clear, simple, and clever navigation you'll find in this book, a geometric beauty. Sections are organized according to color in a two-by-two grid, with the active section occupying most of the browser window; the grid is tucked into the corner opposite the page's content. So, depending on which page you're on, the navigation shifts among the window's four corners. Supporting details are numbered and appear in the active frame when clicked, or open up a new window.

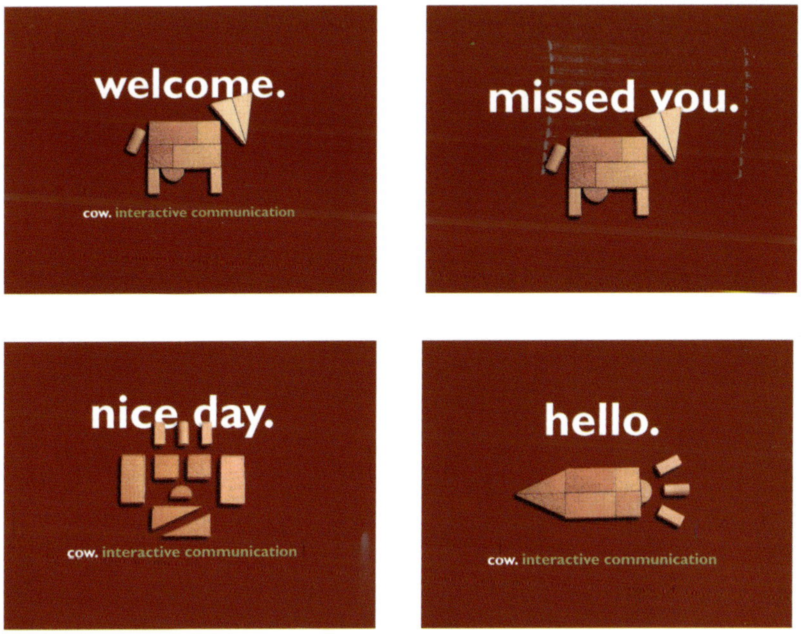

Title
souldanse: Art for the soul
URL
http://www.souldanse.com/melanie/
Designer
Melanie A. Ceraso
Illustrator
paul pearson
Photographer
Dave Siekaniec
Programmers
John M. Carlin, Melanie A. Ceraso
Authoring platform
pc

Moving among the sections of this site is like tiptoeing through rain to dodge the falling drops. The main areas are listed in the right-hand frame with subtle JavaScript rollover effects. Clicking on a theme triggers events in the left and center frames: subdirectories appear to the left, intended content in the middle. This visual movement from right to left to center and back again draws your eyes across the entire page, instead of one or two corners.

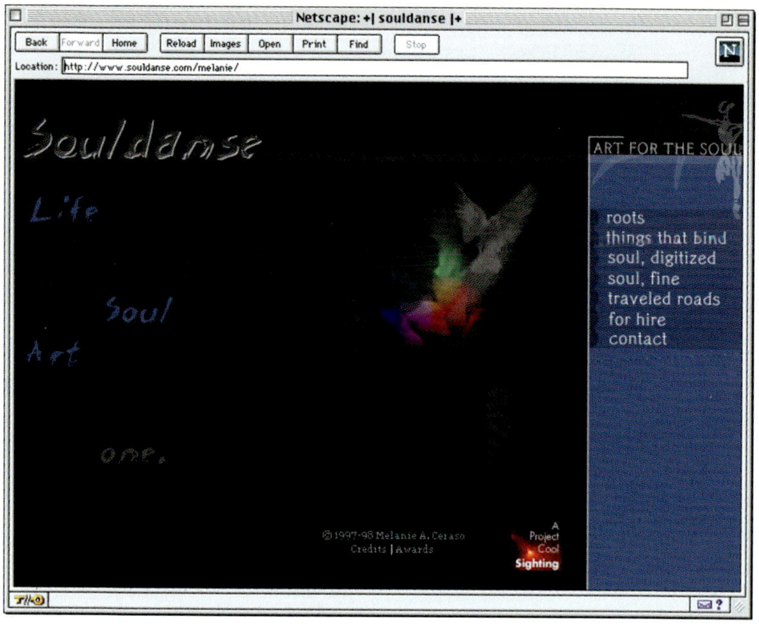

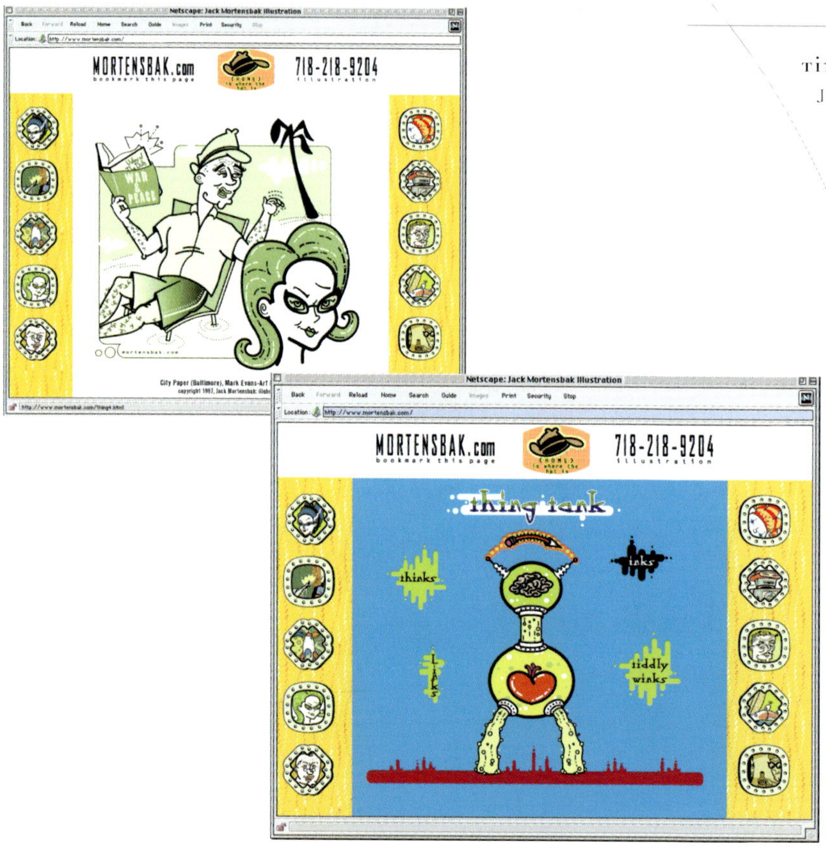

Title
Jack Mortensbak: illoboy!
URL
http://www.mortensbak.com/
Designer, Illustrator
Jack Mortensbak
Programmer
Ben Malloway
Authoring platform
Mac

Some people prefer Web sites with depth, like walking into a large house and exploring its rooms. Sometimes, however, that approach just is not needed. This site provides everything at the outset: links, news, contact information, and artwork samples that all load into the center frame.

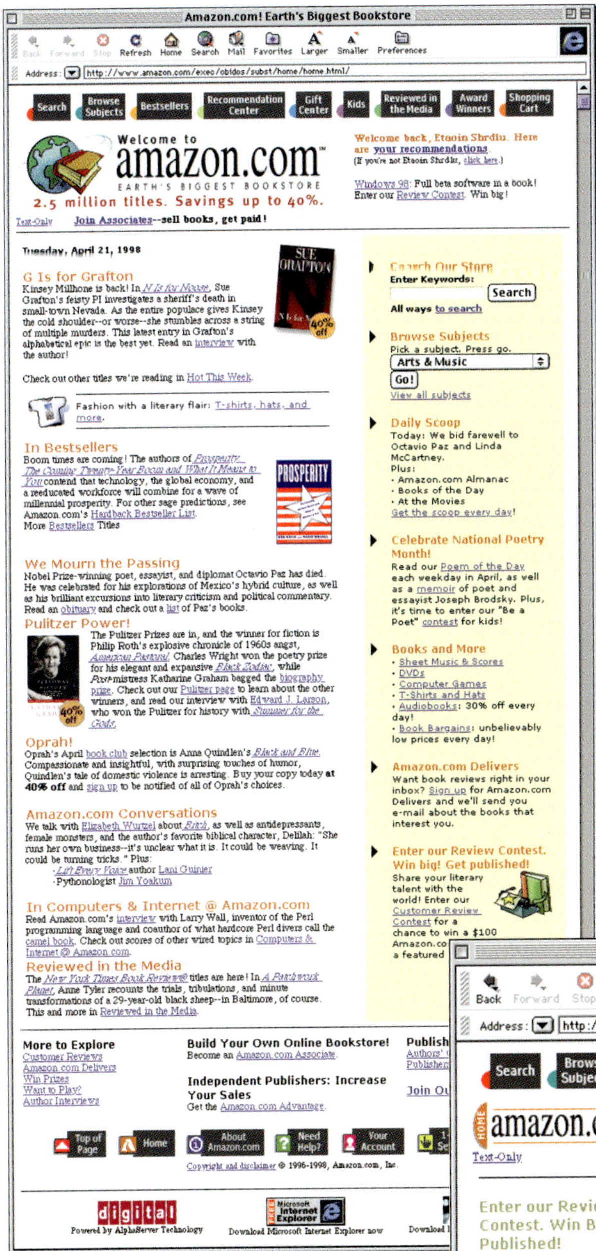

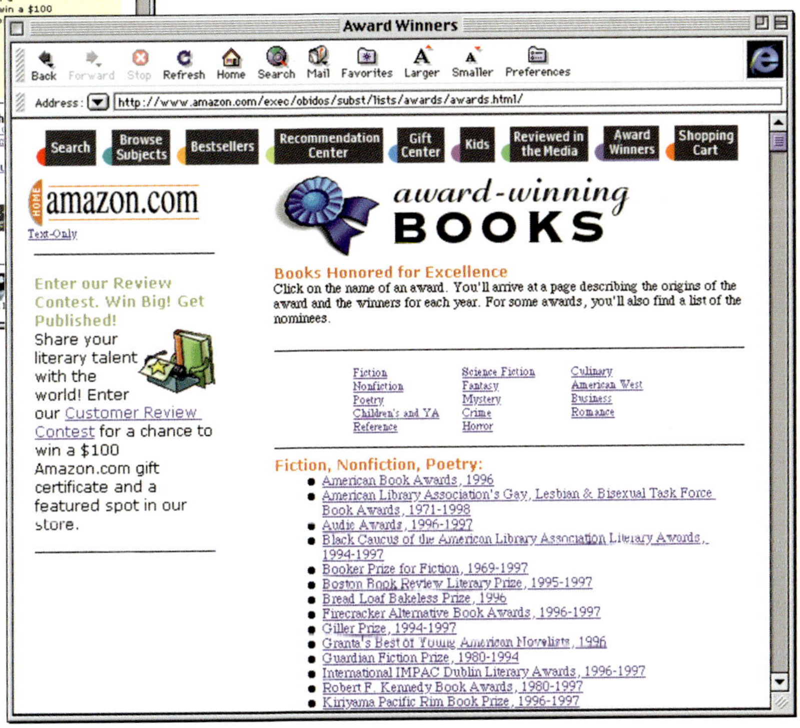

title
amazon.com
URL
http://www.amazon.com/

Each section has both a color, a name, and some custom typography. When you click on any section, the icon on the top navigation bar is underlined in that section's color. A bit of custom type and special graphics add to each section's sense of being a different part of the store. The bottom text navigation differs from the top; the bottom emphasizes customer issues, while the top focuses on editorial divisions.

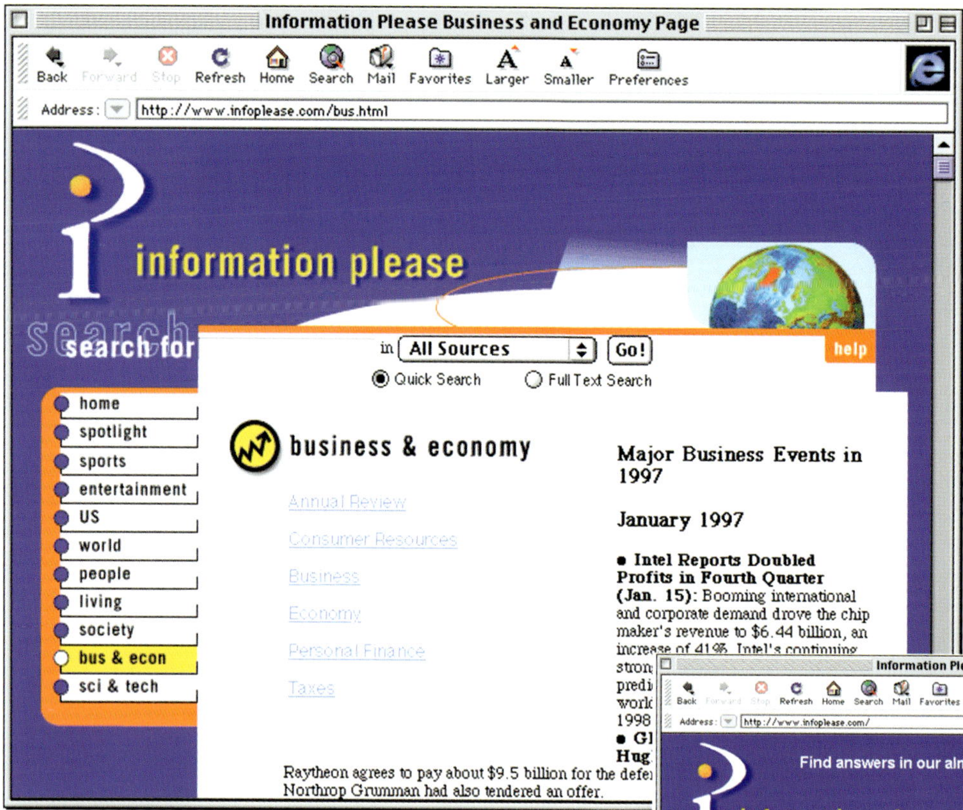

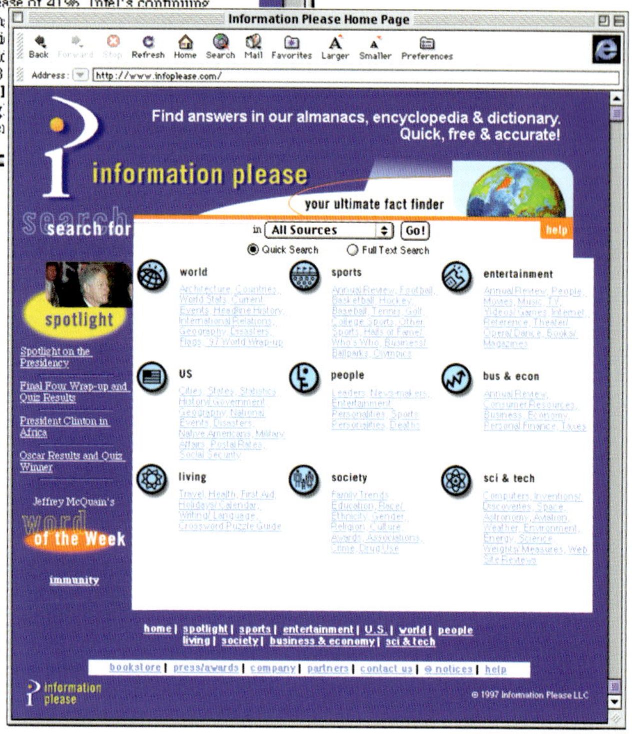

title

information please

URL

http://www.infoplease.com/

design firm

stoltze design

designers

clifford stoltze, susanne hefel,
cynthia patten, rebecca fagan

illustrator

james kraus

programmers

boris goldowsky, paul evenson

authoring platform

mac, pc, unix

Navigating a vast amount of information can be troubling, but Information Please has built a hierarchy that makes it easy to get around. It uses two approaches: major categories are simply identified in a left navigation bar; these include society, business and economics, and entertainment. It then subdivides each category in text links into a finer degree of granularity. However, it does not require drilling down indefinitely; most information is just three or four links deep at most.

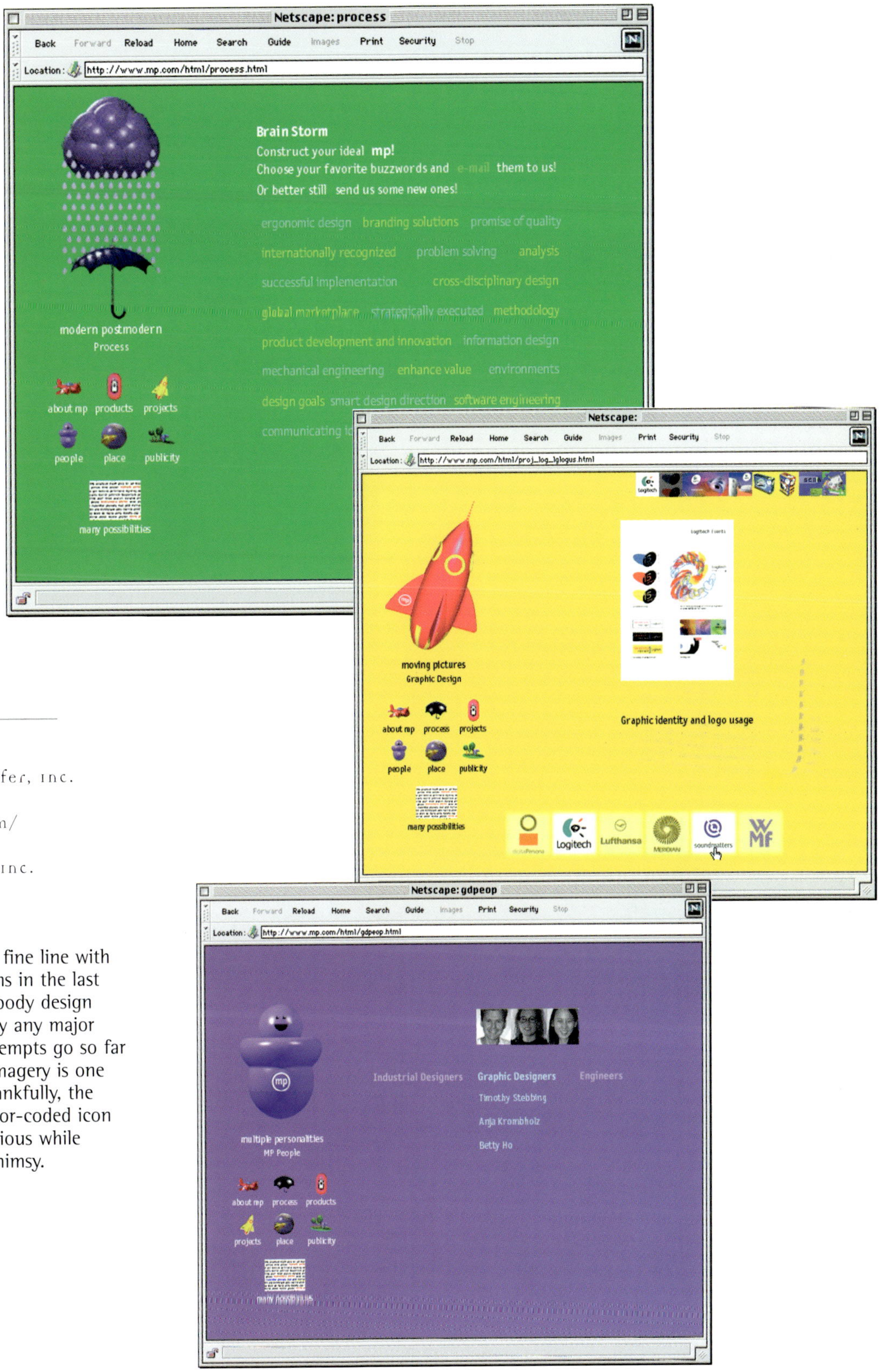

Title
Montgomery Pfeifer, Inc.
URL
http://www.mp.com/
Design Firm
Montgomery Pfeifer, Inc.
Authoring Platform
Mac

Designers have had to toe a fine line with icon-based navigation systems in the last two decades. Some icons embody design ideals—note the signs in nearly any major European city—while other attempts go so far overboard that decoding the imagery is one step short of hieroglyphics. Thankfully, the bright plastic nature of this color-coded icon system keeps your location obvious while injecting a sense of childlike whimsy.

Title
Urban Desires
URL
http://www.desires.com/
Design Firm
Agency.com
Designers/Illustrators
Jean Esquivel (Gateway and TOC/1st & 2nd screen); Chris Alegra (Korean food)
Programmers
Mike Parker (gateway and TOC/1st & 2nd screen); Chris Alegra (Korean food)
Authoring Platform
Mac

Although the technique seems to be used sparingly on the Web, providing links through drop-down menus is starting to take hold as an alternative to long text lists. Using perhaps one-fifth of the space, these menus offer the same amount of direction while making room for other elements.

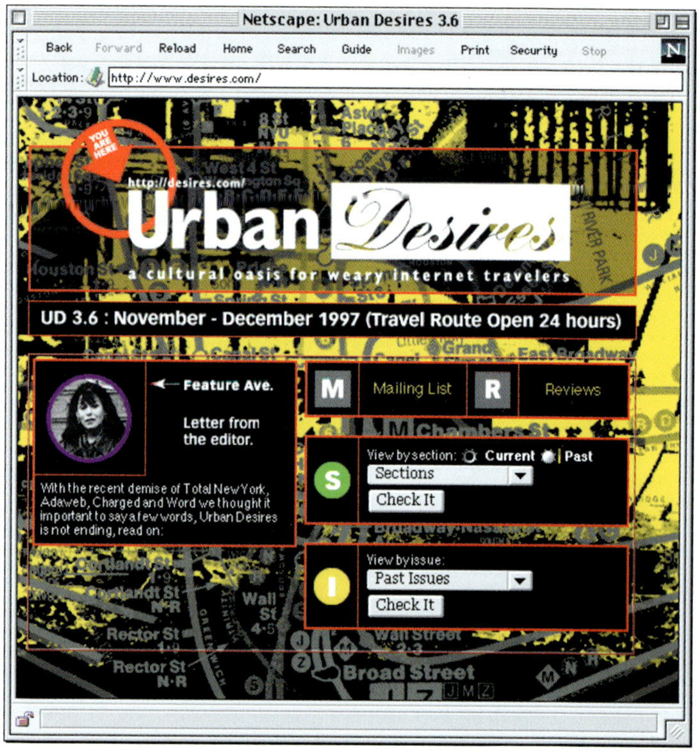

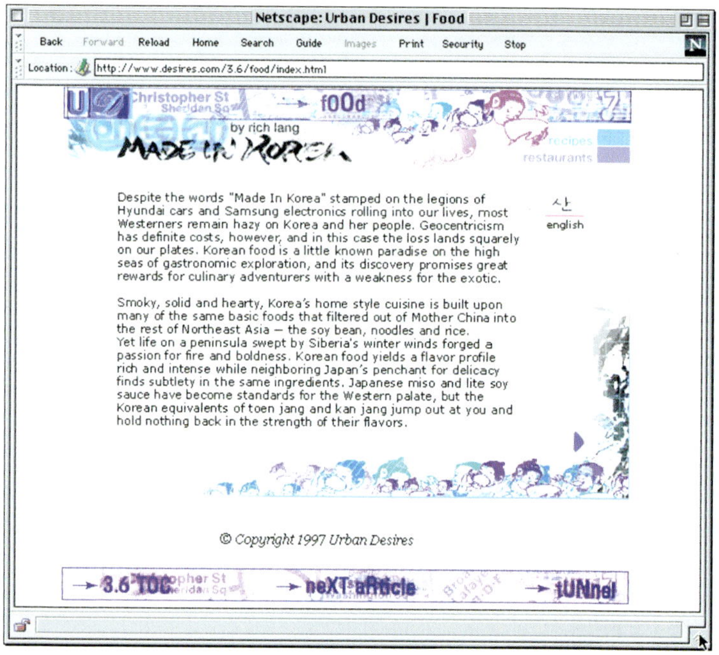

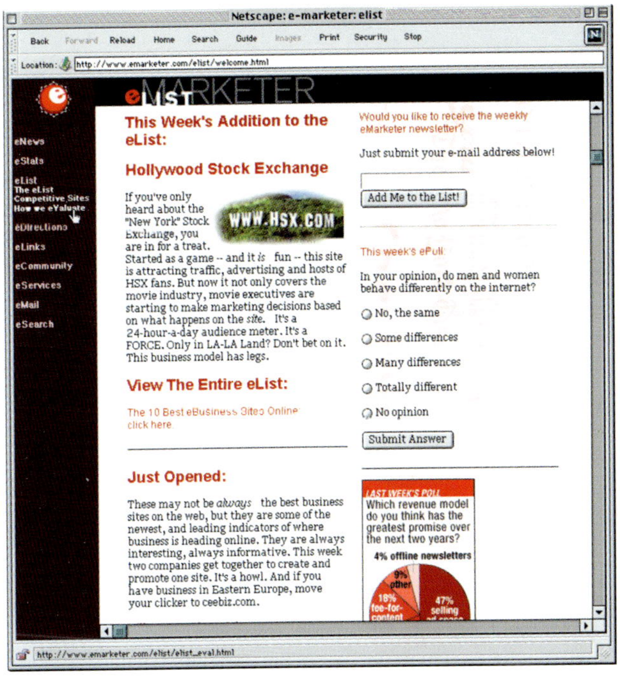

Title
eMARKETER
URL
http://www.emarketer.com/
design firm
TA_G
designers
chuck Moore, Lise Brown, Ben Maloway
illustrator
steve smith
authoring platform
Mac

Visual navigation does not always have to exist solely as a tool for moving from one point to another. Put to creative use, the navigation structure can do a better job of suggesting concepts than some direct imagery. The circular approach on the main page echoes the orbit paths of our solar system, with important satellites of information revolving around the company's logo.

Title
parent soup
URL
http://www.parentsoup.com/
design firm
parent soup
designer/illustrator
christina fredericks
programmers
fay ku, Tom simpson
authoring platform
Mac

Parent Soup has a lot of material it wants to deliver fast, so the designers have chosen to put many links on the home page. But by varying and placing the links, they've made features easy to find. Each category of link has a separate feel: communities appears on the right with a special typographic treatment and with color fields behind them; general sites navigation appears at top and bottom in a simple face with crayon lines between them. Sections take the same approach of grouping links by using a different design scheme.

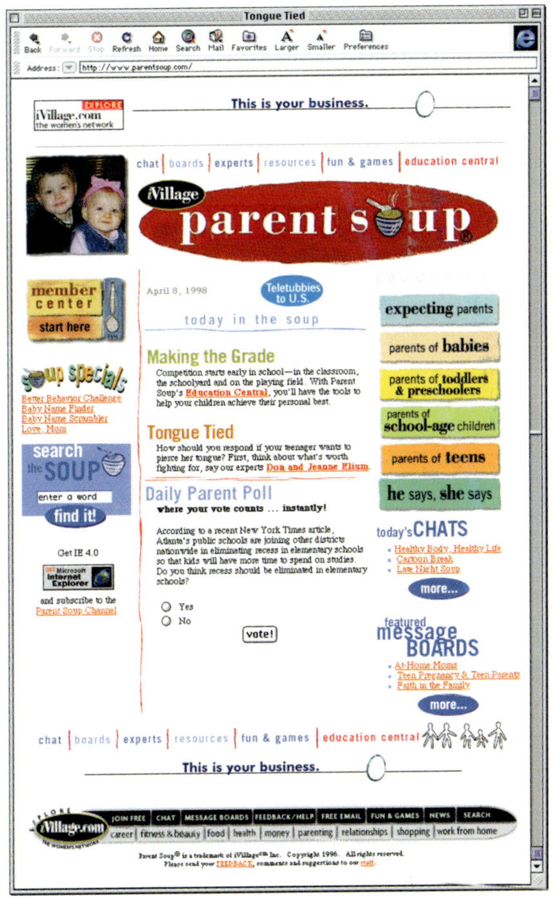

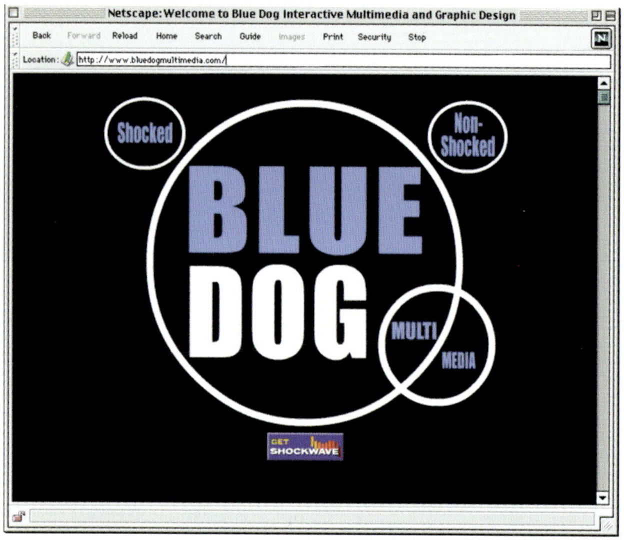

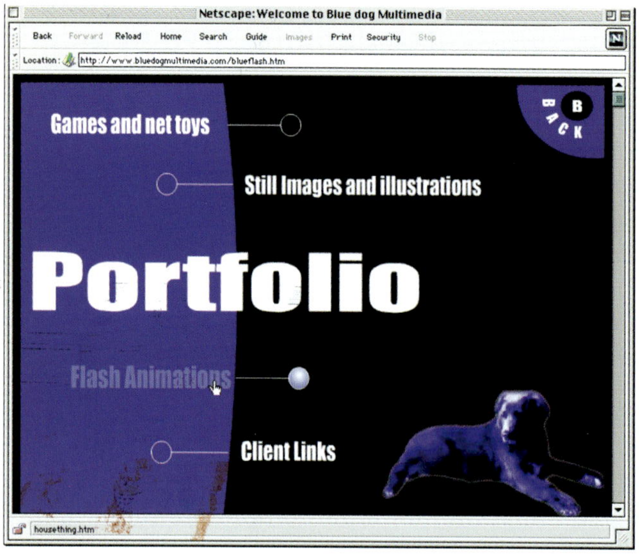

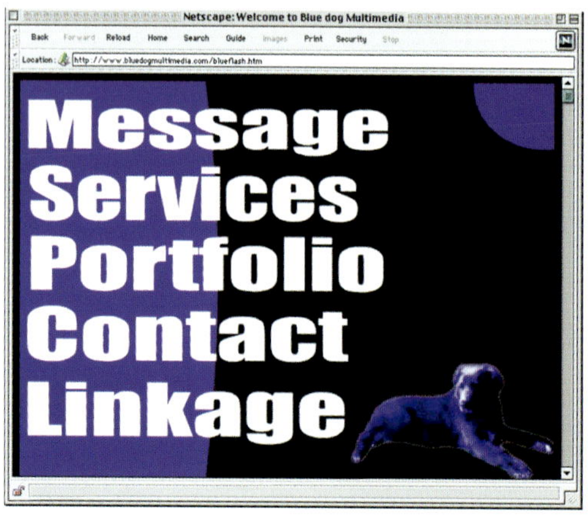

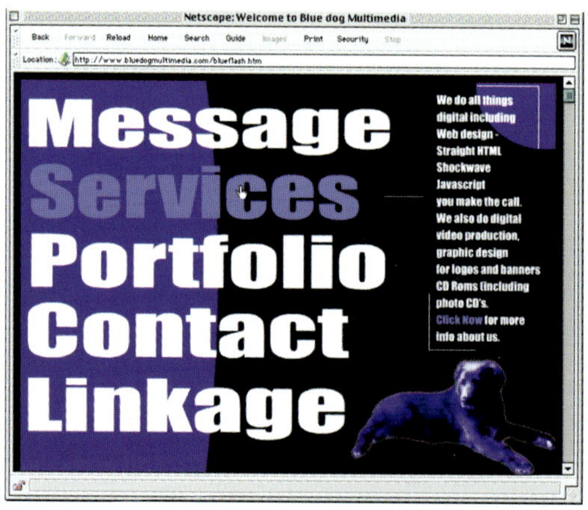

Title
Blue Dog Multimedia
URL
http://www.bluedogmultimedia.com/
Design Firm
Blue Dog Multimedia
Designer/Illustrator/Photographer/Programmer
Mark Underhill
Authoring Platform
Mac

One of the strengths of the Macromedia Flash format is that it does a great job of scaling vector artwork for animations. Since much of the best vector artwork comprises the letters A through Z, it's no wonder that many Flash-based sites, such as this one, heavily employ animated type. The navigation here leaves nothing hidden, and adds audio touches to your choices.

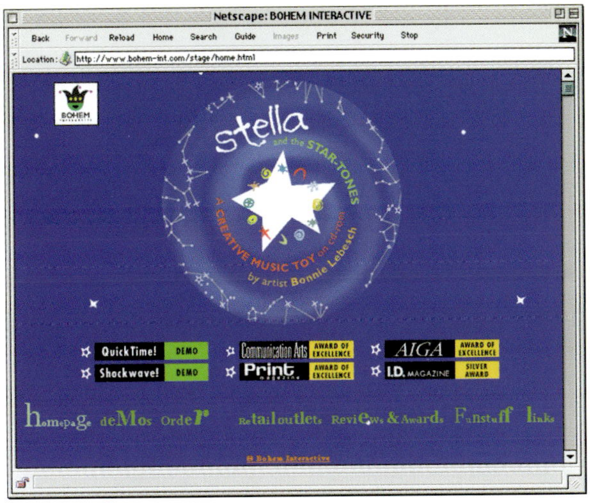

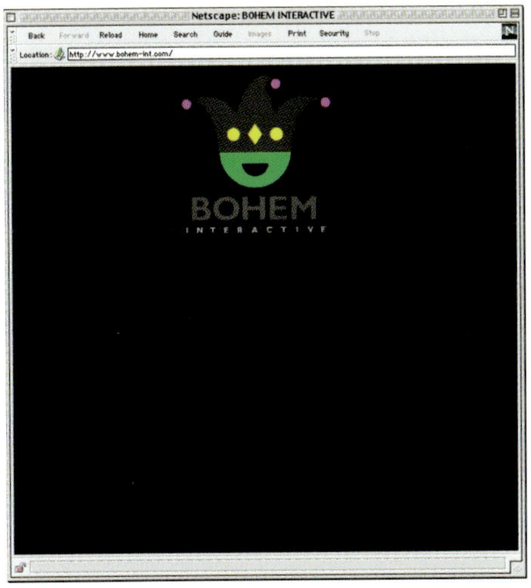

Title

Bohem Interactive

URL

http://www.bohem-int.com/

Design firm

Bohem Interactive

Designer/photographer

Bonnie Lebesch

Illustrators/programmers

Bonnie Lebesch, Don Barnett

Authoring platform

Mac

Despite the push to add stunning graphics to Web sites, often the best way to lead visitors through a site is with plain text links. In this case, the designer has taken advantage of bold and italic styling, plus <FONT> tag controls, to give the links a fun, childlike personality.

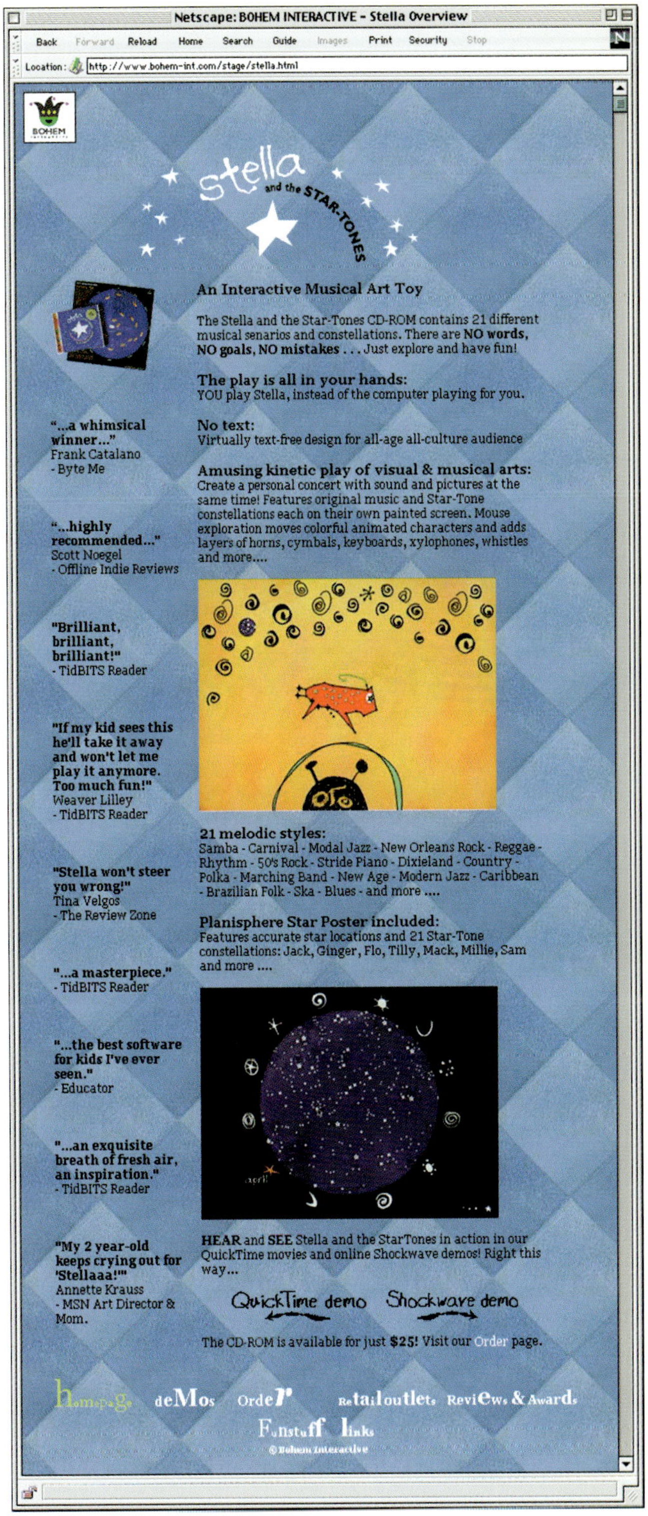

Title
Yale-New Haven Medical Center
URL
http://www.info.med.yale.edu/index.html
Design Firm
Center for Advanced Instructional Media, Yale University
Designer/Illustrator
Patrick J. Lynch
Photographer
Yale University Biomedical Communications
Programmer
Sean Jackson
Authoring Platform
Mac

The straightforward approach to navigation divides items in the top navigation bars into two categories, using tone to help make the differentiation clearer. On top are the facilities that are part of the medical center; on the bottom are subdivisions within the site crossing the facilities. The site uses photographs only as graphics, not buttons (nor does it use illustrations), making the text navigation on the left quick loading and purely functional.

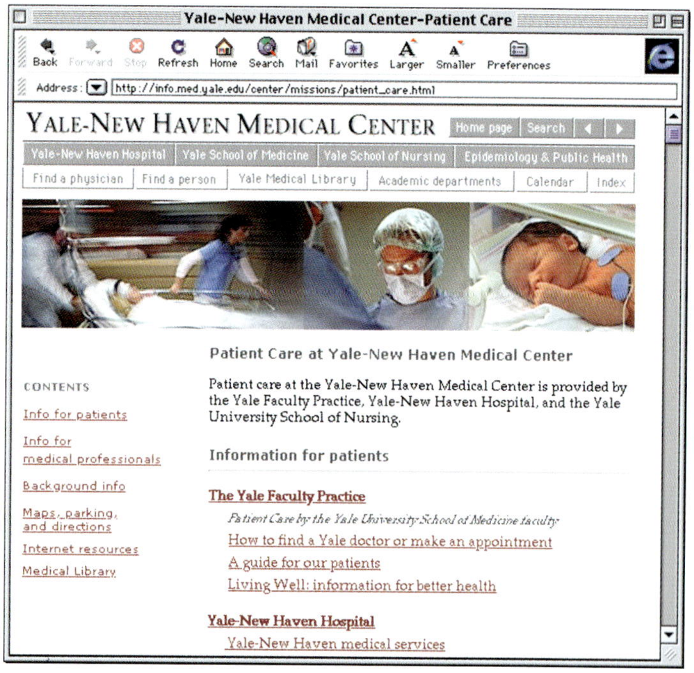

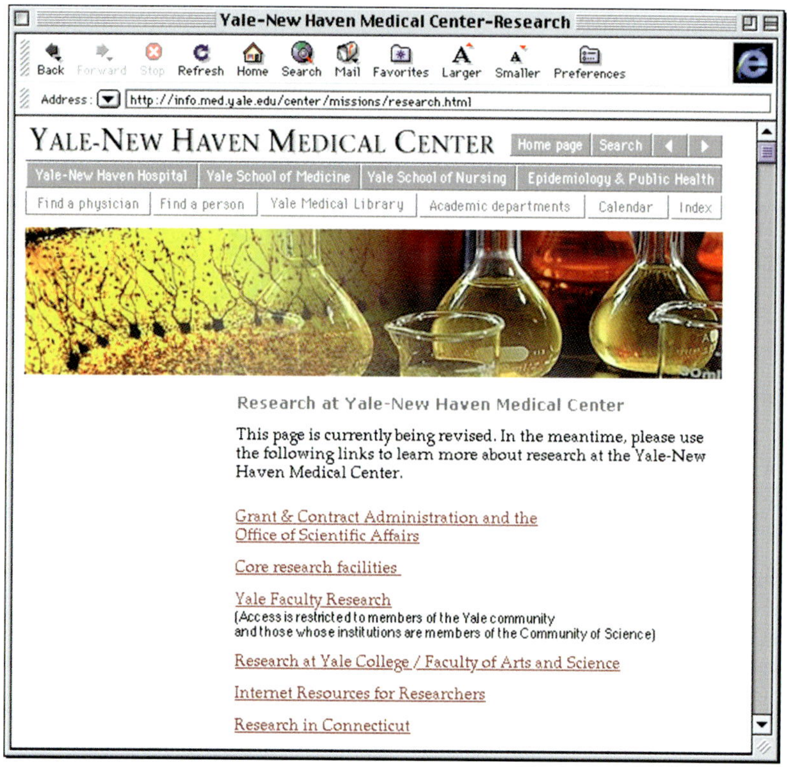

title
typographic.com
URL
http://www.typographic.com/
Design Firm
typographic.com
Designer/Illustrator/Programmer
jimmy chen
Authoring platform
Mac

They make you work for it, but it's not too much of a burden. First, you have to click through four screens to get to the home page. The home page is launched as a separate, small window with no location or status bar. The type representing links is jumbled and screened back at lower left, and in its place arrayed along the bottom are sets of binary numbers. There's no way to know where you're clicking; you have to explore to find anything.

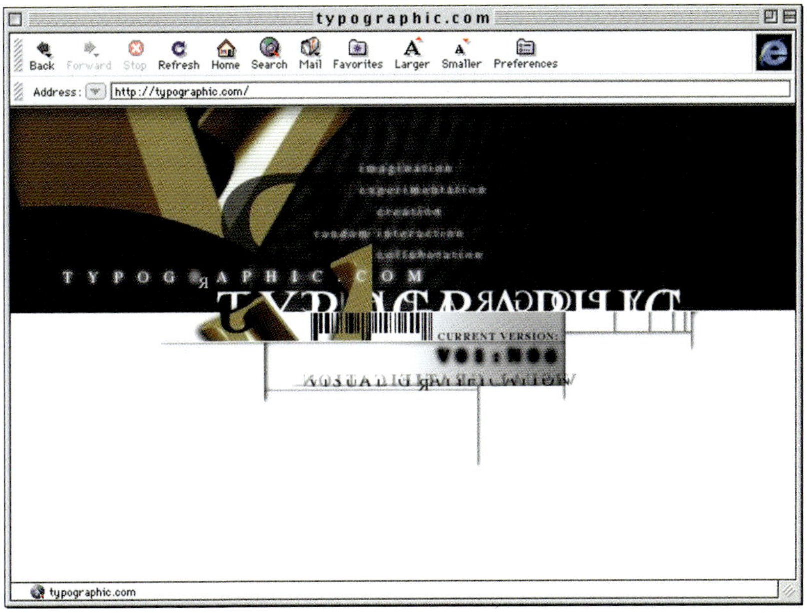

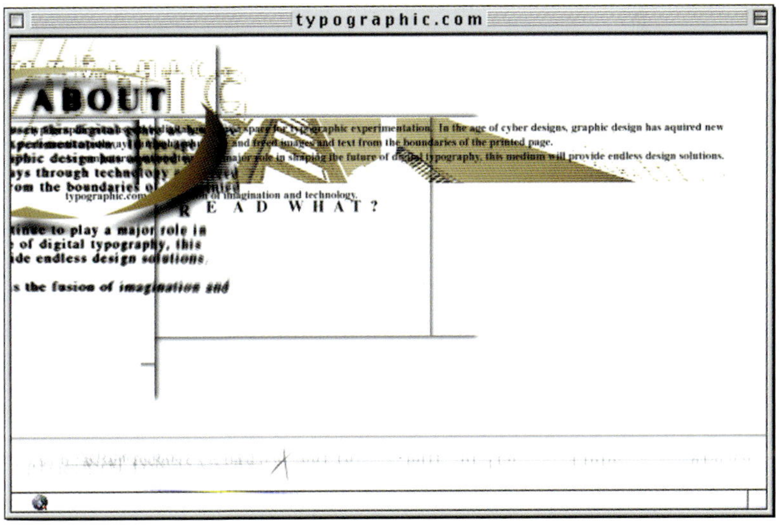

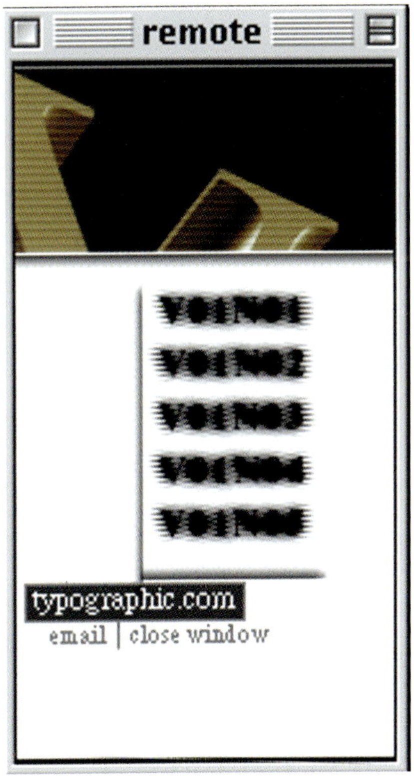

About the Authors

Jeff Carlson

Jeff spent several years doing desktop publishing before jumping into the Web publishing arena by founding and editing *eSCENE*, the Internet's only yearly anthology of the best short fiction appearing on the Web. A stint as Managing Editor at a small Seattle-based book publisher convinced Adam and Tonya Engst that they should tap him for the same position at the widely-read newsletter *TidBITS*. Jeff has published articles in *HOW Magazine*, *Macworld*, and *Adobe Magazine*, and was a contributing editor and columnist for Adobe's online venture, *adobe.mag*. He is also the author of *The Palm III/PalmPilot Visual QuickStart Guide*. In addition to writing and editing, he's an accomplished Web designer and consultant through his company Never Enough Coffee creations. People around him seem to possess strong urges to constantly ask him questions. <http://www.necoffee.com>.

Toby Malina

In 1995 Toby joined Thunder Lizard Productions, a Seattle-based conference production company, as Editorial/Technical Director. At Thunder Lizard, she worked in collaboration with the editorial staff and outside experts in the desktop publishing and Web design fields to develop editorial content for The Photoshop Conference, The Adobe Internet Conferences, and Web Design: HTML and Beyond, amongst many others. In addition, Toby was responsible for the coordination and execution of all conference audio visual including computer systems, lighting, sound, and projection. If it broke, she fixed it. In 1997 she served as product manager for Technique: Digital Artists at Work and The PageMaker Summit.

For the past ten years, Toby has also worked independently as a graphic designer and Macintosh consultant. Her multi-faceted roles have included art director, production artist, MIS manager, software/systems trainer, and mental health professional. Her greatest triumph: wrenching a motherboard from the jaws of a client's basset hound and successfully reseating it.

Glenn Fleishman

Glenn Fleishman has written about technology and its use in several publications, including *InfoWorld* and *NetGuide*. He was a founding contributing editor and columnist at the print edition of *Web Developer* (now only found on the Web), and is a contributing editor and columnist for *Adobe Magazine*, where he writes the Web Watcher column. Glenn was course manager at the legendary Kodak Center for Creative Imaging in Camden, Maine, and later worked doing scanning and color correction at a showcase imaging center nearby, High Resolution Inc. Glenn later worked as a managing editor for Open House, where he technical- and copy-edited several books for Peachpit. He founded one of the first web development companies, Point of Presence Company (POPCO), offering firms Web site programming and hosting. While at POPCO, he helped broadcast the first feature film over the Internet. Glenn worked briefly as a senior manager at Amazon.com Books; while there as catalog manager, he was responsible for increasing the catalog from 1 million to 2.5 million titles. He now works as a consultant, conference chair, writer, and itinerant perl programmer, and recently co-authored the second edition of *Real World Scanning and Halftones*. <http://www. glenns.org>

agi business media productions GmbH
Falkertstrasse 71/2
70176 Stuttgart
Germany

AT&T 1996 Olympic Games
295 N. Maple Avenue
Basking Ridge, NJ 07920

Atlas
1201 B Howard Street
San Francisco, CA 94103

Bau-Da Design Lab, Inc.
480 Canal Street #1102-A
New York, NY 10013

beyondexpress.com
19 Delaware Avenue
Delhi, NY 13753

Bianca Troll Productions
P. O. Box 78097
San Francisco, CA 94107

Blue Dog Multimedia
4001 Riviera Drive
San Diego, CA 92109

Bohem Interactive
2226 Eastlake Avenue E
Suite 61
Seattle, WA 98102

Boxtop Software, Inc.
101 North Lafayette Street
Starkville, MS 39759

Melanie A. Ceraso
Souldanse Digital Design
33 Braxton Lane
Aurora, IL 60504

Ron Chan
24 Nelson Avenue
Mill Valley, CA 94941

Chris Chomick
5248-52nd Avenue North
St. Petersburg, FL 33709

Community Networks Systems
4 Hasadna
Jerusalem, Israel

Construct Internet Design
448 Bryant Street
San Francisco, CA 94107

Core77
561 Broadway
6th Floor
New York, NY 10012

cow. Interactive
Communication
1522 Cloverfield Boulevard
Suite E
Santa Monica, CA 90404

Dartmouth College Curricular Computing
Kiewit Computation Center
Hanover, NH 03755

DDB Interactive
3500 Maple Avenue
Suite 250
Dallas, TX 75219

The Design Office Inc.
1 Bridge Street
Irvington, NY 10533

Disappearing Inc.
45 Wall Street #413
New York, NY 10005

Electric Ocean
53 Wale Street
8001 Cape Town
South Africa

Elliott/Dickens
97 South Second Street
Suite 220
San Jose, CA 95113

eMARKETER
821 Broadway
New York, NY 10003

Emergent Media, Inc.
1809 7th Avenue
Suite 908
Seattle, WA 98101

Enviromedia, Inc.
617 Vine Street
Suite 1336
Cincinnati, OH 45202

Eyescream Interactive, Inc.
17650 NW Gilbert Lane
Portland, OR 97229

52mm
12 John Street
10th Floor
New York, NY 10038

Focus2
2105 Commerce
Suite 102
Dallas, TX 75201

Fractal Cow Studio
2 Achilles Street
Acropolis, Libia
Quezon City, Metro Manila
Philippines, 1100

frogdesign
1327 Chesapeake Terrace
Sunnyvale, CA 94089

Funny Garbage
73 Sprung Street
Suite 605
New York, NY 10012

The Grapevine
321 University Street
Healdsburg, CA 95448

Gr8
2400 Boston Street
3rd Floor
Baltimore, MD 21224

Graffito/Active8
601 North Eutaw Street
Suite 704
Baltimore, MD 21201

Haynes and Boone Web site
901 Main Street #3100
Dallas, TX 75202

Haywood + Sullivan, Inc.
119 Utica Street
Quincy, MA 02169

Hiew, Hon
Q Multimedia
10 Eastland Street
Dianella, Perth, WA 6059
Australia

The Iconfactory
1 Moss Cove Court
Greensboro, NC 27407

Information Please
31 St. James Avenue
Boston, MA 02116

Internet Underground Music Archive
303 Potrero Street, #7A
Santa Cruz, CA 95060

Jack Mortensbak: illoboy!
P. O. Box 2510
New York, NY 10009

The James Gang: Art + Technology
3080 Yonge Street
Suite 5044
Toronto, Ontario
M4N 3N3 Canada

Jason Foundation
395 Totten Pond Road
Waltham, MA 02154

Jessica Helfand/William Drenttel
P. O. Box 159
Falls Village, CT 06031

Jodi.org
Franshalsstrasse 61
2162 CL Lisse
The Netherlands

Kjetil Vatne Graphics + Design
Langarinden 407
N-5090 Nyborg
Norway

KMTT-FM
1100 Olive Way, #1650
Seattle, WA 98101

Knight Errant Design
8948 SW Barbur Boulevard
Suite 168
Portland, OR 97219

Lisa Marie Nielsen Design
601 Fourth Street, #125
San Francisco, CA 94107

Montgomery Pfeifer
461 Bush Street
San Francisco, CA 94108

Nerve Magazine
311 Broadway
Suite 3A
New York, NY 10007

Never Enough Coffee Creations
1619 Eighth Avenue N
Seattle, WA 98109

P2
287 West 4th Street, #10
New York, NY 10014

Pageworks
19 Delaware Avenue
Delhi, NY 13753

Parent Soup
170 Fifth Avenue
New York, NY 10010

Phinney/Bischoff Design House Inc.
614 Boylston E
Seattle, WA 98102

PING Belgium
Interleuvenlaan 5
B-3001 Leuven
Belgium

Pittard Sullivan
3535 Hayden Avenue
Culver City, CA 90232

Pixel Productions UK
39 Ripley Gardens
London SW14 8HF
United Kindom

Qaswa Communications
423 Washington Street
Floor 5
San Francisco, CA 94111

Real World Multimedia
Box Mill, Box
Wiltshire SN13 8PL
United Kingdom

Robot
Kinese 66
S-11122 Stockholm
Sweden

Salon Magazine
706 Mission Street
2nd Floor
San Francisco, CA 94040

Scamper
3100 Benvenue Avenue, #4
Berkeley, CA 94705

Segura, Inc.
1110 North Milwaukee
Chicago, IL 60622

sfstation
3528 17th Street
San Francisco, CA 94110

Simon & Schuster Higher Education
1 Lake Street
Upper Saddle River, NJ

Smallprint
Stereomedia
P.O. Box 262
Fin-00171 Helsinki
Finland

Spoiler Media
3095 SW 15th Court
Gresham, OR 97080

Stagebill
144 East 44th
7th Floor
New York, NY 10017

Studiomotiv
300 Marconi Boulevard
Columbus, OH 43215

Syndetic Design
1302 White Dove Cove
Cedar Park, TX 78713

Tony Shasteen Illustration & Design
1079 Megan Court
Sugar Hill, GA 30518

Tim Trompeter
28 East 10th Street, 9B
New York, NY 10003

Typographic.com
557 Dolores Street
San Francisco, CA 94110

Joshua Ulm
525 Brannan Street
Ground Floor
San Francisco, CA 94107

Urban Desires
665 Broadway
Suite 504
New York, NY 10012

US Web
139 Richmond Street
El Segundo, CA 90245

Vivid Studios
510 3rd Street
San Francisco, CA 94107

Volumeone
654 Metropolitan Avenue
Brooklyn, NY 11211

Yale-New Haven Medical Center
47 College Street
Suite 224
New Haven, CT 06510

INDEX